Photogrammetry for Archaeological Objects

A Manual

TOM AUSTEN BROWN STUDIES IN AUSTRALASIAN ARCHAEOLOGY

Professor Annie Clarke, Series Editor

The Tom Austen Brown Studies in Australasian Archaeology series publishes new research on the archaeology of Australia and the adjacent regions. It aims to develop our understanding of Australasia's human past, with particular focus on the archaeology of Aboriginal and Torres Strait Islander peoples during both prehistoric and contact periods.

Animal Bones in Australian Archaeology: A Field Guide to Common Native and Introduced Species
Melanie Fillios and Natalie Blake

Between the Murray and the Sea: Aboriginal Archaeology in Southeastern Australia
David Frankel

Crafting Country: Aboriginal Archaeology in the Eastern Chichester Range, North-West Australia
Caroline Bird and James W. Rhoads

Jakarda Wuka (Too Many Stories): Narratives of Rock Art from Yanyuwa Country in Northern Australia's Gulf of Carpentaria
li-Yanyuwa li-Wirdiwalangu (Yanyuwa Elders), Liam M. Brady, John Bradley and Amanda Kearney

Photogrammetry for Archaeological Objects: A Manual
Madeline G.P. Robinson

Photogrammetry for Archaeological Objects
A Manual

Madeline G.P. Robinson

SYDNEY UNIVERSITY PRESS

First published by Sydney University Press

Sydney University Press
Fisher Library F03
Gadigal Country
University of Sydney NSW 2006
AUSTRALIA
sup.info@sydney.edu.au
sydneyuniversitypress.com.au

A catalogue record for this book is available from the National Library of Australia.

ISBN 9781743329832 paperback
ISBN 9781761540431 hardback
ISBN 9781743329856 epub
ISBN 9781743329849 pdf

We acknowledge the traditional owners of the lands on which Sydney University Press is located, the Gadigal people of the Eora Nation, and we pay our respects to the knowledge embedded forever within the Aboriginal Custodianship of Country.

CONTENTS

ACKNOWLEDGEMENTS

This book would not have been possible if it weren't for a number of people and institutions. Firstly, to Joseph Frey, who has been my unwavering source of support, thank you for tolerating all my grammar queries and being by my side throughout this project. To Olivia and Tim Robinson, whose support has been the foundation of all my research and work. And thank you, Tim, for introducing me to the world of photography all those years ago. A big thank you to Martin Wright, who has not only put up with me talking about this manual for so many years but has assisted me in teaching photogrammetry and has made me an all-round better archaeologist. And a special thank you to Kotaro Yamafune, Gus Porter, Will Figueira, Januar Harianto and Renata Ferrari for guiding me through the early days of my journey into photogrammetry.

A huge thank you goes to the Chau Chak Wing Museum for allowing me the opportunity to model a range of archaeological objects from the museum's collections and permitting me to include an assortment of them in this book. A special acknowledgement to the amazing duo Jane Thogersen and Eve Guerry, your encouragement means more to me than you know.

Thank you to Annie Clarke and the Tom Austen Brown editorial board, Andrew Wilson for all your help and advice along the way, the Discipline of Archaeology, and the School of Humanities at the University of Sydney. Thank you to Sydney University Press, to Naomi van Groll and Agata Mrva-Montoya, for all your assistance, advice and encouragement in getting this over the finishing line.

To Peter Hiscock, if it weren't for you, this manual would never have existed. Thank you for your contributions and for suggesting the idea of turning my photogrammetry worksheets into a published manual; this opportunity has been an amazing one.

To the ever-supportive, inspiringly passionate and all-round superstar Lauren Franklin. I cannot express to you how much I have appreciated your constant source of help, support and insight. Thank you for everything.

And finally, to all the photogrammetry students that I have taught over the years. Thank you for teaching me how to best teach you.

LIST OF ABBREVIATIONS

AF – autofocus

AWB – auto white balance

DoF – depth of field

DSLR – digital single-lens reflex

EV – exposure value

FPS – frames per second

f/ or f-stop – "focal-length"-stop (the aperture setting of the lens)

GCP – ground control point

ISO – International Organization for Standardization

JPEG – Joint Photographic Experts Group

K – Kelvins (measurement of colour temperature)

MF – manual focus

MP – megapixel, also abbreviated to MPx in *Metashape*

PPI – pixels per inch

SfM – structure from motion

TIFF – Tag Image File Format

WB – white balance

LIST OF FIGURES

LIST OF TABLES

Chapter 1

INTRODUCTION

1.1 Why photogrammetry?

Archaeology is a study primarily focused on *things*. Things whose origins stem from any imaginable human activity – things made from scratch, things produced organically then altered using another sharpened thing, small things stacked together to create larger things for practical or ritual reasons, or simply the inedible things left over from dinner. Things allow us to study the past and attempt to answer questions about how humans navigated, adapted and responded to an ever-changing world. They provide a means to understand how we interacted with each other and the consequences of that interaction: the evolution of culture, language and social practices. The temporal dots are able to be joined by the analysis and assessment of things, allowing us to determine how we inevitably got to where we are today.

It is this focus on things that gives archaeology its unique and enviable capacity to allow its researchers to study anything and everything – the one caveat being that anything under study has an observable relationship with past humans. This means there is an infinite number of objects, features or sites that one archaeologist may encounter in their career. Unfortunately, the time archaeologists have with their subject material is typically limited, possibly due to budgetary constraints, field seasons or deadlines. Additional issues like accessibility can restrict the length or the quality of time an archaeologist has to work with their subject material. Material may be located somewhere too difficult to physically visit, objects may be too fragile to handle, or a museum may reject a request to analyse a specimen. The conversation of accessibility resurrects a profound paradox with the two core foundational aims of archaeology – to analyse and to conserve cultural material – as these two goals can be, and often are, in conflict. The handling and analysis of an object can endanger its conservation, and invasive techniques may impact suitability for potential future examination. Imposing severe restrictions on the handling of historical material, however, will inevitably stymie the progression of research. These decisions are realistic ones that archaeologists have to make; however, fortunately for us, there is a method available that not only gives us access to material 24 hours a day, seven days a week, but also leaves the original untouched. This technique is photogrammetry.

Photogrammetry is the process of creating digital three-dimensional models of objects, features or sites by "stitching" together a series of overlapping, well-exposed and sharp digital photographs. Via this technique, an accurate and measurable record can be created of a subject's surficial texture, colour and detail, as well as its morphology and surface topography. This 3D record immortalises the subject in digital space and allows it to be delivered to anyone with internet access, anywhere on the planet, where it can be inspected, observed, analysed and reanalysed without fear of damage or degradation.

Photogrammetry provides a wealth of benefits for analysis, data extraction, conservation and educational purposes; it is therefore understandable why it has become so popular in the archaeological sciences. It can be used as a method to model any object, feature or landscape, terrestrial or submerged, in controlled lab conditions or in the field. Geometrically accurate, photo-realistic models can aid in preserving material or providing detail that is not evident to the naked eye. Furthermore, photogrammetry works best with material that is detailed, with rough, complex and non-reflective surfaces and is therefore well suited for digitally archiving artefacts made from wood, stone, bone, shell and clay – the common material types archaeologists tend to deal with. Additionally, as digital cameras have become a standard piece of equipment included in fieldwork trips for site recordings and artefact photography, little additional preparation or gear is required to capture data for photogrammetry model-making, as your primary piece of equipment will already be packed.

Photographs have been increasingly relied upon to record archaeological material and sites since their invention. Their photo-realistic nature enables easy interpretations by all observers and capturing image data provides the opportunity for future researchers to develop their own interpretations and evaluations of material. Photographs still present a variety of limitations that must also be considered, however. Images often provide restricted views or perspectives of specimens and frequently have limitations in their resolution, particularly when looking at older documentation. Photogrammetry, on the other hand, extends the qualities of individual 2D photographs by providing observers with a 3D view of an object. Good-quality and accurate models can serve as reliable substitutes for the original for some specific purposes. The interactive nature of digital models allows the viewer to rotate a model in any direction at any distance with close-up inspections of the surface being possible, rendering the model as an effective simulacrum. The nature of photogrammetry allows for the images taken to be wrapped around the three-dimensional model so that the texture and surface variation are captured and presented on the model. Conveniently, these wrapped images can also be switched off, meaning the model's topography can be inspected in a single tone, wireframe, or as a coloured mesh, showing fine fluctuations in the surface. Adding even greater depth to possible analysis, photogrammetry allows measurements to be obtained from models. An accurately generated model will be a 1:1 scale replica of the original specimen, therefore allowing software to provide precise measurements between points, calculate the surface area of an object or a subsection, determine the volume, or calculate geometric morphometric analyses of the object's shape.

There is an unreasonable generalisation, held by some who consider digital models to be a poor representation of the original specimen, that data obtained from a model will automatically be inferior or less accurate than data obtained from the real object. There are a variety of tests, measurements and observations that in fact will be more accurately recorded (and can only be obtained) from a digital model, for example, the dimension of an angle at a junction of surfaces in a cross-section. The limitations of digital models differ from those of the original specimens, so naturally, the opportunities they present are also different – this is why models are such valuable sources of data. There are going to be instances when the original specimen is more valuable; however, for some questions the digital representations may be preferred. Digital models provide new and different opportunities for greater access, display and data extraction compared to the originals. Therefore, as archaeological simulacra, digital models will and do facilitate the development of an expanded field of archaeological questions and interpretations.

An additional characteristic of photogrammetry is the fact that it allows repeatability of analysis. A common problem associated with some traditional methods of examination used in the fields of archaeology is the repeatability of methods to obtain data. When using calipers to measure a specimen or its features, or drawing an object, the results will vary depending on the researcher, their level of skill, and also when the data was obtained. The possibility of deterioration of organic or fragile material means measurements may differ each time it is observed.

In contrast, photogrammetry models are unaffected by time. Models that contain highly accurate three-dimensional and topographic information have the capacity to be reanalysed using identical methods at any point in the future to answer questions or test theories not yet even proposed. This quality means we are able to "future-proof" our archaeological material. In the event that accessibility to a specimen is lost, having a data-rich model that is easily stored and delivered means our investigations can to some degree continue.

The focus in this manual on photogrammetry as a method of generating digital 3D models is born from four convenient facts:

1. almost everyone owns or has access to a camera, even if it is a component of their smartphone or tablet device
2. photography equipment is relatively portable compared to other 3D modelling and scanning equipment
3. photogrammetry is inexpensive compared to other alternative scanning technologies
4. photogrammetry produces a photo-realistic model that can be studied.

With enough skill, knowledge, and a suitable photography setup, anyone can create a photogrammetry model that matches one generated in a more expensive and less portable scanning process. An additional convenient characteristic of photogrammetry is that the two stages of creating a model – capturing and processing – can be conducted at different times and in different places, and even by different people. Data can be captured anywhere across the globe using only a single camera, in a remote location in the field, in a museum or in a lab and then processed into a model in the convenience of your own office or home.

The main concern in practice, however, is that the quality of a photogrammetry model, like the quality of a photograph, is dependent on a large variety of choices regarding procedure. There are choices you have to make when you set up your camera, create a shooting environment, plan the shooting workflow and the camera positions, as well as when selecting the settings to process your models. All these choices affect the success and accuracy of your digital model products. These choices are the subject of this book. This manual will guide you, with helpful photographs and diagrams, through all the considerations you need to progress through the stages of photogrammetry to successfully capture and create a digital 3D model.

1.2 Structure of the book

This book is structured as a manual, with the goal of providing you with the skills that will enable you to begin making photogrammetry models. There is no expectation for you, the reader, to possess any prior understanding of photogrammetry or photography; therefore, a range of concepts and equipment will be introduced to you progressively, as well as photographic and software procedures. Through these chapters, information is provided to help you develop and improve your photography skills, instruct you on how to set up the equipment you might need to take high-resolution photographs, how to edit images, build models, and how to fix issues with the models created. Followed in sequence, these chapters will give you a broad familiarity with the process of photogrammetry, but additionally, each chapter can be used as a reference for specific tasks and problem-solving.

This journey starts in the next chapter, Chapter 2, by explaining the fundamental concepts of photography and how to set up your camera correctly to shoot for photogrammetry. Of course, everyone knows how to take photographs, but taking photographs for the purposes of photogrammetry is a more specialised skill that must be understood to build successful models. In this chapter, instructions on how to monitor the quality of your images to ensure model success are provided, as well as a discussion on the physical limitations of photogrammetry. Chapter 3 progresses to the types of equipment required in the photogrammetry setup and what optional items are useful to improve image quality. With an understanding of the type of equipment used for capturing images for photogrammetry modelling, we can then progress to Chapter 4, where we look at how to set up for shooting in a controlled environment (i.e. indoors using artificial light), how to prepare for shooting in an open shooting environment, how to create your own lightbox, how to position lights, and how to make object mounts. Chapter 4 also outlines how best to take photos when outside in an uncontrolled environment, where you may be relying on the sun for illumination. Chapter 5 covers the procedure of capturing objects for photogrammetry modelling. The necessary steps to conduct before you begin shooting are listed, such as writing an information board, creating a metadata spreadsheet, and setting up your camera to a balanced exposure to suit your particular shooting environment. The order and types of camera positions are then discussed and why they are necessary to correctly capture your objects. This chapter also includes the "golden rules" of photogrammetry. These rules are crucial and must be followed to build successful photogrammetry models. In Chapter 6, the possible methods of editing your images are outlined, how to calibrate the colours of your images, what focus stacking entails and how and when to focus stack your images. A deep dive into processing a model in Agisoft *Metashape* is provided in Chapter 7. Here the stages of creating a model, how to build a batch process, and how to edit and improve the models in *Metashape* are outlined. Chapter 8 presents a range of photogrammetry case studies, showing examples of how different archaeological objects can be modelled in a range of shooting environments. The equipment used and the camera settings for each case study are outlined, along with the final model products and their associated metadata. For beginner photogrammetrists, it is likely that you will run into a range of modelling issues; therefore, several of the most common problems are presented in Chapter 9. For each problem, we discuss what the most likely causes are, how to fix them, and the ways to avoid them in the future. In Chapter 10, we look into a variety of other photogrammetry software currently on the market, both licensed and free open-source. Their current system requirements are presented with a review of their accuracy, processing time and cost, and general pros and cons are compared based on recent published evaluations. A more comprehensive appraisal of the pros and cons of *Metashape* and the open-source program *Meshroom* is also presented in this chapter, followed by an introductory workflow to processing a model in *Meshroom*. Finally, Chapter 11 presents some concluding thoughts on photogrammetry and its use in archaeology and educational outreach.

At the end of this manual a useful "photogrammetry kit" is included to help you improve the success and accuracy of your models. This kit contains two reference guides; the first is a workflow of the steps to set up and shoot an object in a controlled environment, and the second is to guide you through the jobs and associated settings required to process a textured model in *Metashape* at high accuracy. It also includes two scale bars with colour charts, targets of varying sizes to help with model alignment that can be cut out and used in your projects, a "chessboard" pattern to calibrate your lenses (see Chapter 5, Section 5.7), a sheet of white paper to set your white balance (see Section 5.2.2) and a sheet of 18% grey colour to help set your exposure (see Section 5.2.1).

So, grab your camera and let's begin!

Chapter 2

KNOW YOUR CAMERA

2.1 The core elements of taking a great photograph

Creating accurate photogrammetry models requires knowledge of how to capture clear and detailed images. A good photograph is one that is well-lit, with the subject in focus, and filling almost the entire frame. Taking a picture that has enough light depends on having one or more light sources, which can either be artificial, such as studio lights or a camera flash, or natural; that is, the sun. There are also several camera settings that you can adjust to increase how bright an image is. These are:

- shutter speed (the length of exposure time)
- aperture (the size of the hole in the lens that lets in light)
- ISO (the camera sensor's sensitivity to light).

These three settings can all be adjusted to guarantee an image has enough light to capture the detail of a subject.

We also want the object being photographed to be clearly revealed, showing a great deal of detail. Those portions of the object which are clear and detailed are said to be *in focus*. When building a photogrammetric model, the whole subject (or as much as possible) needs to be in focus in the images taken. This can be done by adjusting what is called the *depth of field* (DoF) in the camera's settings. Depth of field refers to the distance between the closest and furthest parts of the object that are in focus. Since you want to have as much of the object in focus as possible, you need to configure your camera settings to give your photograph large depth of field. When only a small section of the subject is in focus; that is called a shallow, or small, depth of field. For the purposes of photogrammetry, this is not desirable. Depth of field is controlled by the aperture of the camera lens and is discussed in greater detail below.

It is also important to familiarise yourself with the settings on your camera and what they mean. Different camera brands and models will arrange the settings differently, and possibly with different icons. In Figure 2.1, we can see the locations of the aperture, ISO, shutter speed, and also the white balance, file size and type, the priority setting and the metering mode of a Canon 80D camera body. All these features will be discussed in this and the following chapters.

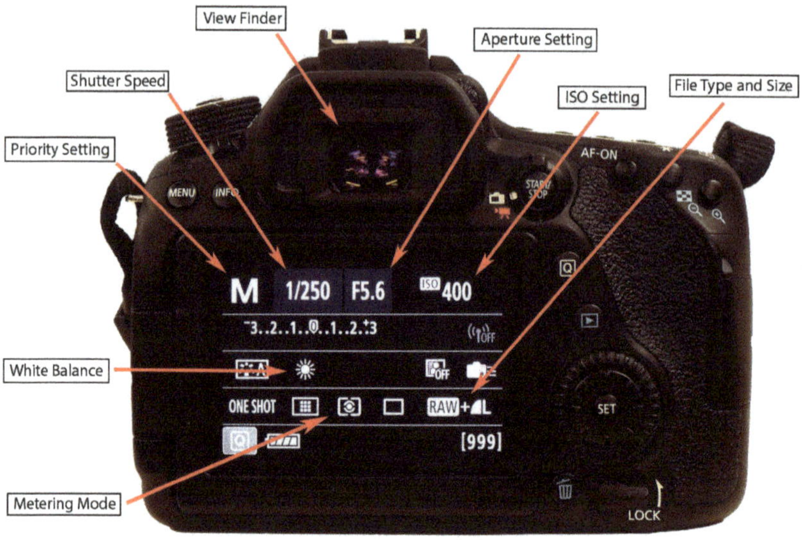

Figure 2.1 Icons and symbols commonly used in digital cameras.

Recognising and understanding the key principles of photography, and how to implement them to take useful photos, improves your skills and the photographs and, by extension, the photogrammetry models they can create. For that reason, we now provide an introduction to the main concepts you will need to understand when shooting for photogrammetry. These principles will help you set up a camera in any environment and take decent-quality images.

2.2 Shutter speed

Shutter speed, or exposure time, is simply the length of time the shutter is open to allow light to pass through and hit the camera's sensor. The sensor detects and "captures" the light funnelled in through the lens, converting the photons into digital signals to be sent to the camera's memory card. Depending on the type of camera you are using (digital single-lens reflex (DSLR), mirrorless, compact or smartphone), the mechanism for this process varies. The concept, however, is universal. Faster shutter speeds (e.g. 1/1000 of a second) allow less light to pass through the lens, creating a darker image, compared to a slower shutter speed (e.g. 1/50 of a second) which generates a brighter image. Every time the shutter speed is doubled (e.g. 1/100 increased to 1/200), the image sensor of the camera loses 50% of its exposure time to light. In photography, this is expressed as losing 1-stop of light. Similarly, slowing the shutter speed by twice as long (e.g. 1/200 slowed to 1/100) doubles the exposure time the sensor has to light, thereby gaining 1-stop. Those settings affect the clarity of the image – when either the camera or the object shakes or moves. That movement can cause what is called *camera blur*, a fuzziness or lack of clarity in the image created. A faster shutter speed not only reduces the brightness of the photograph, it also reduces camera blur; whereas a slower shutter speed will not only increase the brightness of the photograph, it also makes the camera more sensitive to any movement. This means that camera blur is more likely to occur when a slow shutter speed is used, and the blurring can be eliminated by using higher shutter speeds. Figure 2.2 shows the blurring that can occur with slow shutter speeds, compared to the sharpness that is gained with higher shutter speeds, all else being equal.

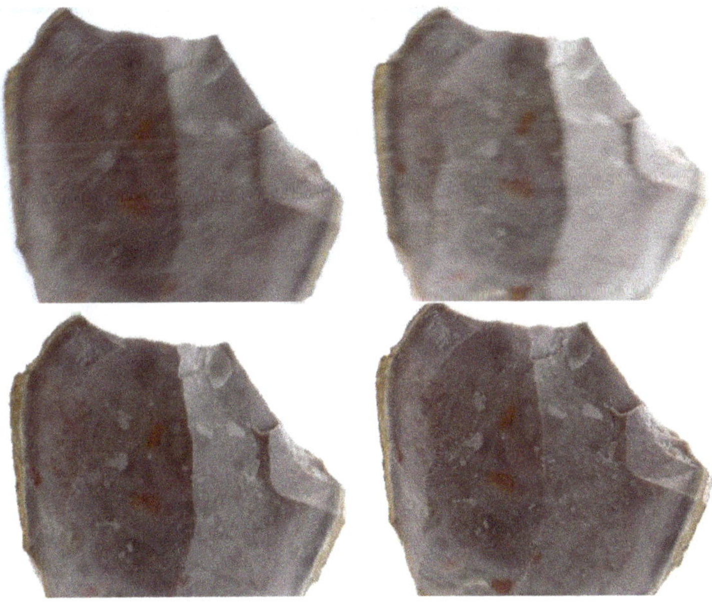

Figure 2.2 Varying shutter speeds of a specimen on a turntable. Top left: 1/4 of a second, top right: 1/25 of a second, bottom left: 1/60 of a second, bottom right: 1/320 of a second. Aperture and ISO have been adjusted to maintain a balanced exposure. Discipline of Archaeology reference collection, the University of Sydney.

2.3 ISO and light sensitivity

ISO stands for the International Organization for Standardization, an international body that standardised the sensitivity to light of film stock, and now applies its rating scale to camera sensors. When the ISO number is higher, the sensitivity of the camera sensor to light is increased. The effect of changing the ISO is similar to altering the shutter speed: doubling the ISO value doubles the light sensitivity by 1-stop of light and inversely if you halve the ISO, the light sensitivity is reduced by 1-stop.

Changing the ISO is an advantage in some situations and a disadvantage in others. An increase in the ISO value gives you the benefit of being able to take photographs in low-light conditions without reducing the shutter speed or widening the aperture. Figure 2.3 shows the effect of altering the ISO values while other conditions are kept constant. However, the cost you pay in increasing the ISO value is that "noise" in your image will increase. Digital noise is electrical interference in a photograph that causes random coloured pixels to appear. Occasionally, pixel changes can appear as coloured streaks called "banding". The result will be that the image can appear less sharp, with spots of colour that are not present on the object itself. Today, there are newer models of digital cameras that sport "low noise" high ISO capabilities; this is perfect for shooting material in an uncontrolled

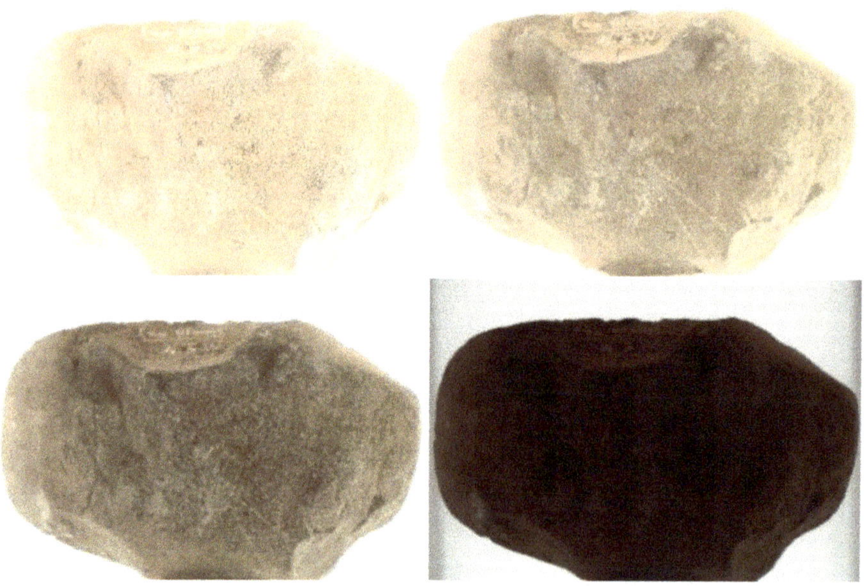

Figure 2.3 Examples of different ISO settings with a fixed aperture of f/4.5 and a shutter speed of 1/250. Top left: ISO set to 1600, top right: 1000, bottom left: 500, bottom right: 100. Private collection, Colin Hornshaw.

environment. This feature, however, may not be available with older camera models so it is important to understand the effects of adjusting the ISO on your camera. To reduce the likelihood of noise, you can use a lower ISO setting and control exposure through adjusting the shutter speed and aperture.

2.4 Aperture

In a camera lens, there is a mechanism called a diaphragm. The diaphragm consists of overlapping metal blades (called the iris) that dilate and contract, adjusting the size of the hole at its centre. This hole in the lens is called the aperture. Much like the pupil of an eye, the size of the aperture controls the amount of light that can pass through the lens, hitting the camera's sensor and affecting the image's brightness. The size of the aperture is described in "f-stops" or "f/" (or occasionally on a camera's LCD screen as simply "f"). The "f" stands for focal length. A low-numbered f-stop, such as f/2.8 or f/3.5, means that the aperture itself is *larger* – and so can let in more light. A higher-numbered f-stop, say f/16–f/32, has a smaller opening, and therefore lets in less light, darkening an image unless you compensate by changing the shutter speed or ISO. The effect of altering the f/ is illustrated in Figure 2.4, which shows images taken with different f-stop values but the same ISO and shutter speed.

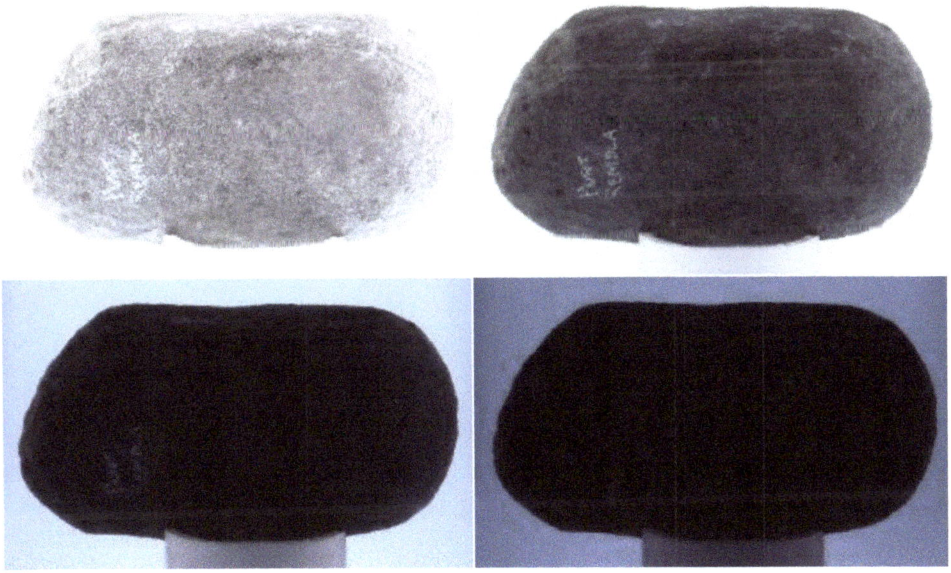

Figure 2.4 Examples of the same image at different apertures. Top left: f/2.8, top right: f/5.6, bottom left: f/10, bottom right: f/16, with ISO 200 and shutter speed of 1/250. Private collection, Colin Hornshaw.

Different lenses have different f-stop values. Common and traditional f-stops are f/1.4, f/2, f/2.8, f/4, f/5.6, f/8, f/11, f/16, f/22. Moving from left to right, from smaller to larger values, the aperture's diameter and consequently the amount of light entering through the lens diminishes. Unlike shutter speed and ISO, stops of light are not calculated by doubling or halving the aperture values, but by multiplying or dividing by 1.41. For example, starting from f/1.4 and moving to the next f-stop, f/2, 1-stop of light is lost because 1.4 x 1.41 is effectively 2. Moving from f/2 to f/2.8 loses another stop as 2 x 1.41 = 2.8 and so on.

While there is a pleasing logic to those traditional f-stop options, you may find yourself using a lens with different options. Newer lenses will likely have a different range of aperture options such as f/3.2, f/3.5 and f/4.5. This is because the diaphragm can contract or expand in fractions of a stop to obtain correct exposure. Hence there are more available ISO and shutter speed settings than just multiples of 1.41.

If you are interested in calculating the diameter of an aperture, simply divide the focal length of the lens being used by the f-stop value set. For example, if a 200 mm lens was being used, and the camera was set to an f-stop of 4, the diameter of the aperture would be 50 mm. Similarly, the f-stop is the focal length divided by the aperture diameter.

Aperture setting is a critical variable in establishing exposure, not only because it affects the brightness of an image but also because it controls the depth of field. Depth of field is particularly important in all photography and plays a special role in photogrammetry.

2.5 Exposure

Exposure is one of the primary concerns when shooting for photogrammetry. Exposure is the amount of light that enters the lens and hits the image sensor. An overexposed image is one that is too bright; that is, too much light has hit the sensor when the photo was taken. Conversely, an underexposed image has too little light hitting the sensor, resulting in darker images.

The image's brightness is controlled by the principle of the "exposure triangle" (see Figure 2.5). The exposure triangle involves the relationships between a camera's shutter speed, ISO and aperture. Together these three factors control how bright an image is.

Increasing the camera's shutter speed will decrease the image's brightness if the ISO and aperture are kept the same. If you decrease the f/ value (i.e. increase the size of the aperture), however, while increasing the shutter speed, you can balance

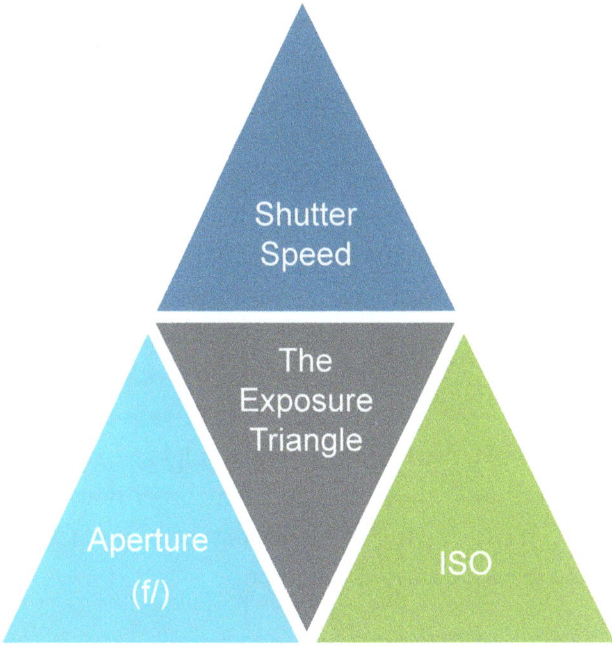

Figure 2.5 The exposure triangle.

out the light lost from the faster shutter speed and achieve a well-balanced image. In another example, if a well-exposed image has camera settings of 1/80 shutter speed, ISO 400, and an aperture value of f/9 and the camera's f/ value was adjusted to f/14, the image will appear darker. By increasing the ISO to 800, however, the image's brightness will be restored and produce a more balanced exposure. If the image becomes too bright, instead of lowering the ISO again, another option would be to increase the shutter speed to 1/100, reducing the amount of light entering the lens. This is how the three relate to one another – adjusting one may require readjusting another to compensate for the change in brightness.

When shooting for photogrammetry, the aperture setting will often be the priority as that controls the image's depth of field (2.6); therefore, normally it is the other two settings that will be adjusted to maintain correct exposure.

2.6 Depth of field

The depth of field, also known as depth of focus, describes how much of what is being photographed is in focus. Sharp images are particularly important for photographs used in photogrammetry modelling. That imperative means you will want to maximise depth of field to make as much of the object in focus as possible.

Depth of field is dependent on three factors: aperture, focal length, and the subject's distance from the camera lens. Lower f-stops provide larger apertures, resulting in a shallow depth of field. With those settings, at least part of the subject is sharp and in focus, but the rest of the image such as the foreground and background will be out of focus and hence blurry. A higher f-stop, representing a smaller aperture, allows more of an object to be in focus, so a greater amount of the subject, the foreground and background will be sharp in the image. The difference is illustrated in Figure 2.6, which shows the same image with two different f-stop settings with all other settings constant.

The sharpness of an image will be influenced by other factors as well, such as the image resolution (2.7) of the camera, but the f-stop can be readily altered to give greater depth of field. All else being equal, higher f-stops are advantageous for the higher depth of field they offer, but remember that choice comes at the cost of lower light. Hence moving to higher f-stops is best achieved with special lighting conditions, as we discuss in Chapter 3.

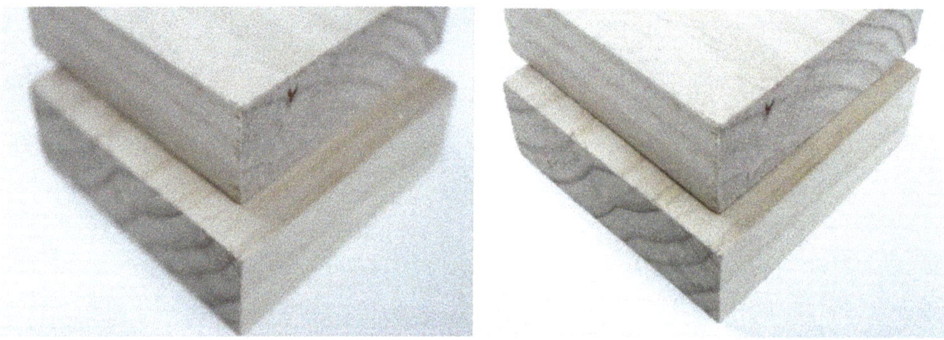

Figure 2.6 Differences in depth of field. The left image has an f/2.8, ISO 500, shutter speed 1/100; the right is f/22, ISO 1600 and a shutter speed of 1/100. Notice the differences in sharpness between the left and right and how much sharper the lower block is in the second image.

Lenses are conventionally divided into a number of categories, such as standard, macro, wide angle or fish-eye. In general, only the characteristics of standard and macro lenses suit the needs of photogrammetry. A macro lens has the ability to produce close-up images with impressive detail, but they typically have a shallow depth of field, regardless of the aperture chosen. The result is they may have only a small portion of the subject in focus. A true macro lens has a magnification of at least 1:1 (meaning that the image is "life-size"; this is further discussed in Chapter 3). This higher ratio (compared to a standard lens) results in the depth of field being smaller, regardless of the aperture chosen – the visual differences between an aperture of f/22 and f/32 are imperceptible for some macro lenses. This is important to keep in mind when shooting small objects and when choosing a macro lens to use for photogrammetry.

2.7 Image resolution

Resolution describes the amount of detail in an image. In photography, resolution is measured in pixels per inch (PPI). A high-resolution image has more pixels than a low-resolution image. The more pixels, the more the image will be crisp and detailed. Resolution is important in photogrammetry as we want as much information as possible to recreate an object or scene accurately in digital space. Resolution is affected by the file format set on your camera. RAW file formats preserve the most image detail, followed by the Fine JPEG file format setting. These formats will, however, produce larger file sizes – a trade-off that is necessary for our purposes in photogrammetry. Some cameras may also offer Normal and Basic JPEG file formats, TIFF formats, and possibly even a range of large, medium and small RAW file formats, whereas some do not offer a choice to change the file format at all, and the images will be captured in RAW or JPEG only. Take note that most camera manufacturers have their own RAW file format with a unique name, such as Canon's CR2 and CRW formats, and Nikon's NEF and NRW. It is therefore recommended to explore the capabilities of your camera so you can capture the best possible images for photogrammetry modelling. For more information regarding selecting the right file format for photogrammetry shooting, see Chapter 5.

2.8 Focal length

The focal length of a lens (measured in mm) is the distance between the optical centre within the lens (i.e. the point of light convergence) and the image sensor when the subject is in focus. Focal length indicates the angle of view and the magnification (see Figure 2.7). It tells us how much of the subject will be captured (angle of view) and how large the objects in the frame will be (magnification). Long focal lengths have a narrower angle of view and higher magnification; conversely, shorter focal lengths have a wider angle of view and lower magnification. Focal lengths are the primary criteria of what distinguishes one lens type from another.

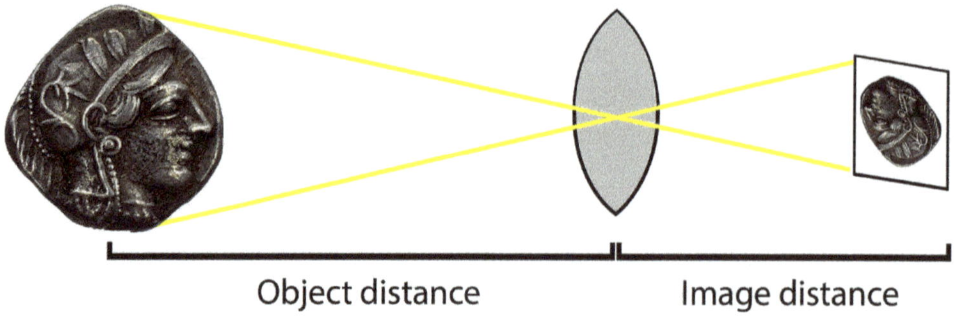

Figure 2.7 Illustration of a lens' focal length. NM2004.655, Nicholson Collection, Chau Chak Wing Museum, the University of Sydney.

2.9 Minimum focusing distance

Minimum focusing distance describes the shortest distance the lens can be from an object when the image is still in focus. When choosing a lens for shooting small objects in a lightbox, this is important to understand as you have limited space to move; therefore a lens with a small focusing distance is often preferred. Note: there is no specific relationship between the focal lengths of a lens and the minimum focusing distance; hence different lenses with the same focal length can have very different minimum focusing distances.

2.10 Field of view

Field of view, or angle of view, is the area that can be perceived through a camera's lens. The field of view depends on the lens type and focal length; that is, a 24 mm wide angle lens will have a much wider field of view compared to that of a standard 50 mm prime (non-zooming) lens. The smaller the focal length, the wider the angle of view (when a sensor of the same size is used); conversely, the larger the focal length the narrower the field of view.

2.11 Focal plane

The focal plane is the point of sharpest focus in an image. The focal plane stretches horizontally across the image and anything situated on this invisible plane is in perfect focus. Objects that are in front of or behind this plane will be out of focus; however, areas immediately surrounding the focal plane will still appear to us as being in focus. These parts of the image that appear in focus make up the depth of field and, as we already know, this can be very shallow or quite deep depending on the aperture f-stop setting (see Figure 2.8).

Like depth of field, the primary factors involved in determining the location of the focal plane are aperture, focal length, the distance between the subject and the lens, and the distance between the subject and the background and the foreground. When shooting for photogrammetry, the focal plane must remain on the subject to keep it in focus, while increasing the depth of field will allow more of the specimen to be sharp. This will improve alignment and meshing accuracy, and the overall aesthetic of the model.

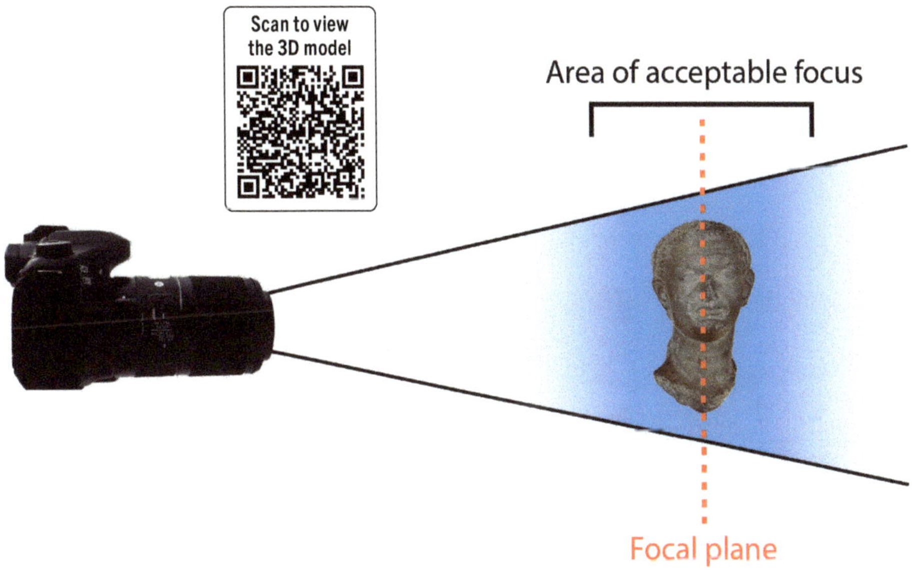

Figure 2.8 Illustrated focal plane of a camera lens. NM64.325, Nicholson Collection, Chau Chak Wing Museum, the University of Sydney.

2.12 White balance

When shooting in different lighting conditions, for example outside in the sun or shade, inside under fluorescent lights or under candlelight, the colour of light will be different. White may not appear white; it may be warmer (more yellow/red) or cooler (more blue). Variation in the colour of light is referred to as the "temperature" of colour or light and is measured in degrees Kelvin (K). If you are building your own photogrammetry setup, it is best to have a light source at a colour temperature of 5700 K, as this is the most "white" light in the spectrum. Controlling your lighting environment may not be possible, however, and the time of day or year, presence or absence of cloud cover and type of artificial light will all result in different colour temperatures in your images. It is therefore essential to know what the white balance (WB) is and how to adjust it on your digital camera to correct for these variations.

White balance is simply a colour-filtering setting to balance the colour temperature in the shooting environment. By adjusting the white balance of an image, the colour cast can be corrected to reflect the true colours within an image. The white balance can be set in your digital camera by selecting your shooting conditions (daylight (~5700 K), shade (~7000 K), cloudy (~6000 K), tungsten (~3200 K), white fluorescent (~4000 K) before shooting. Figure 2.9 shows the effects of using some of these choices on an image. If you are unsure of your conditions, the white balance can be automatically set by selecting the auto white balance (AWB) setting. It is recommended that the white balance of your camera is custom set to obtain the right white balance as this helps to achieve the correct colours for your model. Setting the white balance is outlined in Chapter 5.

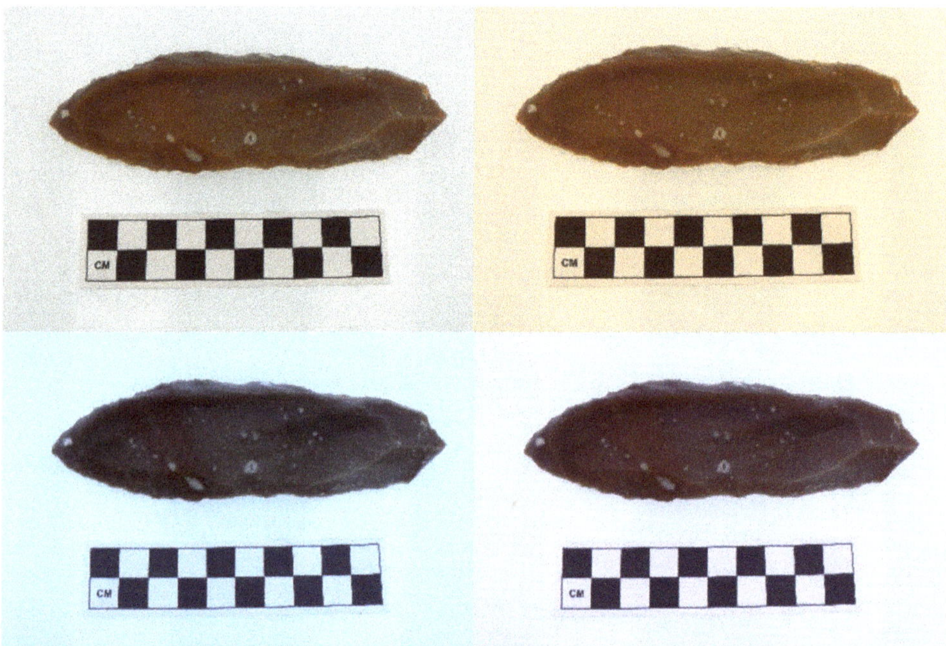

Figure 2.9 Various white balance colour casts. Top left: daylight (~5700 K), top right: shade (~7000 K), bottom left: tungsten light (~3200 K), bottom right: white fluorescent light (~4000 K). Discipline of Archaeology reference collection, the University of Sydney.

2.13 Autofocus and manual focus

Images can be taken using the autofocus function (AF) or the manual focus (MF) function. The autofocus setting means the camera will focus on the subject for you. The autofocus system relies on a sensor on the camera that will focus on a subject depending on variables such as contrast, light, motion and the subject's location; however, these variables will depend on the model of the camera and the type of sensor it possesses. Autofocus can be an incredibly fast and efficient method of capturing images. This is particularly useful for photogrammetry shooting where we try to photograph quickly. In insufficient light conditions, however, the camera can take considerable time "hunting" for something to focus on.

Manual focus means that you, the photographer, have to manually adjust the focus of the lens. This can be achieved in various ways depending on the camera model, but it is most commonly adjusted by twisting the focus ring on the lens. For photogrammetry shooting there may be occasions, such as when shooting small objects like microliths or beads, where manual focus is essential to capture the correct shots; however, for larger objects either way is acceptable. The AF and MF settings are either found on the camera body, the lens, or in the menu of the digital camera.

2.14 Camera shake

Camera shake, camera blur or motion blur occurs when the camera moves while photographs are being taken causing images to appear blurry and out of focus. It is a particular problem that occurs with slower shutter speeds. This is why tripods or monopods (single staff) are important in photography. Using a tripod will prevent camera shake in all but the most extreme conditions. If you are holding the camera in your hand (freehand shooting), the shutter speed must be fast enough to avoid camera shake. A good rule of thumb to avoid camera shake is to set the shutter speed to a figure greater than the inverse of the focal length of the lens being used. For example, if you are using a 50 mm macro lens, the minimum shutter speed should be 1/50 of a second or faster.

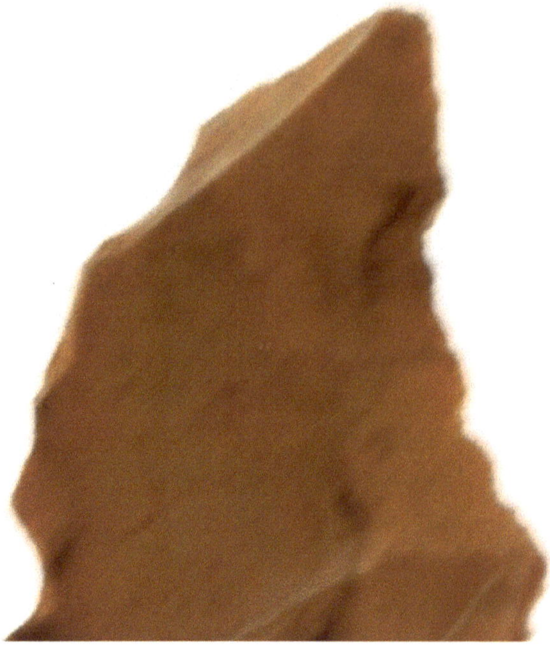

Figure 2.10 Example of camera blur. Discipline of Archaeology reference collection, the University of Sydney.

2.15 Monitoring image and model quality

Ask yourself as you are capturing images: "Are these good photographs?" It is not a difficult task to determine whether an image is good or bad and it is good practice to check on the images after each round of shooting is completed to monitor the quality. Identifying the quality of an image can be brought down to four categories: focus, exposure, frame-fill and colour.

When assessing the focus or sharpness of the image, ask:

- Is the image clear and sharp?
- What is in focus?
- Is enough of the subject in focus?
- Does the shutter speed need to be increased?
- Does the depth of field need to be increased – should the aperture be adjusted?

When looking at the brightness of the image, ask:

- Is the image overexposed or underexposed?
- Does the ISO need to be adjusted?
- Should the shutter speed be adjusted?
- Is the camera focusing on a section that is too dark or too bright, affecting the overall exposure?

When looking at the content in an image, ask:

- Is the subject filling the entire frame?
- Should the lens be closer or further away from the subject?
- Is the correct lens being used? Should a macro lens or a different lens be used?

When assessing the colour of the image, ask the following:

- Has the white balance been correctly set?
- Are the colours correct or is a colour correcting chart needed?
- Is the detail coming out or does the light need to be adjusted?
- Is there too much reflection off the subject's surface?
- Do the lights need to be dampened?
- Is a flash required to gain more detail from the surface of the subject?
- Is the appropriate background colour being used, considering the shade of the subject?

These questions will help you as the photographer understand how to improve image quality and consequently a better model will be produced. Colour and exposure of an image can be modified in image editing software, such as Adobe's *Creative Cloud*; however, it is better practice to monitor and capture decent photos to speed up the model-making process.

These questions above can also be asked of the photogrammetry model once it has been rendered. Evaluating whether the final product has sharp, clear texture, the right colour caste and brightness is another way of determining whether the model has been created successfully.

2.16 Limitations in photogrammetry

A camera is a passive sensor (i.e. the camera detects the reflected light from an object's surface); therefore the primary issues faced in photogrammetry are caused by the refraction, distortion or absence of light. If there is a significant amount of light bouncing off an object causing the surface to be distorted or even hidden by the light, photographs taken will capture the reflected light and not the true surface complexity. This is an issue as the photogrammetry software processing the model will not reconstruct the surface accurately. It may distort the surface of the model (made up of small triangles called the mesh layer) or create small unattached fragments of mesh in the model called "artefacts" (a somewhat unfortunate term for archaeologists). Similarly, issues will arise if there is insufficient light in the shooting environment. If the camera cannot clearly detect the surface detail due to the object being underlit, it will not be rendered in the 3D model and inaccuracies may occur in the model's morphology.

Objects being photographed for photogrammetry must be well-lit, ideally with even, dampened light, so photographs clearly exhibit the surface detail and morphology of the object. There are several ways to improve the quality of images of a specimen when lighting is an issue, such as including additional light sources in the photography setup, changing the intensity and direction of the light, adjusting the camera settings to balance the exposure, or positioning the object in a lightbox where the lighting and intensity can be controlled.

Materials that are not ideal for photogrammetry modelling include highly reflective or glossy objects, or ones that are transparent or translucent. Objects made of glass, or glassy stones such as clear quartz or obsidian, pose a problem to photogrammetrists as photographs will capture detail or structure that is *within* the object and not the actual surface. This will result in the photogrammetry software rendering the interior features onto the surface of the model instead, possibly even distorting the morphology of the model too. Featureless, very smooth surfaces or objects that are consistently one colour with no other details (i.e. something made of plastic) are also problematic as there is insufficient surface detail that can be detected in the images. The most successful models are made of materials that are rough in texture, have significant detail, and are unreflective. Such materials include stone, cement, textured fabric and wood.

2.17 Next steps

Having a basic understanding of the principles of photography will help produce suitable images for photogrammetry models. The most important rule to remember is the exposure triangle: the relationship between a camera's shutter speed, aperture and ISO settings. Knowing how these interactions work and how they can affect the image's depth of field is essential to correctly setting up a camera.

Although image quality can be manipulated by adjusting the camera's settings, the photography equipment will affect the image quality as well. In the next chapter, we discuss the equipment required to shoot objects for photogrammetry models. The photogrammetry tool kit can include a variety of different pieces of equipment and is flexible depending on your budget. A range of camera types can be used, and the following chapter discusses the positives and negatives of each type, with an introduction to the relationship between sensor size, pixel size and image resolution. An overview of lenses and lens accessories is also provided, with a discussion on what focal lengths are and which are the most suitable for capturing objects of different sizes. This chapter also covers additional equipment needed in close-range object-based photogrammetry, such as lightboxes and other light sources, the importance of background sheets and their colour, tripods, monopods and turntables. Additionally, the chapter provides the necessary information for you to understand how each piece of equipment works as this will help you capture better images which will, in turn, create more successful and accurate photogrammetry models.

Chapter 3

EQUIPMENT

The main piece of equipment needed for photogrammetry shooting is, unsurprisingly, a digital camera. Camera types range in price and usability but for photogrammetry, it is necessary to use a camera that has adjustable settings. There are many different camera options that can be utilised; DSLR, mirrorless, compact, action and smartphone can all be used to create photogrammetry models. Below, each of these camera types is discussed along with some directions on how to get the most out of the camera you have on hand for shooting for photogrammetry (3.1).

What is also necessary to understand for photogrammetry modelling is lenses. In this chapter (3.2), we discuss the different types of lenses and how to determine which lens is the most appropriate for your own projects based on their dimensions. We then list a variety of lens accessories that can be very helpful for shooting small artefacts.

Aside from camera gear, there is a range of other pieces of equipment that you can include in your photogrammetry tool kit. In Section 3.3, we discuss a number of different items that will improve your shooting workflow; from lightboxes through to camera rails, there is a variety of gear that you might find useful to improve the speed of capturing your images, as well as the quality of your models.

It is not vital to have the best or most expensive pieces of equipment to create accurate photogrammetry models. One of the benefits of shooting for photogrammetry is that it can be successfully conducted on either a small or larger budget. Fortunately, there are many options available today that can fit a variety of budgets. If you are in a tight squeeze, you can make your own inexpensive supplementary equipment; guidance on this has also been included in this chapter. Familiarising yourself with your photography equipment will improve the quality of the models generated and the pace at which you work – it is better to understand how best to use the equipment you have on hand than to purchase expensive gear and not know how to use it properly.

3.1 Camera types

The ideal camera to use for good-quality photogrammetry models is one that permits manual control of settings, allows for interchangeable lenses and can shoot in RAW format. Such cameras are DSLR or mirrorless digital cameras. The choice of camera body type, however, may be dependent on financial constraints or the photographer's proficiency and understanding of photography. DSLR and mirrorless cameras are further identified by the size of their sensors; that is, full-frame or cropped. Full-frame cameras have a light sensor the size of the standard 35 mm film frame (24 x 36 mm) and will produce the highest quality photographs; however, they, and their corresponding lenses, are more expensive. Cropped-sensor cameras have sensors that are smaller than the full-frame 35 mm. These include the APS-C or APS-H (Advanced Photo System type – C and H, respectively) cameras, the Four Thirds (4/3) standard and Micro Four Thirds cameras. Cropped-sensor cameras are very reliable and a favourable alternative to a full-frame at a reduced cost.

All the major camera brands, Canon, Nikon, Panasonic, Sony, Fujifilm, Leica and Pentax, produce exceptional ranges of camera types – most offer full-frame, cropped-sensor, DSLR and mirrorless models that can be used for successful photogrammetry modelling at a range of prices. If you want to purchase a camera, shop around and compare costs, quality and specs from several brands. There are some brands (e.g. Leica) that are considerably pricier than others. This can be due to the quality of their mechanisms and superior materials; however, there may be equivalent alternatives available from other brands with similar specs with a lower price tag.

3.1.1 DSLR and mirrorless cameras

Both DSLR and mirrorless cameras are suitable for photogrammetry shooting, despite ongoing debates regarding which is better. Both allow for manual control over settings and for interchangeable lenses, which is key. Without digressing into the variations of camera mechanics, the primary difference between DSLR and mirrorless cameras is that light entering the lens of a DSLR bounces off a mirror and through a glass prism (hence its name "digital single-lens reflex") to the optical viewfinder. What you see when you look through a viewfinder in a DSLR is what the lens is seeing (although cropped to some degree). In a mirrorless camera, however, light entering the lens hits straight onto the image sensor. Digital previews are sent to the LCD screen on the back of the camera and, unlike the DSLRs, what you see in the viewfinder is electronically created and therefore given the name electronic viewfinder (EVF). Alternatives to DSLRs and mirrorless cameras are compact cameras, smartphone cameras and action cameras.

3.1.2 Compact cameras

Compact or "point-and-shoot" cameras can be a cheaper and lighter alternative to DSLR and mirrorless cameras, and there are some models on the market that can take excellent photographs. Without the option of having interchangeable lenses and usually a limited aperture and ISO range, however, compact digital cameras are not the most ideal choice for object-based photogrammetry. The macro setting on a compact camera cannot match the quality or capabilities of a dedicated macro lens and will generally have a maximum magnification of 1:2 (see 3.2). The sensors on compact cameras are also smaller, meaning that image quality will not be at a similar standard. Compact cameras also tend to have less sophisticated software compared to a DSLR or mirrorless camera (except for high-end brands, which also come with a higher price tag). It is possible to purchase decent compact cameras that will certainly create useful models of larger objects or sites, but if you believe that photogrammetry will be a practice that you or your institution will employ frequently, it might be an idea to invest in a good-quality camera body and a variety of appropriate lenses.

3.1.3 Smartphone cameras

Smartphone photogrammetry (SPP) is a popular method of generating photogrammetry models from apps that run on smartphone and tablet devices. The popularity of smartphone photogrammetry is rapidly growing due to its ease of use, speed of model generation, and accessibility on handheld devices. This technology can be a powerful tool for archaeologists during fieldwork if you want to create fast, approximate models of an object or terrestrial feature found in situ. It is also useful for photogrammetry beginners to explore these apps to familiarise themselves with the SfM (Structure from Motion) process and the method of data acquisition. For analysis purposes, however, it is recommended that DSLR or mirrorless cameras are prioritised over smartphones or tablets for image capture. Despite smartphone camera technology rapidly improving, there are still a number of drawbacks that users should be aware of. Depending on the smartphone model or brand, manipulation over certain camera settings such as aperture, ISO, shutter speed, white balance or metering may be limited or not possible. They also have fixed focal length lenses that are not interchangeable. Additionally, the lenses may not have the minimum focusing distance required for macro shooting, which is necessary for close-range object modelling. Depending on the make and model, the resolution of the images may also not be at the standard that full-frame or cropped-sensor DSLR and mirrorless cameras have due to the sensor size in smartphone cameras. It is these factors that can affect the accuracy, success and overall appearance of the photogrammetry models produced. Due to their popularity and the frequency with which smartphone devices are used for photography, however, it is likely that future developments in the technology will make them comparable alternatives to other digital cameras. For the moment, for high-resolution and accurate models of archaeological material, DSLRs and mirrorless cameras should be prioritised.

3.1.4 Action cameras

Although action cameras are relatively inexpensive high-definition cameras, they really should not be prioritised as your primary camera for artefact photogrammetry. The reason is that they are simply not designed for it; adjusting the exposure settings is not easy, the cameras are very sensitive to light, they quite often produce photos that have camera shake, and they have wide angle lenses. The only instance in which they are useful is when modelling topography or underwater structures due to their water and pressure resistance and high sensitivity to light. This, however, should not deter you from bringing one into the field as they are useful as a backup camera as they are lightweight and portable. If an action camera is your only option, rest assured that they do allow for different lens attachments, and it is possible to calibrate the camera to eliminate lens distortion caused by the wide angle lens.

Action cameras do have the benefit of being able to capture difficult and hard-to-reach areas (being small and having a wide angle lens). After taking stills of the object you want modelled, it is wise to do a second run using the 4k video function, following the same camera positions and path used in taking the stills. This acts as a backup if you are having reconstruction issues or have missed an area when taking photographs. If you do use an action camera, it is advisable to use a colour rendition chart afterwards to control white balance as action cameras do not have this function.

If the only camera you have access to is either an action, smartphone or compact camera, do not despair, as image editing software, discussed in Chapter 6, can improve the quality of the photographs to some degree, which will improve the overall aesthetic of the model. Prioritise using a DSLR or mirrorless camera if you can, as model quality will drastically improve when they are used correctly. Camera settings and how to shoot for photogrammetry are outlined in Chapter 5.

3.1.5 Pixel size, sensor size and resolution

The image sensor is fundamentally the core element of the camera that determines the quality of the photographs, the depth of field and light sensitivity range, the image size, and the types of lens that can be attached to the camera. The mechanism of an image sensor is incredibly complex; therefore, a simplified explanation of how they work is provided here. Image sensors are a solid device positioned inside the camera body, towards the back. Sensors are covered in cavities called photosites. These photosites capture photons (light energy) that enter the camera via the lens when the shutter is open. Photosites themselves cannot differentiate between colours; thus each photosite is covered with either a red, green or blue filter to collect light within that specific range of the electromagnetic spectrum. This is called a colour filter array (CFA). Once the photons hit the sensor, the energy is then converted into varying strengths of electrical signals based on the intensity of photons hitting the photosite. The camera's processor interprets the signals and colours, and stitches together the information to form an image. The important thing to note here is that the photosite number is directly related to the pixel number and size of an image. A pixel is created from a combination of red, green and blue photosites, once the information collected from the sensor is converted from analogue to digital values.

When looking at the specs of a digital camera, the first spec listed is most commonly megapixel size. A megapixel (MP) simply means a million pixels, and cameras can range in MP size between 16 MP up to 60 MP in high-end full-frame cameras. It is a common misconception that the MP size of a camera will indicate the quality of the images taken. A high MP count does not automatically mean that the images are of better quality. Image quality depends on two other factors as well as pixel count: the sensor size and technology, and the quality of the lens.

There are several camera sensor sizes available on the market. The most common are full-frame 35 mm 36 x 24 mm sensors, APS-C sensors which range in crop factors between 1.35x, 1.5x and 1.6x depending on the manufacturer, and the Micro Four Thirds that have a 2x crop factor. If a sensor has a relatively higher photosite count, the photosites are smaller to fit on the sensor. Smaller-sized photosites do not pick up light as well as larger ones, which is why having more packed onto a smaller sensor is not going to produce a better image. A sensor that is capturing less light will more likely produce an image that has more noise as well as decrease the image's dynamic range (the range between the maximum and minimum differences in brightness the sensor is capable of). If you have three cameras with the same MP count and sensor technology, but one has a full-frame sensor, one has an APS-C sensor, and the last has a Micro Four Thirds sensor, the largest sensor (the full-frame) has a greater area to capture light and also a larger photosite size compared to the smaller sensors. This is why you should take into consideration the sensor size *and* the MP count of your camera to understand its resolution quality.

The other consideration is sensor technology. There are two primary types of light sensors. There are CMOS (complementary metal-oxide semiconductor) sensors and CCD (charged-couple device) sensors. CCD sensors used to be the primary sensor type used as they produced sharp, less-noisy images. As such, they were and are still utilised in remote sensing scanners, microscopes and barcode readers; however, they have been slowly usurped by CMOS sensors in the field of photography due their superior power efficiency, faster processing time, and lower cost.

There are three varieties of CMOS sensors: basic CMOS, Back Side Illuminated (BSI) CMOS sensors, and stacked CMOS sensors. Basic CMOS sensors are found in low- to mid-range cameras, whereas BSI CMOS sensors are an improved version becoming more common in modern digital cameras. The general components of BSI CMOS sensors are configured differently to basic CMOS sensors: the wiring that delivers information is positioned on the rear of the sensor to allow an increase of light hitting the sensor and the photosites are further forward. This allows for significantly reduced noise in images. Stacked CMOS sensors are a further improvement on the BSI CMOS sensors. While the configuration of the key components is the same, the image signal processor is stacked. This allows for incredible shooting speeds, faster autofocus speeds and subject recognition, with maintained superior standard of low noise in low-light situations. This, unsurprisingly, comes with a considerable price tag, so unless your budget allows it, the BSI CMOS sensors are probably the sensor to aim for. Another consideration to take into account is lenses, as the type, manufacturer and quality chosen will also influence the quality of your images.

3.2 Camera lenses and accessories

The primary purpose of artefact photogrammetry modelling is to correctly capture a specimen's morphology and surface detail to recreate it in digital space for analysis, cataloguing, exhibition or educational purposes. It is therefore important to use the correct lens type for object-based photogrammetry that will capture as much information as possible. To take accurate and highly detailed photographs of artefacts, the ideal lenses are prime macro lenses. Macro lenses allow the shooter to take good-quality photographs of very small objects from a close distance, so the frame is filled by the artefact with no distortion. "Prime" lenses are non-zoom lenses and have a fixed focal length. A prime macro lens with 1:1 magnification is ideal for photogrammetry as the object is life-size on the frame. Most macro lenses have 1:1 (X:Y) magnification where X represents the number of mm on the sensor frame and Y represents the actual object being captured in mm: that is, 1 mm of an artefact's surface takes up 1 mm of the sensor frame (hence "life-size"). Anything less is not considered "true macro" and will not produce as useful images compared to a 1:1 or 5:1 magnification. The reason why prime lenses are preferred over zoom is due to a couple of factors. Firstly, it is important to refrain from changing the focal length during the photographing process as this changes the distortion. Prime macro lenses are also not only more common than zoom macro lenses, but they are usually faster, have a wider aperture and produce sharper images. For these reasons, they are the ideal choice for photogrammetry photography.

What is also necessary is to opt for a lens that has a focus motor. This is particularly important if you want to shoot in auto-focus and your camera body does not have an in-built autofocus function. Lenses without a focus motor are not common, and they are quite tricky to use, especially for photogrammetry shooting. Some very powerful macro lenses on the market do not have an autofocus function (e.g. Canon's incredibly powerful MP-E 65 mm macro lens that has a 1-5x zoom capacity) and are not ideal for fast shooting, particularly if the subject is positioned on a moving turntable. Without the autofocus function, using photogrammetry software that has an automatic shooting function will not work if it cannot focus on the subject. It is very easy to take hundreds of photographs in one photogrammetry shooting session. If you are a novice photogrammetrist and not used to manually focusing the lens for each image, this stage of the process can take a considerably long time and therefore may not be the ideal method. Manual focus is better suited for the photogrammetrist who has grown accustomed to the speed of shooting on a turntable and knows which areas to focus on while the specimen is rotating. When working with smaller artefacts it might be beneficial to use a manual focus setting and and then focus stack your images. Focus stacking can be a useful shooting method for macro photogrammetry (photogrammetry modelling of very small objects) with a high surface complexity, further discussed in Chapter 6.

When purchasing a lens, remember to take note of what mount the lens has. Lenses are designed for either full-frame or cropped sensors, either mirrorless or DSLR bodies, and are typically brand-specific. Lenses rarely possess mounts that are compatible with both sensor types, and an adapter is needed if you want to interchange a lens between a mirrorless and a DSLR camera body. Some brands such as Tokino, Tameron and Sigma, however, offer the same lenses with different brand-specific mounts. So remember to confirm whether the lens you are buying is compatible with your camera body.

It should also be mentioned that a lens filter is an accessory that must be purchased for your lens. Lens filters are attachable discs that screw onto the front of the lens and protect it from dust and dirt, smears and scratches. The size of a lens filter (denoted in mm) is sometimes written on the side of the lens for some brands and, if not, a simple search online will tell you what filter to buy. They are inexpensive and will ensure the longevity of your lens so should be included in every photography tool kit, especially those that go into the field.

3.2.1 What lens to use?

Using the right lens type for photogrammetry photography will make camera positioning easier, decrease the shooting time, and most importantly, improve the quality of the model produced. Lenses come in a variety of sizes so choosing the right one might be a difficult task at first. The millimetre description of a lens, its focal length, refers to the distance from the camera's sensor to the point of light convergence within the lens. It is this that will change how the photograph will look and how big or small the object will appear in the image. Simply put, the shorter the focal length, the wider the field of view. As mentioned before, a macro lens is the most suitable lens for artefact photogrammetry, so this should be your starting point in searching for a lens.

There are several considerations you must think about when choosing a lens for photogrammetry. The first is the size of the artefacts you are shooting. If you are working with artefacts that are all roughly similar sizes, then it will be easier to choose the right lens type. Lens type becomes particularly important if smaller artefacts such as microliths, bone or pottery fragments are being modelled, as difficulty in model processing can increase as subject size decreases. Table 3.1 is a rough guide to what lens is suitable for various artefact sizes.

Table 3.1 Suitable focal lengths for various artefact lengths.

Artefact length (cm)	Appropriate macro lens focal length (mm)
<3 (e.g. microlith, bone or shell fragment)	70–120
3–10 (e.g. retouched flake, shell or pottery sherd or small vessel)	35–70
10–20 (e.g. hand axe, pottery vessel)	35–50
20–50 (e.g. grindstone, pottery vessel)	~35

Artefacts that are less than 3 cm in length can be difficult to accurately model and you will attain greater mesh accuracy by using a lens with a longer focal length such as a 70 mm. How to model an object less than 3 cm is outlined in Chapter 8, where the steps on how to achieve accurate models at this size are detailed using a 90 mm lens with a microlith as an example. The advantage of using a lens with a longer focal length is that the higher magnification and the narrower field of view is perfect for small objects. It is possible to use a wider focal length lens on small objects (an example is a 35 mm macro lens to model a tetradrachm shown in Case study 8.8); however, be aware that detail on the surface may not be captured as accurately or as clearly and it may produce texture that is not as sharp or precise compared to a lens with a longer focal length of 70 or 90 mm, for example.

Artefacts that are between 3 to 10 cm would benefit from a slightly shorter focal length macro lens – between 50 to 70 mm is suitable, although a 35 mm will also do the trick. Larger specimens that are at least 10 cm in length are perfect for a shorter focal length macro lens, around 35 mm. These lenses have a wider angle allowing more of the artefact to fill the frame. Again, lenses with a shorter focal length will also allow you to be closer to the specimen; this is advantageous when working in a lightbox.

For any material that is larger than 20 cm, opt for a short focal length around the 35 mm range; a 50 mm lens is still usable although it may take longer to shoot the object. Ultra-wide or fish-eye lenses should be avoided due to the amount of distortion created, but it is also unnecessary to have such a wide angle lens for artefact photogrammetry. When shooting a site on land or underwater, however, ultra-wide lenses can be used, with distortion corrected in the photogrammetry software. In these cases, it can be useful as more of the topographic or bathymetric information is captured in the images. Having a wider angle will also cut down on the number of images required to photograph the entire area.

If there are a variety of objects that you want modelled, ranging between small specimens to large-scale sites, having a few different suitable lenses is helpful. If you are unable to purchase a variety, having a standard kit lens on hand (the lens that usually comes in the box when a camera body is purchased) and a low- to mid-range (35–50 mm) macro lens is a decent starting point. Opting for a lower to mid-range focal length lens is a safe choice as they can be used to model both larger and smaller artefacts. A great option is Canon's 35 mm macro lens for DSLR (EF-S) or mirrorless (RF) macro lens. These are fast and versatile lenses that can be used to photograph objects less than 10 cm in diameter due to the short minimum focusing distance. It is possible to photograph larger artefacts with a longer focal length, but there are two things to be aware of. The first is that you will likely take more photos to capture the entire subject's surface, and secondly the photographer will have to be further away from the subject to capture the entire subject within the frame (for the wide shots). This becomes problematic if you are shooting in a lightbox, as the lens may have to be a considerable distance outside of the lightbox, thereby increasing the possibility of experiencing light fall-off. Light fall-off is the loss of light intensity over distance, meaning that the images may be susceptible to being underexposed.

To visually exhibit how focal length affects an image, Figure 3.1 shows two images of the same object (a shell adze) being photographed using the same camera body with the tripod positioned at the same distance from the object. The first image was taken using a 35 mm macro lens and the second using a 90 mm macro lens. The first image shows the entire shell's surface on a black background with a scale bar underneath. In the second image, however, all that is in the frame is a fraction of the shell's surface. Due to its longer focal length, the image appears zoomed in compared to the 35 mm lens. These images also show why it is so useful to have a longer focal length lens to model small objects.

Many people will ask, "Why can't we just use a standard lens but set the camera to macro mode?" The simple answer is that a standard zoom lens put on macro mode will not achieve the same results as an actual macro lens as there are physical limitations of the lens that will not allow for true macro photography (1:1 magnification). It also restricts manipulation of the camera settings, meaning the aperture and shutter speed may not be set to the ideal settings. While the "macro mode" feature of a DSLR or mirrorless camera is a nice one to have, it is not effective in producing the necessary photographs needed for photogrammetry.

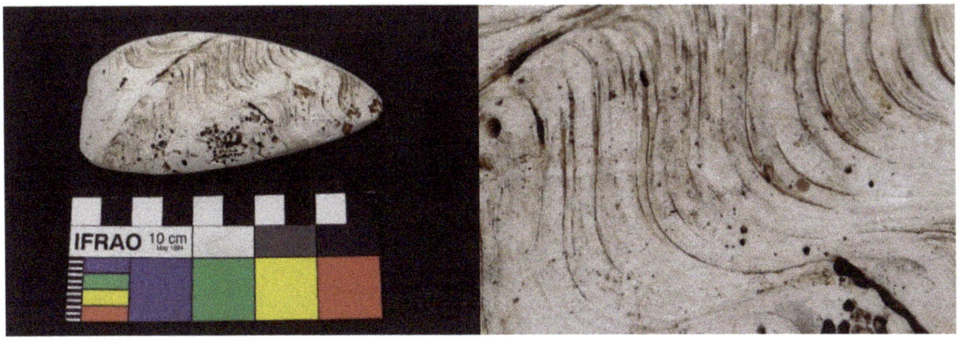

Figure 3.1 Image taken using a 35 mm macro lens (left) compared to one using a 90 mm macro lens (right); both cameras are in the same position. Object from Iatafu Village, West Futuna, Rob N. Williams.

3.2.2 Attaching lenses

When attaching or changing lenses, ensure that the environment is clean and dry, preferably in an indoor setting. This is to reduce the likelihood of dirt or dust entering the camera. If you are changing lenses, it is good practice to lay out your lenses on a flat surface, lens facing down with the lens cap on to allow for a quick exchange of lenses. It is not advisable to put a lens on its side as it will likely roll away from you, off a table or into another object. Never place the lens with the lens mount (the silver part of the lens that attaches to the camera body) facing down if the rear lens dust cap is not on.

To change over a lens, place the camera on its back (where the LED screen is) on a table or something sturdy, press the button next to the lens on the body, grip the lens firmly and twist the lens off moving anticlockwise. Secure the rear lens dust cap on the mount so that both ends are covered and put down, again on a flat surface with the lens pointing down so it doesn't roll away. Take the rear lens dust cap off the other lens, align the coloured marker on the lens mount to the corresponding coloured marker on the camera body, press the button down on the body and place the lens into the camera body. Once it feels that it is in correctly, release the button and twist the lens in a slow clockwise direction. When twisting in the lens, the mechanism should feel smooth. If there is any resistance, take the lens out and check to see if the thread is aligned and the lens is not being forced in at an angle. If it feels like there is a gritty sensation or if there is a grinding sound coming from the lens, dirt or sand may be in the thread so take the lens off and inspect both the body and the lens. If the dirt cannot be removed easily with a microfibre towel or soft-bristle brush, you may need to take the equipment to a camera shop to be properly cleaned.

Just remember you cannot use more than one focal length when shooting an object for photogrammetry modelling. This is because the distortion between lenses varies. Changes in distortion in the photographs will affect the accuracy of the 3D models and the models will not reflect the true three-dimensionality of the object. This is the same reason why you do not want to zoom into an object when photographing it – the distortion for each focal length is different and will alter the true shape of the model. So when you start a shooting session with an object, stick with the same lens until you finish.

There are a number of other pieces of equipment that can be used for macro shooting that can also be utilised for photogrammetry of smaller artefact material. These include teleconverters, extension tubes and bellows, reversing and coupling rings, and close-up lenses.

3.2.3 Teleconverters

If the majority of the specimens you are shooting are larger than 10 cm but you have a few that are smaller than 3 cm, a teleconverter is a handy addition to your photography kit. Teleconverters are useful devices that alter the focal length of the prime lens you are using. They attach between the camera body and the lens and increase the focal length by a specific factor, depending on what type of converter you purchase. Essentially, they act as a magnifying glass; if you are using a 50 mm prime macro lens with a magnification of 1:1, with a 2x converter the focal length is doubled turning the 50 mm lens into a 100 mm lens with a 2:1 magnification. Instead of buying a range of different lenses, a teleconverter is a useful and light alternative to quickly increase your focal length. The disadvantage of using converters is that photographs will have reduced image sharpness, the speed of the lens will be slower and you will lose brightness – around 2 stops of light for a 2x converter and about one stop for a 1.4x converter.

3.2.4 Extension tubes

Extension tubes are devices that fit between the camera body and the lens; however, unlike teleconverters, extension tubes are hollow and do not contain any lens. Extension tubes increase the distance between the lens and the image sensor and as such decrease the minimum focusing distance. This allows you to move much closer to a subject, remain in focus, and obtain a much larger magnification (particularly when using with macro lenses as it can increase the magnification beyond 1:1). The increase in magnification can be determined by dividing the extension distance by the focal length of the lens. For example, a 50 mm standard lens with a 25 mm extension tube will increase the magnification by 0.5x. If the original magnification of the 50 mm lens was 0.21x, the new magnification would be 0.21 + (25/50) = 0.71x.

Extension tubes are also able to be stacked, further increasing the magnification of the original lens. Having a 12 mm and a 25 mm stacked onto a 50 mm standard lens with a native magnification of 0.21x will bring it up to 0.21 + ((12+25)/50) = 0.95, which is almost 1:1 magnification on a standard lens. The disadvantage of using an extension tube is that the photographer is considerably closer to the subject. Being so close may make managing even illumination difficult if the camera is obstructing the light source.

3.2.5 Bellows

Bellows are similar to extension tubes as their function is to increase the distance between the lens and the image sensor. Unlike extension tubes, however, bellows are flexible and can be gradually increased in length, extending past where extension tubes can, which are a fixed size. The magnification can be 1:1 and even beyond life-size; therefore they are frequently used for macro photography. Bellows, however, tend to be more expensive and require a studio setup with a tripod as they are relatively bulky. They are therefore a less prudent choice when shooting in an open environment.

3.2.6 Close-up lenses

Close-up lenses are an easy, cheaper alternative to improving image quality using a standard lens. Close-up photography is not macro photography; it is simply the ability to position the camera closer to the subject to increase the magnification while remaining in focus. Close-up lenses screw onto the filter thread (the front) on the front of a lens to shorten the effective focal length of the lens. This allows the primary lens to focus on subjects close to the lens; that is, they reduce the minimum focusing distance. Being closer to the subject means the sensor will be filled with more of the subject and reduces the amount of negative space. This is very helpful for photographing artefacts for photogrammetry.

Close-up lenses come in a range of magnification powers, known as diopters, which are expressed positively and in metres. The higher the diopter, the greater the magnification, with +1 being a slight increase and +10 being a significant increase.

To work out the maximum magnification from adding a close-up lens, simply multiply the focal length of the primary lens by the diopter value of the close-up lens. For example, coupling a +4 close-up lens onto a 200 mm lens will increase the maximum magnification to 0.8x, as 0.2 x 4 = 0.8. As diopters are expressed in metres, remember when calculating the magnification to convert the focal length to metres. For higher magnification, use a lens that has a longer focal length as this will increase the magnification power of the close-up lens.

3.2.7 Reversing rings

Reversing rings are attachments that screw onto the filter thread (the front) of a lens, allowing the lens to then be attached to the camera body backwards. Mounting the lens backwards increases the magnification; as the glass is now facing towards the camera, the subject is magnified instead of being made smaller. What is interesting is that the shorter the focal length of the lens used, the higher the magnification. This is why wide angle lenses are commonly used with reversing rings. The focusing distance, however, is sacrificed, and you need to move closer to the subject. Although this can be useful for photogrammetry purposes, being closer to the subject may be problematic as the photographer may cast shadows over the object. The other issue with using reversing rings is that the camera body loses its communication with the lens; therefore, autofocus settings such as aperture have to be set manually.

3.2.8 Coupling rings

Coupling rings are similar to reversing rings in that they screw onto the lens being used. With coupling rings, however, another lens can be further attached, face-to-face, to the first lens, creating one very long lens. By so doing, the magnification increases, creating a macro image. The first lens that is attached to the camera body must be the one that has the longer focal length of the two. To calculate the magnification, divide the two focal lengths of the lenses. For example, if the first lens was 100 mm and the second was 18 mm, 100/18 = 5.55x. While this is a very powerful tool, it is not the most ideal setup for photogrammetry shooting for a number of reasons: the magnification will likely be too powerful to produce images useful for photogrammetry purposes, the lens will be so long that manoeuvrability will be awkward and limited, focusing will be difficult, and the length of the lens may obstruct the light from hitting the subject.

3.3 Other photography equipment

3.3.1 Lightboxes

The best setup for artefact shooting includes using a lightbox. A lightbox is exactly as it sounds – it is a large empty container that can be easily flooded with light. Lightboxes can be made from plastic, cardboard or metal. Lightboxes made from lighter fabrics such as nylon or polyester are typically referred to as light tents. Lightboxes have an opening at the front (and occasionally the top) where the camera is positioned, and the subject sits directly inside in the centre of the lightbox surrounded by the ambient light. Some lightboxes that come with either accessory or in-built lights allow for the colour temperature and the intensity to be adjusted. A turntable can also be positioned inside the lightbox to make photographing the subject easier; therefore, some lightbox manufacturers have a turntable built into the lightbox. The benefits of using a lightbox are that they limit shadows and provide a flat, monocolour background – a crucial asset for photogrammetry shooting.

Lightboxes vary in size and design and come in a range of costs – from a cheaper light tent setup under AUD$50 up to the large metal lightboxes with in-built lights, turntable and software that range around the AUD$20,000 mark. The crowdfunded Foldio line from Orangemonkie is a great place to start for photogrammetry professionals and beginners. Portable and lightweight, with in-built LED lights and an app-controlled turntable, these are affordable lightboxes that are really useful for photogrammetry shooting (see Figure 3.2). They come in a range of sizes and are a great investment for any archaeology department for conducting field or lab photogrammetry – all you need is a power source. For a more heavy-duty alternative, you can opt for a rigid lightbox such as the Ortery PhotoBench series (see Figure 3.3). With in-built software that synchronises shooting and turntable controls, automatic background masking, light intensity, direction and temperature, they are more of a professional standard of lightboxes and are useful pieces of equipment. These also come in a range of sizes depending on the dimensions of the artefacts that need to be photographed.

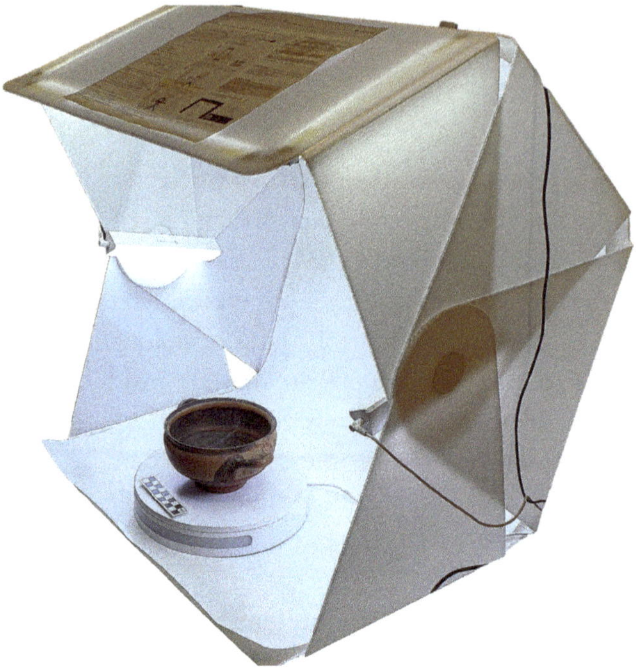

Figure 3.2 The Foldio lightbox and Foldio360 turntable. NM73.3, Nicholson Collection, Chau Chak Wing Museum, the University of Sydney.

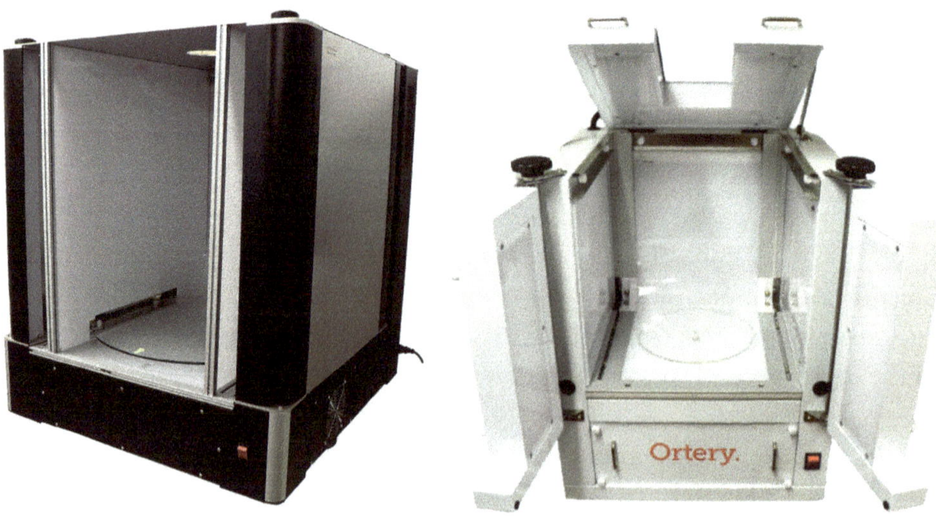

Figure 3.3 The Ortery 3D PhotoBench series, the 260 and 80.

3.3.2 Backgrounds

When shooting in either an open photography setup or a lightbox, it is essential that the background is seamless and has no interruptions or obstructions. This reduces the likelihood of any problems in the alignment stage or any background features being incorporated into the mesh or texture of the model. Having an uninterrupted background also reduces the likelihood that you will need to mask before or during the processing stage. Masking is where the background or other unwanted features are masked out of images so only the object is analysed by the software. This is further discussed in Chapter 7.

Background colour is typically either black or white and the choice is dependent on the colour of the object being modelled. A good guide to follow is artefacts that are light in colour are better captured with a black background and darker artefacts with a white background (Figure 3.4). This is so the photogrammetry software can clearly identify the boundary edges of the object as it rotates so they are not lost in the background. Black backdrops work best when fabric is used, such as muslin or velvet, as the light is absorbed. Black paper or cardboard can be used if that is the only option; however, shiny or glossy paper or plastic are not ideal for black backgrounds as they create reflections which can be captured in the images.

For all darker artefacts, a white background will work; however, you must remember that white backgrounds can introduce shadow as they reflect light as opposed to absorbing it. A white background can also add brightness to the

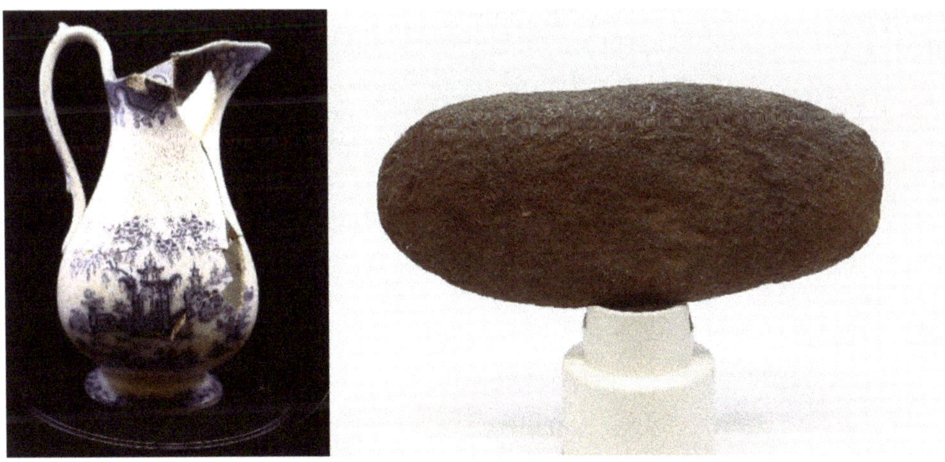

Figure 3.4 Lighter objects should be photographed with a black background (left) and darker ones with a white background (right). Discipline of Archaeology, Regentville collection (right) and reference collection (left), the University of Sydney.

specimen's surface, however, which may be favourable. Choosing the right white material can greatly reduce lighting and shooting issues. Sheets of matte white paper, cardboard, plastic or canvas are ideal.

Coloured backgrounds should be avoided as the colour of the background will bounce onto the specimen giving it the corresponding incorrect colour. This will be captured in the images and create a textured model that is the wrong colour caste. Photogrammetry software will find it difficult to determine what is the background and what is the subject when there are similar shades of the same colour in the background and the specimen and, as a result, it will likely incorporate the background into the model too.

3.3.3 Turntables

Turntables are not a necessity when it comes to shooting artefacts; however, they will make the process smoother and faster. Turntables are rotatable plates that can be either manually or electronically rotated 360° in either direction. As we need to take 360° images around the object, turntables will rotate the artefact for us. Manual turntables will not be as fast as electronic turntables; however, they are still preferable to physically rotating the object after every shot, or the photographer walking around the object taking photographs at every step. There are a variety of electronic turntables on the market that automatically rotate when the switches on the base are turned on. The turntables recommended for photogrammetry purposes are those that are controlled by a smartphone app. These turntables, such as the Foldio360 turntable, created by Orangemonkie, allow the user to manipulate the rotation direction, degrees of rotation and rotational speed, and they have an in-built light source for additional illumination.

3.3.4 Flashes and diffusers

On-camera flashes are separate accessories that are attached to the camera's "hot shoe" (the slot on top of the camera). If you do not have access to a lightbox or the lamps you are using are not providing enough light, an on-camera flash with a diffuser can help enormously in the lab or in the field where there is insufficient light. On-camera flashes are particularly useful for smaller artefacts with finer detail. Fine surface detail must be captured for accurate modelling and illumination is one of the primary ways in which it can be captured correctly. Another alternative to a flash is an LED panel that also slots into the hot shoe. Like a flash, the intensity can be manipulated; however, instead of flashing when the shutter is open, LED panels may be simply "continuous" light – once on, the light is always on.

There is a range of on-camera flash types on the market, but for photogrammetry, a ring flash is preferable. The light source circles the lens (see Figures 3.5 and 3.6) so it is less directional than a panel or gun flash. When setting a flash, it is possible to adjust the intensity of the flash by increasing or decreasing the power by thirds of 1-stop of light. The flash's screen will have a range of modes to choose from, namely E-TTL (evaluative through the lens), Manual and Multi. In E-TTL mode, the recommended mode, the intensity of light can be controlled by thirds of a stop, increasing from 0 to +0.3, +0.7, +1 etc., and decreasing by thirds of a stop, -0.3, -0.7, -1, etc.

If you are unable to obtain the right intensity or the flash is too directional, a diffuser will dampen the flash's intensity effectively. The point of a diffuser is exactly as its name suggests – it diffuses light and limits directional light and by so doing reduces intense shadows and reflection. This is crucial when photographing shiny artefacts – aligning issues may occur due to unwanted reflections on the subject's surface.

There is a variety of diffusers on the market; however, if you are on a budget, they can be made from a range of materials that you are likely to have in a lab, office or classroom. The easiest way to make a DIY diffuser is to tape paper directly over the light source. The types of paper that are effective are baking, wax, tracing or tissue paper. If standard A4 paper is the only paper available, rest assured it

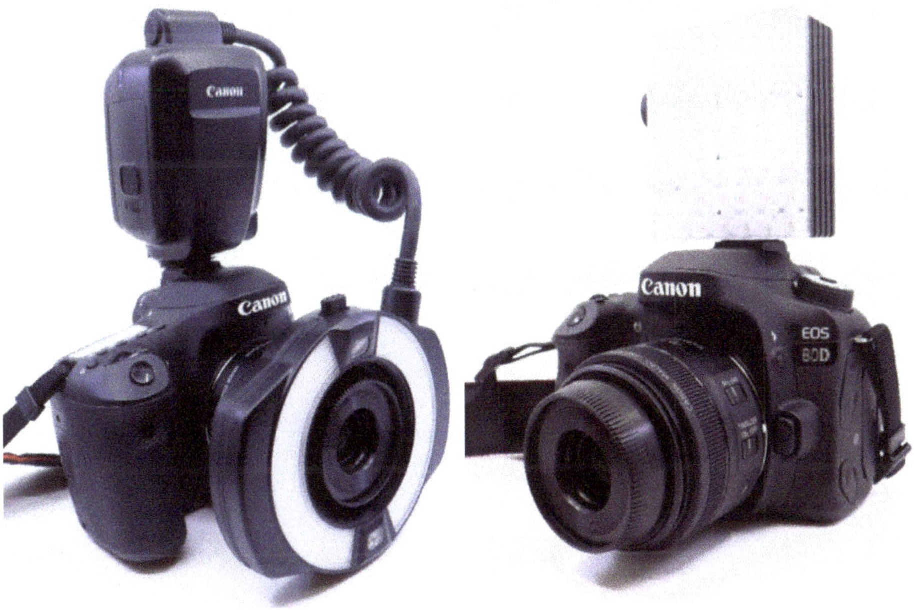

Figure 3.5 Ring flash and LED panel.

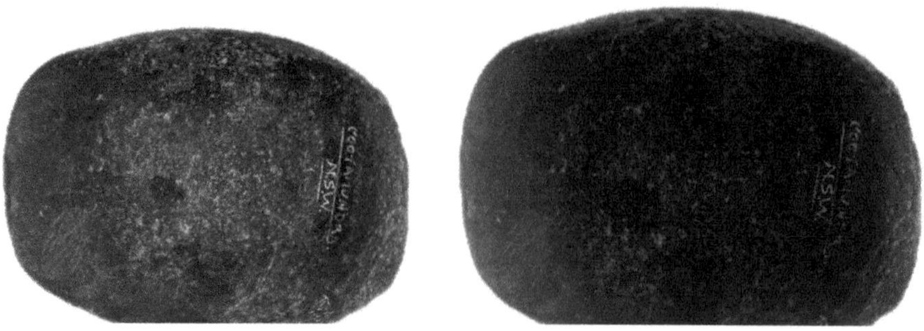

Figure 3.6 Shooting with a ring flash (left) compared to without a ring flash (right). There is significantly more detail in the left image when using a ring flash. Private collection, Colin Hornshaw.

will work; however, it will cut out significantly more light compared to the other types listed here, so you may have to increase the intensity of the flash. Other materials that can work include cut-up shower curtains, white fabric such as rayon or nylon, or simply sticking strips of masking tape over the light. For LED panels or studio lamps, placing a white shower cap over the light source can also act as a great diffuser at a very low cost.

It is rarely advised to use the pop-up in-camera flash as you cannot control the direction or intensity of the flash and so this flash is seldom useful. If you are in desperate need of more light, and the pop-up flash is your only choice, a simple addition to your camera can quickly improve the photographs. A paper tube such as a Pringles tin cut and fitted on top of the flash with paper taped over the opening is a quick and easy way to control the light's direction and dampen the intensity. Pringles tins are preferable over a normal cardboard tube as the interior of the tin is covered in reflective silver paper, which will reflect the light through the tube and not absorb it.

3.3.5 Tripods

A sturdy tripod that has a decent height range and a mobile head is ideal for photogrammetry shooting. Lighter carbon fibre tripods are best for travelling and going into the field as they do not weigh much and typically can fold down into small portable sizes. For photogrammetry conducted inside a lab or studio, heavier studio tripods are a better choice as they reduce the possibility of camera shake, allowing the photographer to work with slower shutter speeds. Be aware that heavy foot traffic around a photography area that does not have a solid floor can contribute to camera shake; this can also be mitigated by a heavier tripod.

Depending on the height of the table on which your lightbox is situated, an ideal tripod has a centre column (the central adjustable pole) with an adjustable height range of at least 20 cm. Depending on the object being captured, the photographer may need a wide range of heights and it is more time-efficient to adjust the central pole than having to readjust each leg every time you change camera position. Therefore it is advised to set the legs at an appropriate height before you commence shooting as this will allow the camera to reach the lowest and highest positions required to completely capture the object being photographed.

Tripod heads come in a range of designs, but the most reliable in terms of ease of adjusting and precise positioning are three-way heads (Figure 3.7). The separate levers are easy to use and allow complete control over each independent axis, with several brands having in-built spirit level bubbles to ensure that images are level. While ball heads are cheaper and do allow good freedom of movement, they are not as accurate nor great for quick minor alterations and can be a bit clumsy during fast shooting. Tripod head design, however, does come down to personal preference and budget.

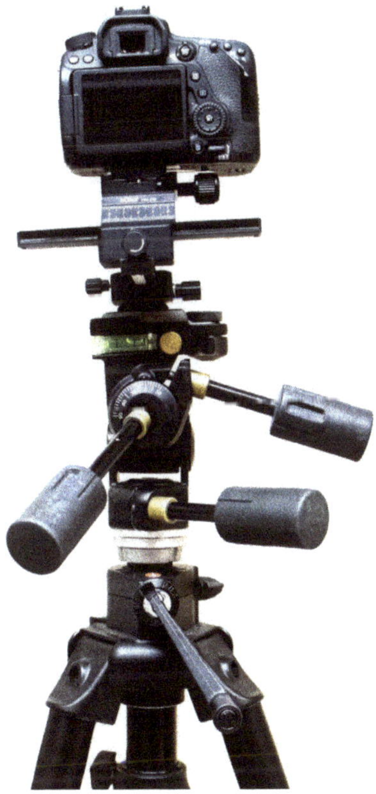

Figure 3.7 Tripod with three-way head and rail.

3.3.6 Monopods

Monopods are a singular pole that the photographer can hold and, like tripods, support the camera on top of a mount. Monopods are a great way of ensuring you have consistently level shots while also taking the weight of the camera. Monopods are light, easy to move, and will rarely get in the way. Monopods, however, are unable to be freestanding so you must hold them at all times. Monopods are best used when taking photos of a topographical site as they allow for easier manoeuvrability compared to tripods. They are extendable and therefore very useful when aerial images are required at a site where drones are not permitted; simply extend the pole out to its maximum length. A shutter release remote will allow you to take shots from a distance (via a Bluetooth or wireless connection or with a cable) or you can utilise the camera's interval timer. If you are using a digital camera with a rotatable LCD screen, you can swivel it to face you or even download the camera manufacturer's app that should allow for live-view shooting on your smartphone, tablet or computer.

3.3.7 Camera rails

The processes involved in photogrammetry shooting for archaeological artefacts require the tripod to be adjusted frequently – not just up and down on the Y axis but on the X and Z axes. For fine adjustments of the camera's position along the X and Z planes, a rail is a great addition to a photography kit (Figure 3.8). The camera is screwed onto the rail and the plate at the bottom of the rail can be attached to the tripod. The camera can be adjusted incrementally along the X and Z axes on rails for very fine and controlled movements. If you are modelling very small objects, such as microliths or beads, incorporating a camera rail into the setup will significantly improve the quality of the images as it allows you better control of the camera's position. It also decreases time spent shooting as by adjusting the rail you do not have to nudge the tripod or adjust the artefact or turntable to capture the correct shot.

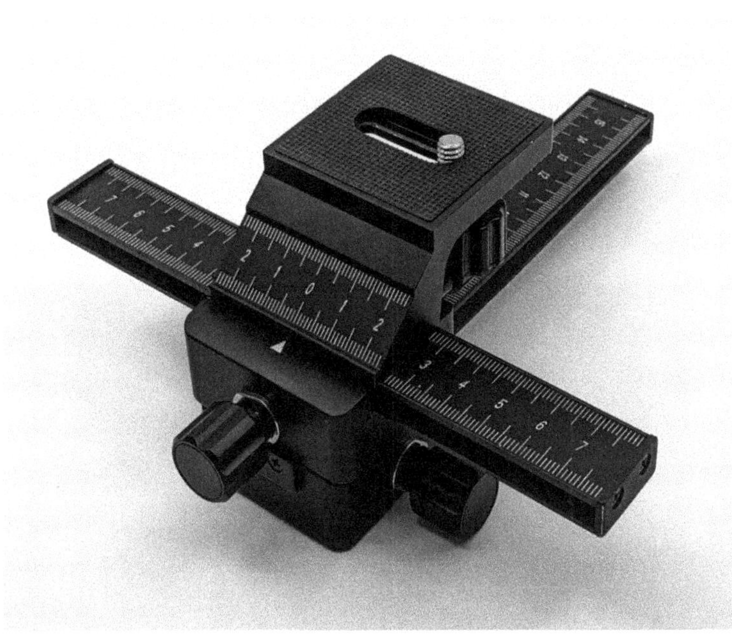

Figure 3.8 A camera rail that has an X and Z axis rail. A camera rail allows for fine adjustments of the camera.

3.4 Next steps

Now that the range of equipment needed for object-based close-range photogrammetry has been discussed, the next stage is to know how to design the photography setup. The photography setup will depend on the environment you are working in; that is, are you shooting inside in a sheltered room? Are you outside, capturing an object that is exposed to the elements? Chapter 4 provides steps to help you design a space to capture your objects for photogrammetry modelling in a sheltered, controlled environment and outlines how to prepare for shooting archaeological material or sites in an uncontrolled environment.

The importance of designing an effective photography environment should not be underestimated. A decent photography setup will affect the quality of the photogrammetry models produced and can take the pressure off you, the photographer, as correct exposure is easier to obtain. Capturing high-quality photos for photogrammetry becomes more challenging in uncontrolled or low-light environments. Therefore, it's essential to familiarise yourself with different types of gear available and learn how to set up in both controlled environments and in uncontrolled or open settings. Your choice of equipment will depend on the shooting location and the subject being photographed.

Chapter 4

SETTING UP TO SHOOT

Wherever you decide to photograph archaeological material for photogrammetry model-making, you will need to plan how you are going to shoot the objects and what equipment you will require to capture them successfully.

For archaeologists, photogrammetry setups are either going to be located in a controlled environment or an uncontrolled one. A controlled environment is one that is inside, protected from the weather, and where lighting direction and intensity can be manipulated. An uncontrolled environment, on the other hand, is exposed to the elements, shelter is minimal, and the photographer may have to rely on sunlight as the sole light source. For example, this could be in the field at an archaeological site or excavation. Different conditions mean different equipment will be needed and this chapter presents the type of equipment necessary to use in either scenario.

Firstly, how to create a photography setup in a controlled environment is discussed (4.1), with additional instructions for making your own lightbox (4.1.1) and how to design an "open" shooting environment; that is, a shooting setup that is not within a light box (4.1.2). How to position lights (4.2), create mounts for heavy and small objects (4.3), and correctly position an artefact for photogrammetry shooting are also covered (4.4). Matting powders and sprays are then discussed (4.5) with a look into why they can be useful for some modelling projects. The second half of this chapter outlines how to combat working in a variety of different weather conditions when shooting in an uncontrolled environment (4.6). We discuss what time of day is the best time to shoot, how to deal with the sun, rain and shadows using a polariser filter, and when to use a monopod or freehand shoot (4.7).

For any type of photogrammetry shooting, the ideal setup is sheltered, organised and with ample space to move. Moving and positioning artefacts onto mounts and turntables and adjusting tripod heights and camera positions raise potential issues regarding the safety and security of the specimens and the camera gear. You do not want to contribute to possible hazards by having unnecessarily wide tripod legs or a mess of cables waiting to trip you up. Having a well-organised system will also allow you to move faster through the shooting process, regardless of whether you are in a controlled environment or in the field.

4.1 Setting up a controlled environment

A controlled environment is one where you have complete control over the area in which you are photographing an object. The area is sheltered, lighting is sourced from artificial lights and, if possible, their intensity, temperature and direction can be manipulated. A controlled environment is protected from the weather, and typically, power sources are easily accessible. This is the ideal situation in which to be photographing archaeological artefacts as you, the photographer, can take your time (as you are not dependent on the sun for illumination), you can be precise in the adjustments of the objects and camera gear, and the safety of the equipment and specimens is ensured.

Equipment in a controlled environment can include the following:

- camera body
- lens
- tripod
- camera rail
- lamps
- flash and diffusers
- lightbox
- background sheet
- turntable
- object mounts
- colour calibration target and scale bar
- laptop or desktop computer.

Find a desk or table that is at a height at which you can sit or stand comfortably, that has space around it to move and position your tripod, that is close to a power outlet and, if possible, away from any windows letting in direct sunlight. This will be the place where you can set up the lightbox, or create an open shooting environment (instructions are outlined in 4.1.2). If you want to shoot straight to a computer, ensure you have enough space on the desk for a computer or laptop so you can easily see the computer screen from where you will be at the camera. Once you have set up the lightbox or the open shooting setup with lights positioned, place the turntable in the centre of the lightbox or the background sheet, and the tripod in front of the desk. Extend the central column to its greatest length first and then adjust the legs – it is easy to take up unnecessary space if tripod legs are too high or wide. If you are using a flash, connect the flash onto the camera's hot shoe before attaching the camera to the tripod's head. Connect the camera to the computer (if you are shooting to one) and ensure that no cords from the camera or the lightbox are in the way of the photographer or near the legs of the tripod. The computer should be close enough that any cables or cords reach the computer easily without tension. Turn the lights and camera on and make any minor adjustments. An example of a controlled photography setup is shown in Figure 4.1. It is at this point that the white balance should be set (how to set the white balance is outlined in Chapter 5).

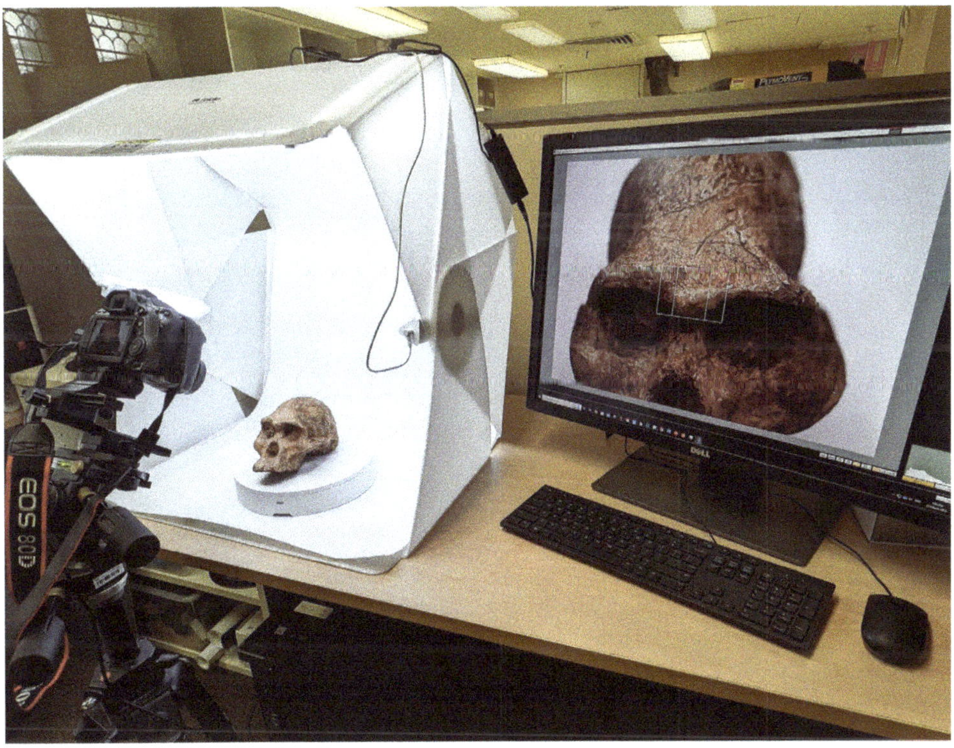

Figure 4.1 A photography setup for shooting photogrammetry models. Discipline of Archaeology reference collection, the University of Sydney.

The last step is to place the mount in the centre of the turntable (if using one) and then position the archaeological object. More information on how to make a mount is detailed in 4.3. It is good practice to make sure everything else is in place and working before the artefact is placed on the turntable.

Take note that lightboxes, lights and camera flashes can generate a lot of heat throughout a shooting session and can become quite hot. If the lightbox has LEDs glued to the panels, these lights may unstick when they heat up and may become too hot to touch. Shooting in an air-conditioned room away from direct sunlight is ideal but if this is not possible, turn off the lighting equipment every couple of hours and let them cool down. Flashes are known to become hot quite quickly and will stop working if you are shooting rapidly so you will have to let the flash cool down before using it again.

The most crucial piece of equipment to have in a controlled photography setup is a decent light source as light quality will ultimately determine the quality of the model. All other items are not absolutely necessary (apart from a camera and lens), but they will help considerably in the shooting process and the success of the model products. Luckily, a number of these items above can be made yourself with material you can typically find in an office or local hardware store and can significantly improve the success of your photogrammetry models.

4.1.1 How to make a DIY lightbox

If you are unable to purchase a lightbox, or you find yourself in need of one in the field due to working in an environment with insufficient lighting, a makeshift DIY lightbox can be constructed quite easily from material you might find in an office. All you need is:

- a cardboard box
- three sheets of baking paper, parchment paper or normal A4 paper
- a long sheet of A3 paper
- penknife
- ruler
- masking or sticky tape
- 2–3 lamps, torches or any other light source.

The following steps outline the process involved in creating a DIY cardboard box lightbox and are shown in Figure 4.2.

1. The first step in making a DIY lightbox is to remove the flaps from the opening of the cardboard box. Once they are off, position the box so that the opening is facing towards you. Place one of the pieces of paper onto the top panel, mark out the corners with a marker or a pencil then remove the paper.

2. Draw a 5 mm line from each marked corner towards the centre and join these up with a ruler to create a smaller rectangle.

3. Using the penknife, cut out the inner rectangle. Repeat these steps for the two side panels of the cardboard box.

4. Once each panel has been cut, place a piece of paper over the window and secure it with masking tape.

5. Sticky tape the A3 piece of paper at the back of the box and drape it forward, securing it with some tape. It is best to position the tape in a location that cannot easily be seen at the front, as tape is reflective and may show up on some images. Another option is to use double-sided sticky tape.

6. Position a lamp on either side of the box facing towards the windows, and one behind the box, with the light angled down. The lamp may need to be placed on top of something to reach the top window.

7. The subject can then be positioned inside the box and the setup is now ready to be used to take photos.

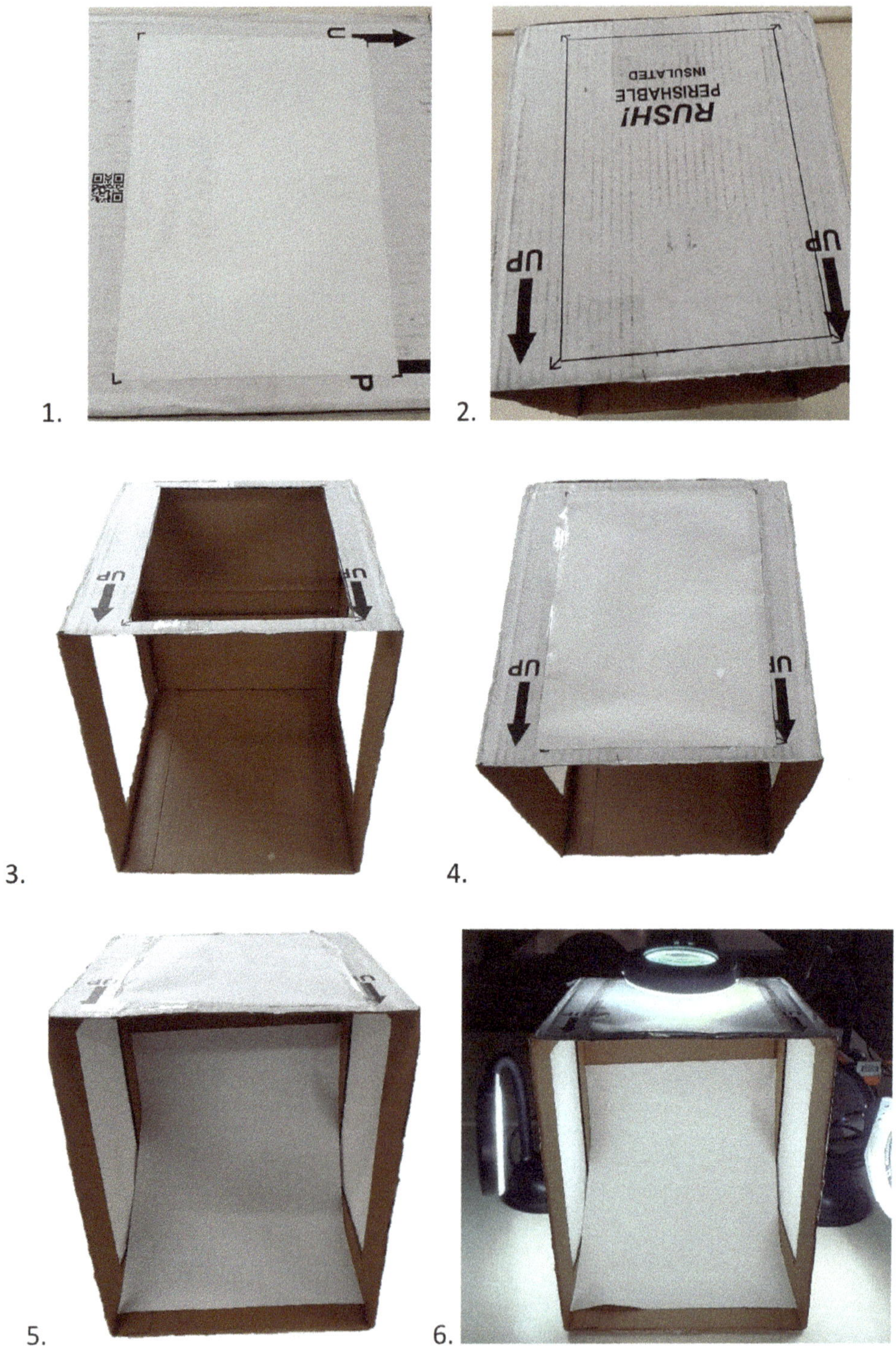

Figure 4.2 The stages of preparing a DIY lightbox.

4.1.2 How to make an open photography setup

Another easy and quick way of building a photography setup that does not involve cutting up cardboard boxes is to have an open photography setup. Although it is harder to control the lighting this way it is easier to construct compared to a DIY lightbox. All you need is:

- a sheet of black or white material
- a desk against a wall or backing board
- baking paper or parchment paper
- duct tape or alligator clips
- 2–3 lamps, torches or any other light source
- turntable or plate
- tripod and camera.

Firstly, the sheet of material needs to be secured to the wall or the backing board with either duct tape or alligator clips. Drape the material over the desk. Depending on whether you have a tripod or not, you might need to adjust the height of the artefact being photographed by stacking books underneath the material. Position the lamps on either side of the artefact and the tripod in front. If the light is too intense, tape baking paper over the lamp to dampen the light. If you are using a manual turntable or a plate on which you are going to photograph the artefacts, marking out the degrees around the circumference can help to maintain consistency in your shots and ensure coverage. For example, if you want to shoot every 10°, measure and mark these out so you know how much to rotate the turntable or plate. Figure 4.3 shows an open photography setup that uses a black turntable and background sheet made of a velvet-like material as the object is so light. Two lamps have been positioned on either side and one overhead to create even illumination of the subject.

4.2 Positioning lights

Where you position the lights for an open shooting environment will affect the amount and location of shadows on the subject being photographed. As outlined before, the ideal lighting is ambient and distributed evenly over the object's surface. This means you will need to have light coming from several different directions around the subject. Depending on how many lamps are available and what your photography setup is like, the ideal location of the light sources is to have an overhead light and one on either side of the subject, similar to the arrangement of lamps in Figure 4.3. This arrangement is also favourable when using a light tent or

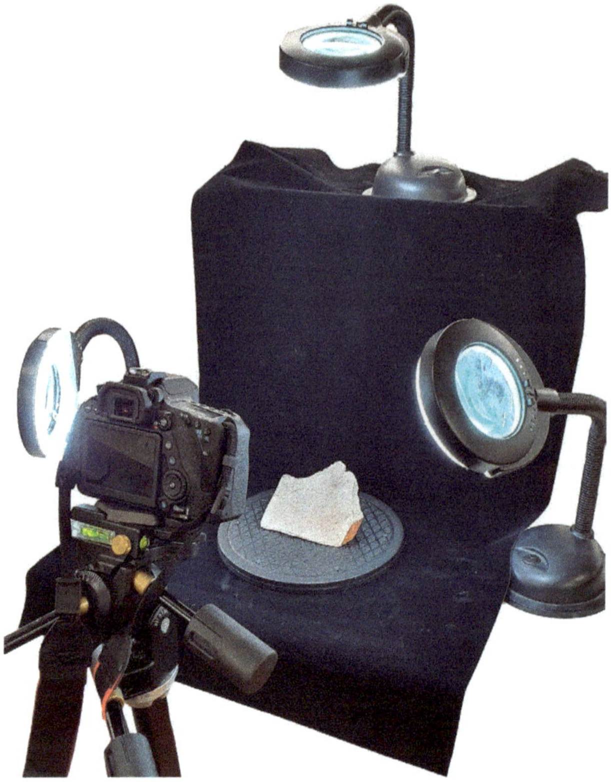

Figure 4.3 An example of an open shooting environment. Note the positions of the three lamps around the subject.

lightbox with paper walls. This is to avoid directional lighting. For some objects, such as pottery vessels with particularly rounded bellies, having an additional light source below the object with the light pointing up underneath the belly can drastically help with eliminating shadows cast here.

If you only have two lamps, there are several configurations that you can try for the best results (see Figure 4.4). The first position can include both lamps on either side of the object pointing towards the object, or they can be slightly in front of the object and pointing towards the object. These two configurations can be at the same height or at two heights – one light that shines on top of the object, and one directly at the front, looking up underneath the object. Another configuration is having one light behind the object, as is shown in Figure 4.3, pointing directly down on top of the object and another in front and to the side, facing the object at a 45-degree angle. It will be trickier to achieve even illumination with two lights but not impossible; simply try out a few positions until you are satisfied with the results. When using only one lamp, obtaining even illumination is more tricky so, if possible, move the object into a space that is well-lit so you can rely on the ambient light as well. Dampen the light source of the lamp (to limit any obvious shadows) and trial a few positions around and in front of the object to see which one effectively illuminates the face of the object; just ensure that the light source is not in the camera's angle of view.

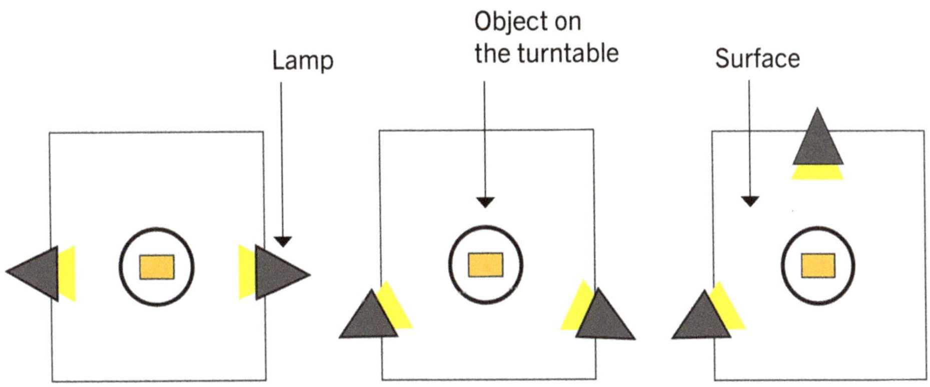

Figure 4.4 Three different arrangements of light sources using two lamps.

Other forms of artificial light, such as ring or gun flashes, or attachable LED panels (all covered in Chapter 3), are also useful as additional light sources. Light that hits directly at the object must be used with caution, however; intense light will bounce off the surface straight back to the lens, causing glare. Glare is problematic for photogrammetry model-making as it will be incorporated into the model. Glare inhibits the camera from seeing the surface of an object, causing issues with the mesh of the model and may result in the creation of unattached clumps of mesh "artefacts". If the subject is even slightly reflective, the flash or light source will need to be dampened or the brightness reduced.

4.3 Object mounts

Object mounts or stands securely hold the artefact and keep it safely positioned when being rotated on a turntable or on a flat surface when it is being photographed. Mounts can be made from a variety of materials and can be designed in a number of ways. They can have a central column with either clasps or wire prongs on top that hold smaller, lighter artefacts or they can have a wide base made of plastic or wood that has been cut to support larger objects.

The purposes of using object mounts for artefact shooting are to orient the artefact correctly, reduce the intensity of any shadows produced, and provide additional height so the camera can fit in next to or under the archaeological object. Mounts can be fashioned from any material that has a sturdy base that can take the weight of the specimen and can hold it securely in the desired position for as long as is required. Some photogrammetrists use metal clips or pegs to secure the object, but it is important that whatever is chosen will not damage the object either. It is also important to avoid any mount material that is transparent. Shots including a transparent mount may distort the specimen, create unhelpful reflections, and may reduce the success of running automatic masking if the software cannot determine what is the mount and what is the subject.

4.3.1 DIY PVC pipe mount

Plastic PVC piping or fittings work well for mounting heavier artefacts. Piping is cheap and easily sourced from any hardware store, and it also comes in a range of sizes. Piping that has one end with a larger diameter than the other increases stability and is more reliable.

These types of fittings are particularly useful as they also allow you to stack them together. Adjusting the height of the specimen can make it easier to position the camera to get the right shot, particularly the parallel shots. If the turntable or desk is in the way of the tripod, increasing the height and camera angle can avoid such issues (see Figure 4.5).

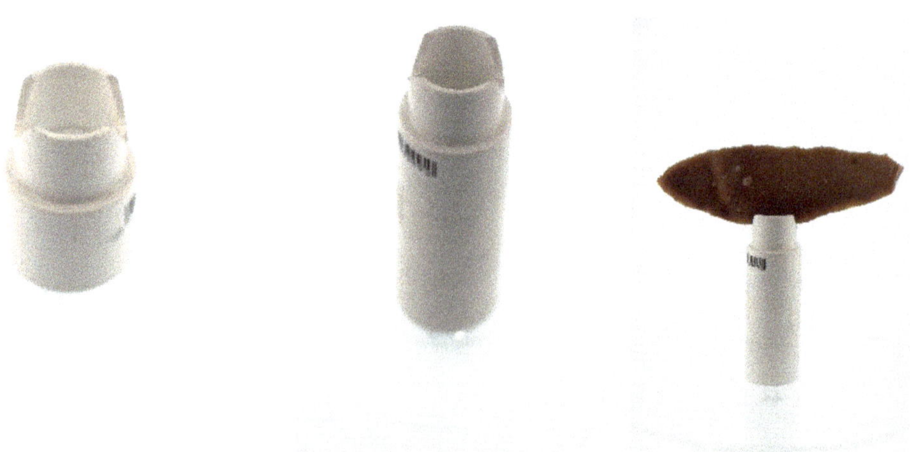

Figure 4.5 Stackable pipe segments make useful mounts. Discipline of Archaeology reference collection, the University of Sydney.

To make a mount from PVC piping, measure the width of the artefact and cut out a section of the piping of the same size using a saw. Depending on the shape and how soft the artefact is, cut out either a "V" shape or a square cut, ensuring that there are not any sharp protrusions or edges. If you are shooting several artefacts of varying sizes, a good idea is to have several pipe mounts with various-sized cut-outs to fit them. If there is only a small collection or they are consistently the same size, measure the width of the thickest specimen in the collection and cut out a "V" shape to that size, but have a long taper to the point of the "V" so smaller specimens can fit securely as well.

After cutting out the sections of the piping, sand down the edges to reduce the likelihood of any scratching. If the specimen is fragile or soft, attaching felt is a good idea; however, this could potentially reduce the stability of the artefact. Fitting foam or polystyrene into the centre of the piping can further aid in stabilising the artefact. Simply make an incision through the centre of the foam for the artefact to sit in.

If a specimen is particularly tricky to stabilise, and the only option is to hold it with a tack-like substance, refrain from attaching it directly to the artefact and cover the tack or putty with cling wrap (or something similar) to create a barrier between the tack or putty and the artefact. If there is the possibility that the specimen may undergo a residue analysis, be sure to keep the specimen from coming in contact with any material or substance that might contaminate the object's surface or structure.

4.3.2 DIY block and wire stand

A block and wire stand is a quick and relatively easy DIY mount for small artefacts, such as microliths. All that is needed is a block of heavy material such as wood, a wooden stick such as a chopstick, a kebab stick or even a paddle pop stick, and some wire. Drill a hole into the centre of the block to put the wooden stick in and glue it around the base for extra stability. If the block is too obvious and needs to be disguised, cut a hole out of a large piece of paper (in whatever colour matches the background) and place it on top of the block. Twist two lengths of wire around the wooden column at the top and leave 1–2 cm untwisted. Bend these two pieces into loops so that they are parallel to each other. The loops are what hold the artefact in place (see Figure 4.6). For fragile objects, glue some felt onto the wire to further protect the object. An alternative to this method is to use a small clip on the end of the central column, like a small alligator clip. For any clips, glue felt to the insides of the clasps to ensure that the clip will not scratch or damage the artefact. It is imperative that you also ensure that the object will not break from the pressure of being held within the clip. If in doubt, opt for a wire clasp instead.

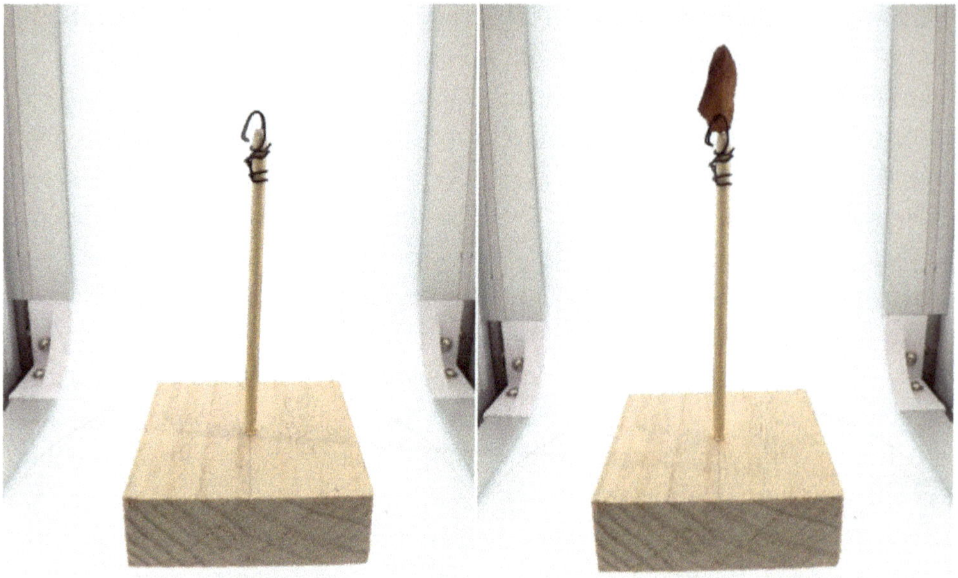

Figure 4.6 A block and wire stand. Discipline of Archaeology reference collection, the University of Sydney.

4.4 Positioning the artefact

It is important to consider the best way to position an object before photographing it. Depending on whether the artefact is on a mount or lying flat on a turntable, the camera positions will change, and the number of shots per round may differ, as will the number of shooting rounds needed to cover the entire object. Positioning the artefact for successful model shooting will be dependent on the artefact's size and shape and there is no hard and fast rule to this process. Some objects may align more successfully in a horizontal position rather than in a vertical one, so it might be ideal to experiment with the object in various positions and compare the model products to see which position produces the most successful model.

Smaller artefacts such as lithic material, pottery sherds or shells are modelled well if they are secured on a tall stand, such as the block and wire stand shown in Figure 4.6. This allows the photographer to position the camera correctly to capture the right photographs and reduces the likelihood of shadows occurring. Additionally, using a tall stand with the object placed in a vertical position reduces the likelihood of the mount appearing in the images as there is more of the object's surface above the mount. The stability and security of the object, however, is the most important factor so prioritise stability over ease of photography. It is not worth the risk of standing an artefact if it is likely to fall when it is being rotated.

Having the artefact in a less desirable position simply means you, the photographer, may have to take more photos to ensure it aligns correctly.

For larger material that is mounted, the orientation of the artefact is less of an issue. Depending on the size of the artefact, the mount is likely to be smaller than the artefact in which case orienting the artefact in either a standing or a horizontal position will work (see Figure 4.7). If you are unsure which orientation to choose, look for any shadows that might occur in both orientations and opt for the one that produces fewer shadows. If no shadows occur in either orientation, choose the more secure orientation.

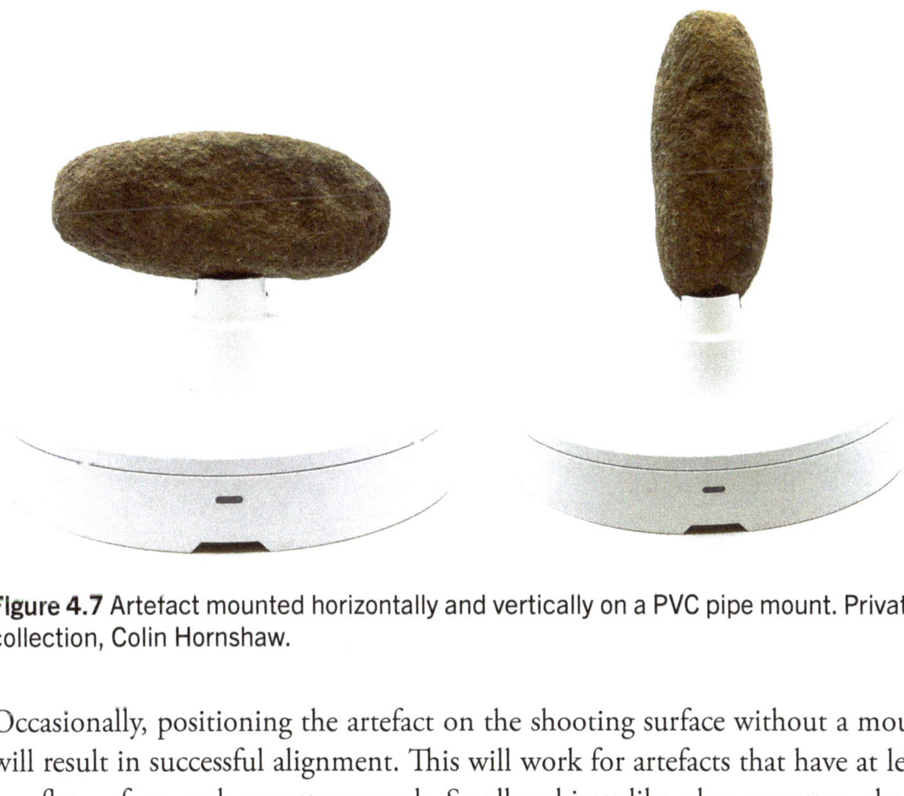

Figure 4.7 Artefact mounted horizontally and vertically on a PVC pipe mount. Private collection, Colin Hornshaw.

Occasionally, positioning the artefact on the shooting surface without a mount will result in successful alignment. This will work for artefacts that have at least one flat surface, such as pottery vessels. Smaller objects like adzes or pottery sherds can also be placed on a surface without a mount but you will only likely obtain a correct model if they have thick edges that do not cast shadows onto themselves, and the edges are wide enough that the software can identify the different sides of the artefact and accurately align them. Spherical objects like rounded hand axes and bivalve shells should be mounted, as curved edges will cast shadows when turned upside down and capturing the nature of the curves is easier when the object is elevated off the turntable.

There may be times in which you will need to shoot an artefact both on a stand as well as lying flat to ensure complete coverage and successful alignment. Very thin objects are a lot harder to model as there is less surface area on the thin edges for the software to connect one side to the other and it is likely that you will need to shoot these objects both on a stand and lying flat to ensure the software can piece together each surface (see Case study 8.3).

There is helpful terminology to describe positioning an artefact. If the artefact is being turned upside down so the underside can be captured, the object is divided into "hemispheres" – the northern and the southern hemisphere. Defining sections of the subject material makes organising the shooting process easier, enabling the photographer to focus on a particular section at a time. If the artefact needs to be repositioned on its side to capture these areas, they would be referred to as the eastern and western hemispheres. Some objects might require their images processed in two hemisphere chunks and then aligned and merged later in the process. In this case, it is a good idea to label the folders with their respective hemispheres so you know which images are to be merged together. Merging model chunks in *Metashape* is further discussed in Chapter 7.

4.5 Matting sprays and powders

If you want to model a highly reflective object, many photogrammetrists use matting sprays manufactured specifically for 3D scanning purposes. A range of these products will evaporate several minutes after being sprayed, while some must be wiped off. Cheaper alternatives include talcum or baby powder; the most effective product for matting is aerosol deodorant (see Figure 4.8). For archaeological artefacts or any cultural material, this process is not advised. If you have permission or the subject is not an archaeological object, then applying a matting spray or powder might be a good option to avoid capturing any reflection. If applying a powder, use a brush to dust the powder on evenly and either brush off with a clean brush or microfibre towel or use a dust blower. If you are using a matting spray, spray from a distance while rotating the object and avoid touching it with your fingers.

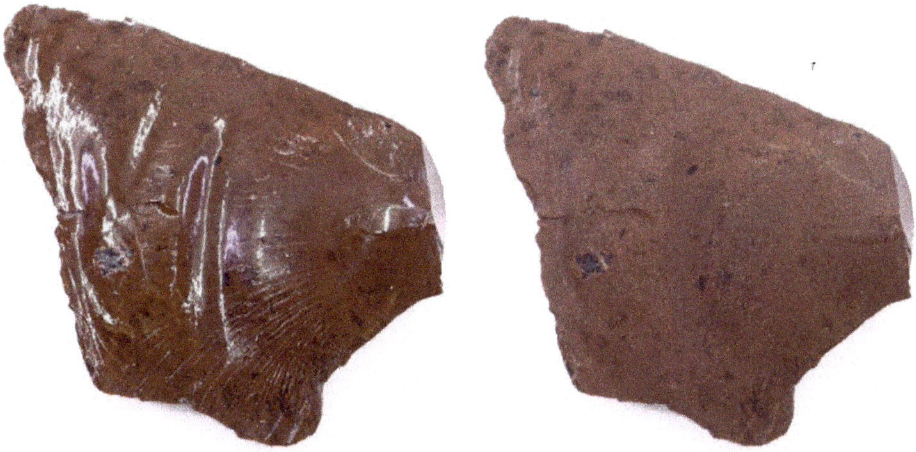

Figure 4.8 A flake before being sprayed with aerosol deodorant and after. A few coats make a difference which is very effective for removing surface reflection. Discipline of Archaeology reference collection, the University of Sydney.

4.6 Shooting in an uncontrolled environment

If an archaeological object, site or excavation is situated in an environment that is exposed to the weather, is without easily accessible power, the photographer is reliant on the sun for illumination or there is considerably limited availability of artificial light, it is considered to be in an uncontrolled shooting environment.

For archaeologists, this may be a scenario that occurs frequently during field seasons. Photography for photogrammetry can become considerably trickier in these cases. Therefore, preparations must be made to ensure this part of the photogrammetry process runs smoothly, but more importantly that the images captured are suitable to make photogrammetry models. The main problems to contend with will be rain, shadows, the sun, and photographing without any shelter. Listed below are a few ways to navigate shooting in an uncontrolled environment to obtain the best possible images for processing a photogrammetry model.

4.6.1 Creating shelter

A tent, marquee or gazebo can be a great addition to your fieldwork kit, especially if photogrammetry is being planned, as it provides a quasi-controllable environment. A marquee can be erected around a topographical feature or can be set up to house a table and lamps for artefact shooting. This enables the lighting to be controlled, provides the photographer with a protected area in which the setup can be designed to their preference, and most importantly protects the photography gear and the photographer from the elements and the sun. A tent with a couple of mounted LED panels, either battery-operated or running from a generator, positioned around the object is a great way to control the ambient light; just ensure you have a way of recharging the batteries.

Having a shelter also means that you have a safe space to exchange or clean camera lenses. It is important to limit the number of times that camera lenses are removed or exchanged when in an unprotected environment as this provides an opportunity for dirt and dust to enter the mechanisms. If you need to clean the camera or the lenses, or change lenses, try to do it in a protected area – even inside a car is better than outside! If no shelter is available to you, the following tips can be adopted to ensure decent images are captured for photogrammetry modelling.

4.6.2 Rain

When working in the field, you should prepare for all weather conditions. This is particularly difficult when you are using equipment that is easily damaged by dirt, wind and rain. It is not advised to shoot when it is raining if the site or subject is unsheltered as most digital cameras are not waterproof and water will damage your equipment; additionally, water on your lens will appear in images. The rain can be contended with, however, if you have access to a waterproof housing or camera rain covers, a good lens hood, and store your camera gear in a waterproof bag. In fact, overcast days are the perfect condition for photographing in an uncontrolled environment, particularly if the archaeological site is in an unsheltered space, as there is no direct sunlight or shadows, and reflections are minimised. Shooting for hours in the sun can also be hazardous to your health; therefore, take advantage of any overcast and cloudy days to do your photogrammetry shooting in the field.

4.6.3 Shadows and the sun

If cloud cover is looking unlikely, the morning or late afternoon are reasonable times to plan to do some photogrammetry shooting in an uncontrolled environment as there is considerably less harsh directional light from the sun, resulting in less intense shadows. Remember, if you photograph shadows, they will be incorporated into the model unless they are removed from your images before processing. If you are shooting an object or site over a long period of time in the sun, the moving shadows may reduce the success of image alignment. If possible, plan to shoot at the same time each day if you are working on a large site to maintain consistent lighting throughout all the photos. If no artificial light is available and you are entirely reliant on the sun for illumination, shooting when the sun is at its zenith will minimise shadows. It is advised to check both the weather conditions and what time the sun will be at its zenith before you head out into the field, so you can prepare your day accordingly.

4.6.4 Limited sunlight

If the sun is the only source of light available to you and the feature you want to shoot would benefit from a bit more light directed to certain places (or you want to reduce intense shadows), a light reflector may help. These can be purchased online or at any camera store. If you do not have a photography reflector or the ability to purchase one, the shiny metallic side of a car windscreen sunshade will do the trick or even sheets of aluminium foil if you are really desperate. If you have another person handy, position them with the reflector on the side which needs added illumination and angle the reflector to catch the sun's rays and direct them towards the subject being photographed. Just remember to not include the reflector or the other person in any of the images.

4.6.5 Polariser lens filters

If you are shooting in the field and relying on the sun for illumination, a polariser filter can improve images, especially if the subject is shiny or reflective. A polariser filter cuts out the glare from the sun, reduces the amount of reflection, and increases the contrast and colour saturation of the images (see Figure 4.9). By rotating the filter, which is screwed onto the end of the lens, the amount of polarised light can be increased or decreased – adjusting the lens' effectiveness. Polariser filters only work on polarised light, however, so will not be affected by unpolarised light. Linear

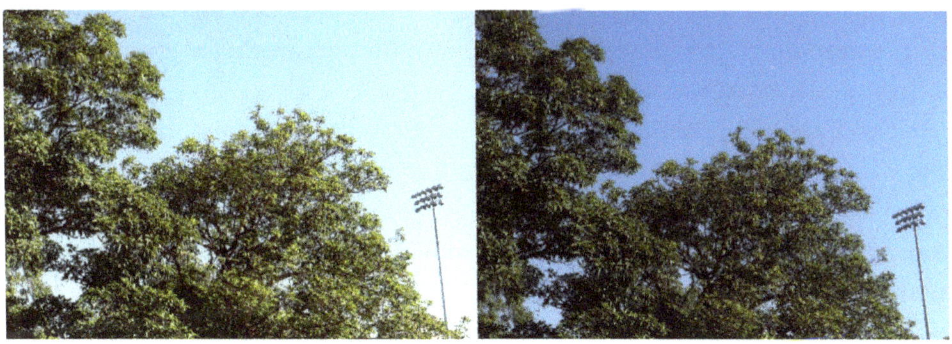

Figure 4.9 An image of the sky without a polariser filter compared to one with a polariser filter. Note the sky is darker and the colours are more saturated with a polariser filter.

polariser filter film can also be purchased to put over flashes and lights to polarise the light. This is useful if you want to cut out light from these sources as well.

4.6.6 Shooting with a monopod

When modelling archaeological sites, fixed objects or archaeological material that cannot be placed on a turntable or rotated securely, the photographer will have to walk around the subject taking photographs. A monopod can be a great asset in this situation. Monopods will ensure each image is level while taking the weight of the camera. This can be handy if you are shooting with a heavy DSLR or a large lens and are shooting for extended periods of time. Monopods are light and do not take up space in your shooting environment; however, unlike tripods, they have to be held as they are not freestanding support structures. Tripods are not ideal in these situations as they can be cumbersome and do not allow for quick movements, especially over rugged or uneven terrain. Tripods also inhibit the photographer's mobility and may prevent them from setting up the correct position of the camera, especially if the object is immovable. As such, monopods are a better choice.

With the benefit of shutter release remotes, you can also easily take aerial shots of the subject by extending the pole out to a longer length. Another option is to use the interval timer shooting feature. By enabling this function (found in the camera's menu options), setting the interval time (e.g. 2 or 5 seconds) between each shutter release and the total number of shots you want to take, you can simply walk around the site or feature and the camera will take a series of images without you having to control the shutter. Just remember to put your lens onto autofocus, not manual focus, otherwise the lens will not focus on the object being captured. Most digital camera companies will have an app that allows you to live-view on your smartphone too, or if your camera has a rotatable LCD screen, swivel the LCD screen down to face you while you position the camera for the aerial shots so you can see what you are shooting.

If you are taking aerial photos with an extended monopod, have someone else with you as a spotter. Walking around, taking photographs, adjusting the camera's position and consistently looking up at the camera's LCD screen or at your phone means you are less likely to be looking at the ground or any obstacles around. This is known as "cognitive tunnelling". This is a state where intense focus on a task at hand can make a person unaware of their surroundings, potentially affecting their ability to react promptly to unexpected events. It can therefore be dangerous, especially when the heavy weight of a camera at the end of a monopod can become unbalanced so easily. Having someone follow you around to monitor you and check for obstacles could save you from falling over and hurting yourself and damaging the camera equipment or archaeological object or site.

4.7 Shooting freehand

Shooting freehand is the fastest way to photograph an object. Without any tripod or monopod, you, the photographer, have the freedom to move quickly around the object and adjust the camera's position with ease. The images will be less level compared to those taken with a tripod or monopod, but as long as the object is being captured correctly, this is not a major issue. Freehand photography can be conducted when shooting in a lightbox, open shooting environment, or in an uncontrolled environment – it is up to the photographer and their preferences.

When freehand shooting, hold the lens of the camera with your left hand and the right side of the camera with your right hand with your index finger resting on the shutter release button on top (see Figure 4.10). With your right hand in this position, you can quickly change the settings on the dials while you are shooting as your thumb should be on the back of the camera. Your left hand on the lens allows you to change the focus of the lens if shooting with manual focus. Remember to always have the camera strap around your neck when freehand shooting – in case you drop the camera, it's not going anywhere!

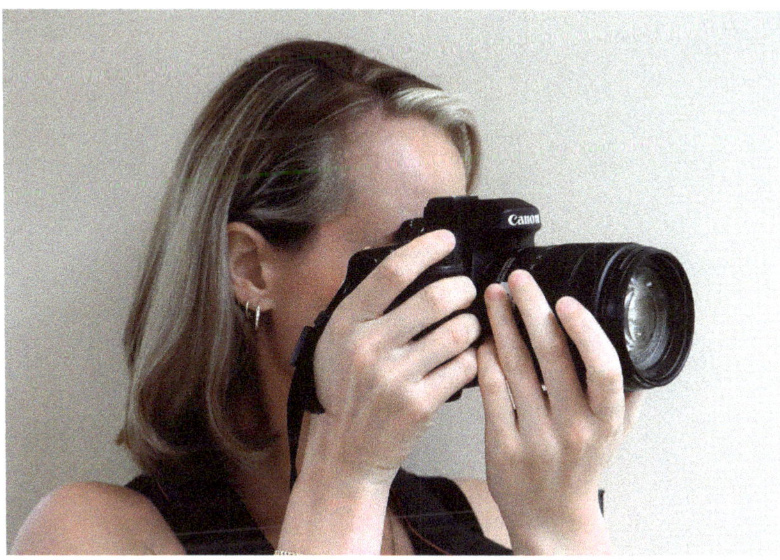

Figure 4.10 How to hold a camera. Image: M. Wright.

When walking around and photographing a fixed feature or site in an uncontrolled environment, always look where you are walking. Having your eyes glued to the viewfinder, with your attention focused on the object and not where you are putting your feet or the monopod can be quite dangerous to yourself, the camera gear and the subject. If possible, remove any obstacles such as backpacks, other equipment or branches to reduce the likelihood of tripping over, and always wear enclosed shoes.

4.8 Next steps

In this chapter we explored how to set up the photography kit in a controlled environment and how to navigate taking photos safely in an uncontrolled one. This is essential information to know before moving on to the next step: setting up the camera and capturing images for photogrammetry modelling. In the following chapter, we outline what the necessary actions are before progressing to the shooting stage, from creating an information board and designing a metadata spreadsheet, to correctly setting up the camera to shoot. The primary focus of the next chapter is the order of camera positions required to capture an object completely, followed by the crucial "golden rules" of shooting for photogrammetry.

Chapter 5

HOW TO SHOOT

It is generally understood that a major benefit of photogrammetry is that it is a practice that requires little expertise to produce useful data (Davis et al. 2017). While you do not need to be a professional photographer to do photogrammetry, the overall success of photogrammetry models is heavily dependent on the quality of the photographs taken and what they exhibit. For photogrammetry modelling, the camera needs to be adjusted to certain settings to control depth of field and exposure. The number and arrangement of camera positions also needs to be considered to ensure the entire surface area of the subject is captured. What is also imperative for photogrammetrists to understand is that organisation and preparation are *essential*. Although you do not need any prior expertise to do photogrammetry, there is a lot to think about when it comes to the shooting stage of the modelling process. This chapter therefore breaks down this process and guides you through each step to make the procedure easier to understand.

It may help to think of photogrammetry as broadly a two-stage process. There is the active stage where you need to set up and take photographs of the object being modelled, then there is the passive stage where the software stitches the images together to create the model (although manually editing models can be a lot of work too!). It is possible to take hundreds, if not thousands, of photos in a shooting session capturing numerous objects with perhaps more than one camera or lens. It is therefore crucial that preparations are made to organise images and metadata to avoid running into problems down the track when you are processing. This chapter therefore begins with an outline of how to manage files and photos (5.1.1), discusses the importance of having an information board (5.1.2), and explains why a metadata spreadsheet to track progress is essential for any photogrammetrist (5.1.3).

To produce accurate photogrammetry models suitable for archaeological analysis, the camera needs to be set up correctly with specific settings to manipulate the depth of field and the exposure. This chapter instructs what aperture to aim for when modelling objects and how to select an appropriate corresponding shutter speed and ISO to balance exposure (5.2.1). Setting the white balance is also discussed (5.2.2), as well as what metering mode should be chosen (5.2.3), what the differences in file formats are, and which ones should be chosen for your projects (5.2.4). There is also some information on the benefits of tethered shooting (shooting to a computer, 5.3), the pros and cons of video shooting (5.4), and some discussion on the question that is often asked – how many photographs to take (5.5).

With the camera set up correctly, you can move on to the primary focus of this chapter – the types of camera positions required to completely capture the surface area of an archaeological object (5.6). Positioning the camera correctly is essential for creating successful and accurate photogrammetry models, so you must know which positions to use and in what order. In this chapter, the types of camera positions are discussed with descriptions of their purpose, where the camera is in relation to the subject, when to use them in the shooting process, and examples of what the resulting images should look like. This is to help you with your own modelling projects so you can plan what camera positions are necessary to successfully capture your object. This chapter also provides an overview of lens calibration (5.7) and when it might be required for your modelling projects. This chapter supplies you with the "golden rules" of shooting for photogrammetry. These are crucial rules that must be adhered to that will improve your photogrammetry models and make the editing process considerably easier (5.8).

5.1 Before you shoot

5.1.1 Organising photos

Before you begin photographing, you should have a clear idea of how you intend to organise the photographs, what to label them, and where they will be stored. This step should not be overlooked as you may find yourself dealing with thousands of photographs after your first shooting session. You cannot afford to lose track of where photographs are or what information the images contain, especially if you are shooting with multiple cameras. The first thing to remember is to never delete anything off your SD card (if you are shooting to one) until you can confirm that all your photographs have been saved to a hard drive, backed up to a cloud-based storage folder, or both.

In terms of organising the photographs, having a master folder is recommended. This folder will hold everything – the images, models, and the metadata of the collection or site – and is clearly labelled identifying the contents. Within the master folder, each artefact should have its own folder that contains the associated images of each trial run and the models.

Labelling the folders should follow a consistent system that identifies exactly what is inside the folder. Avoid using spaces in folder names but have an underscore to separate words or numbers, as spaces can cause issues in processing and exporting data. One method of labelling folders is by identifying the trial run number, for example: "Trial1", "Trial2", "Trial3", followed by what section of the artefact or site was specifically photographed (see Figure 5.1). An example of this when shooting artefacts is to include which hemisphere was photographed in the folder name. For objects that can be turned upside down to form a complete model, the top half is identified as the northern hemisphere ("N"), and the underside, the southern hemisphere ("S"). Regardless of whether you split up these photographs and process the northern and southern hemisphere shots separately and intend to merge them later or leave them as one batch of photographs to process as a whole, it is important to identify what hemispheres the folder contains. For example, if separated on the first trial run of shooting, the filename could be "Trial1_N" or "Trial1_S". If both hemispheres are included in the folder: "Trial1_NS". By following this system, you can have several folders that include different runs and sections. For example, if you want to conduct a second trial run of the southern hemisphere of a specimen as the first trial was not successful, identify the folder as "Trial2_S". If you need to orient the artefact on its side, you can continue this method of designating hemispheres and label one side the eastern hemisphere ("E") and the other the western hemisphere ("W").

If you create your own labelling system that identifies folders and their contents, just remember to continue the same method throughout a collection to avoid confusion or losing data or images. If several trials were attempted in one session of shooting, there must be a clear way to identify which photos are part of which trial run and what the images are of. This is why including an information board is so crucial when shooting multiple trial runs, multiple artefacts or with multiple photographers.

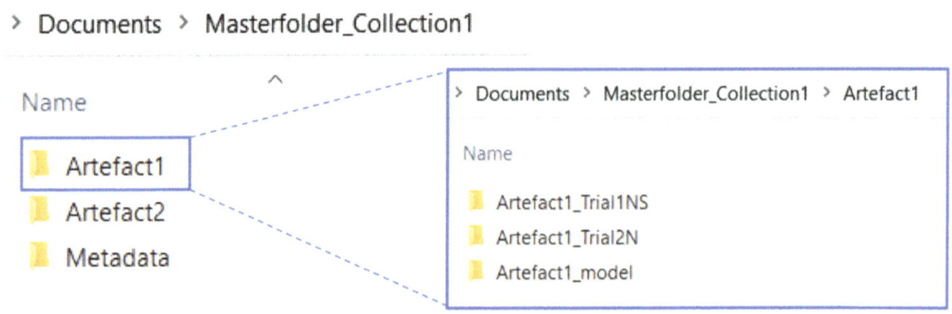

Figure 5.1 Organising photos and models within a master folder.

5.1.2 Information boards

It can be quite difficult to organise photographs if you are struggling to identify what photographs belong to what artefact, to what hemisphere, or trial run number, particularly if you have amassed hundreds to thousands of photographs. A great way to keep track of what artefacts were photographed, what settings were used, the camera and lenses used, and who the photographer was is to write down all these details on an information board and photograph it a handful of times before you begin photographing the specimen. The information board can be a whiteboard or a piece of paper, whatever you have on hand that can be written on and clearly photographed. What these images of the information board will do is define the sections in the stream of images uploaded to a computer. These images will delineate one batch of artefact images from another and provide a quick reference to the specimen being photographed and how it was photographed, so you can select all the relevant images and move them to an appropriate folder. It is good practice to use an information board before every artefact is photographed or before any repeat of a section.

The key pieces of information to include on the information board include the collection name or fieldwork name, date, time, photographer's name, location, artefact ID or site name or ID, trial number and hemisphere/s, priority setting, aperture, ISO, shutter speed, camera and lens type (see Figure 5.2).

There are several reasons why a whiteboard is preferable to a piece of paper. The main reasons are that whiteboard markers are bolder and can be seen from a further distance and using whiteboards means there is less paper wastage. Whiteboards are also not ruined by water or dirt and therefore can be taken into the field where they can also be useful for other tasks.

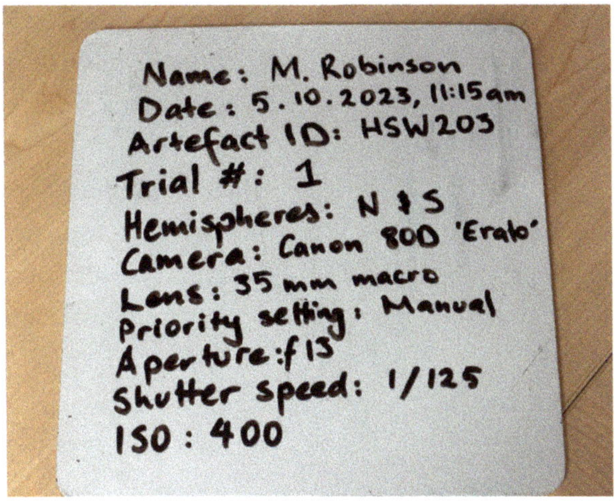

Figure 5.2 Example of a photo of an information board.

5.1.3 Metadata spreadsheet

Having a metadata spreadsheet is essential when creating photogrammetry models. A metadata spreadsheet is a reliable way of keeping a record of what artefacts or sites were shot, the gear, and what settings were used. It is also used to show what camera or software settings were successful and thereby you can conduct comparisons on different shooting techniques, software types or lighting sources. Recording this data can also help direct you on how to improve the shooting or processing of models in the future. A simple Excel spreadsheet can keep a record of all the important information. An example of the type of information that could be recorded is:

Artefact or site identification:

- Artefact ID, site ID, excavation unit, location name or object type
- Dimensions (if necessary)
- Weight (if appropriate)

Equipment used:

- Lens type and focal length
- Camera body type
- Light source used (on-camera flash, lightbox, lamps or none)
- Computer or laptop used for processing

Camera settings:

- Priority setting
- Aperture
- ISO
- Shutter speed

Trial runs and area of focus:

- Trial number
- Shooting date
- Object's hemispheres (if artefact)
- The subsection of area (for landscape photogrammetry)

Model settings:

- Model processing start date
- Image editing
- Colour corrected
- Masking
- Alignment accuracy
- Point cloud or dense point cloud quality
- Mesh face quality
- Post-processing edits

Processing outcomes:

- Number of photographs uploaded
- How many were successfully aligned
- Tie point cloud count
- Mesh face count
- Overall model quality
- General comments

5.2 Camera settings

There can be a lot of buttons, symbols and information on a camera that can at first appear intimidating. Try not to let this stop you from learning how to properly set up a camera as the process is straightforward and is the same for all camera types, even those that have fewer features such as some compact cameras and smartphones. If you are unsure how to manipulate an image by changing the aperture, ISO or shutter speed, go over Chapter 2 to gain an understanding of how images can be manipulated to adjust brightness and depth of field, as this is crucial to setting up a camera correctly. This section uses the information discussed in the previous chapters to prepare your camera for photogrammetry shooting.

5.2.1 Setting the aperture, shutter speed and ISO

The first step in setting up your camera is to choose what Priority mode to shoot in. If you are using a DSLR, mirrorless or compact camera, the most useful setting for photogrammetry shooting purposes is the Manual exposure mode, typically represented as an "M" on the camera's settings dial. This mode allows the photographer to configure the aperture, shutter speed and ISO independently, giving them complete control over the exposure levels and the depth of field. The benefit of Manual mode is that none of the settings automatically readjust while you shoot. This means that in a controlled environment, with even, ambient lighting, the exposure will not change between shots – this is important for successful photogrammetry model-building. The standard camera mode alternatives are Aperture Priority (usually shown as "A" or "Av"), Shutter Priority ("S" or "Tv"), Program Priority (a useful setting that looks for the best balance between shutter speed and aperture, usually represented as "P") and Auto mode. The Aperture, Shutter and Program Priority modes allow the photographer to adjust these settings quickly, offering some control. The Auto mode gives very little control over the settings and should be avoided for the purposes of photogrammetry modelling.

If you are using a camera with adjustable settings, the aperture setting will be your first consideration when shooting for photogrammetry. This is because the aperture affects the depth of field and having a wide depth of field is crucial for successful object-based photogrammetry model-building. A larger depth of field means the camera is set to a higher aperture (f/ number), so start by selecting a mid–high f/ number.

Depending on the type of digital camera and lenses you have, the range of aperture choices will differ. Some lenses have a narrow aperture range, while others have a larger range. Some compact cameras only go to f/11 while more expensive equipment can go up to f/32. Saying that, if you are working with a camera that only goes up to around f/11, this is still a relatively upper mid-range aperture setting and will still produce images with a useful depth of field for photogrammetry modelling. Although it is tempting to choose the highest possible aperture setting to increase the depth of field as much as possible, remember that the amount of light entering the lens will decrease considerably at every stop that the f/ is increased. Due to the nature of macro lenses, the difference between the depths of field of an aperture setting of f/16 compared to f/32 is imperceptible. Setting a mid–high range aperture, between f/11 and f/16 (depending on lighting conditions), will not only ensure you have a decent depth of field but will also let sufficient light into the lens, allowing you to have a more desirable ISO setting and faster shutter speed.

Whatever aperture you decide on, you will have to set the shutter speed and ISO accordingly to maintain correct exposure. Start with setting the shutter speed around 1/100 to 1/125 of a second and take a shot of the object being modelled with the ISO set to Auto to see what the camera automatically sets the ISO to. Ideally, the ISO will be under 800 with optimal shooting conditions yielding an ISO value between 100–400. This means that there is ample brightness in the photography setup and there will be minimal noise. You can then manually set your ISO to the reading the camera automatically provided. If the ISO reading is within this lower bracket (100–400), consider increasing the ISO so you can increase the shutter speed or the aperture value, or both, to maintain a balanced exposure. For photogrammetry purposes, it is preferable to sacrifice a low ISO setting for a faster shutter speed and greater depth of field as your images will be sharper with more of the object's detail in focus.

If the ISO is slightly higher than you would like, say over 1250, set it slightly lower around 800 to 1000 and consider reducing the aperture or the shutter speed by a stop to reach a balanced exposure or add more light sources if possible. To maintain clarity, avoid having an ISO over 2500; however, newer high-end camera models are less affected by high ISO values. If you lower the aperture too much to compensate for the high ISO setting, however, you will reduce the depth of field, so avoid sacrificing the aperture too much to maintain exposure. If reducing the shutter speed, do not lower it below 1/60 on a tripod and it is not advisable to go under 1/100 if you are freehand shooting. Generally, the shutter speed should never be lower than 1/100 to ensure that photographs do not have camera blur.

Take note: when shooting in an uncontrolled environment, it might be a better option to set your ISO to Auto. This means that if light conditions change, the camera will balance the exposure automatically via the ISO setting but maintain the aperture and shutter speeds. If this option is chosen, continually check on the images produced to ensure the exposure field is well balanced.

A very useful tool to keep in your photography kit is a neutral grey target, also known as 18% grey. This coloured sheet is a shade of grey that reflects 18% of the light that hits the target, hence the name. In the same way as photographing a colour checker, before you begin to shoot an object for photogrammetry, position the grey target in the photography setup with all the lights on and the camera set to Aperture priority with the f/ set to an ideal setting for close-range photogrammetry shooting. Half-press the shutter to focus the lens and then take a shot. The in-built light meter in the camera will detect the amount of light reflecting off the target back to the camera and the camera consequently adjusts the shutter speed to reach balanced exposure. This shutter speed is an indication of the exposure time required for this particular shooting environment and can be used for the rest of the shooting session and as a guide to setting the ISO. If you do use a grey target to set the exposure, just remember to set the camera back to Manual priority afterwards to set the shutter speed and the ISO.

It is crucial that you find a balance between the aperture, shutter speed and ISO, so it is advised to play around with these settings until you are comfortable in recognising how each affects the others and in turn the image quality. Favouring one setting over the other two will result in a sacrifice of brightness, depth of field, clarity or sharpness. It is not advisable to degrade the visual clarity of the photographs by setting a ridiculously high ISO (which will result in grainy photographs) to save from having a slow shutter speed, nor is it recommended to risk having motion blur in the photographs by decreasing the shutter speed to save the images from any noise. Finding this balance can be difficult and time-consuming, but it will be one of the most important steps in this process. So take your time in adjusting the settings until you are happy with the brightness levels and clarity of the images and rest assured that it will become easier with practice.

If using a smartphone camera, the ability to adjust the camera's exposure is limited. For a range of smartphone models there is the option to adjust the ISO, shutter speed and the "EV" (exposure value); however, some models have simple editing features such as brightness, contrast and temperature without greater professional control, or have no changeable settings at all. For most smartphone cameras, the ability to adjust the aperture and depth of field is limited as these cameras have fixed lenses (immovable diaphragms) and typically the aperture values of the lenses tend to be quite low (meaning depth of field is shallow). Smartphone cameras are therefore not the most ideal for photogrammetry shooting; however, if it is your only option, try to set the camera to an exposure that is well-balanced by assessing the picture quality on the screen and increase the ratio of the angle of view to a large setting to capture as much information as possible.

5.2.2 White balance

White balance readjusts the colour cast of your images and can make colours more realistic if the ambient light temperature has a high or low Kelvin value. This step does not need to be undertaken every time you photograph a new artefact, only when the shooting environment or lighting is different. Just remember to set your camera's settings before you set the white balance. Depending on the camera model you are using, the most reliable way to ascertain the correct white balance is to use the "Custom White Balance" option in the camera's menu. There are other choices available to you that will alter the colour cast automatically such as Daylight (~5700 K), Shade (~7000 K), Cloud (~6000 K), Tungsten (~3200 K) and White Fluorescent (~4000 K). The effect they have depends on the number of Kelvins the ambient lights are producing. If you do not know the light temperature of the setup, manually set the white balance.

To manually set the white balance, you need to photograph a white balance target in the shooting environment. The easiest option is a piece of plain white paper. The Calibrite X-Rite *ColorChecker Passport Photo 2* includes a white target which can also be used. For Canon cameras, position the paper or target in a location that avoids any shadows and set the camera to "auto white balance" (usually displayed as "AWB"). Adjust the camera's position so that the piece of paper or target takes up as much of the frame as possible or is as close to the focal plane as possible. Take a photo, then change the white balance setting to "Custom

White Balance" in your camera's settings. The camera should prompt you to select an image – select the image of the piece of paper. All your images from then on will have an adjusted white balance that is set to that image. If you think that the white balance is not correct and the colour cast is off, set the camera to auto white balance again and reshoot the piece of paper from a different position, letting in more light so the camera can correctly detect the ambient light temperature. For Nikon cameras, set the custom white balance through the "PRE" setting (for "Preset Manual"), and again shoot the piece of paper or white balance target filling the frame, or as close to the focal plane as possible. For convenience, there is a piece of white paper at the end of this book that can be used to set the white balance.

When taking an image of the white balance, it is good practice to take a shot of the colour rendition chart too, if you have one. Set the camera to RAW and position the chart in the photography setup so the camera has a clear view and is not at an angle. Colour charts and how to correct colour casts are discussed further in Chapter 6.

5.2.3 Metering mode

Most digital cameras will have a function called "Metering Mode" or "Exposure Metering". Metering is how the camera determines the overall brightness of the subject within the frame. The camera's in-built metering sensor does not measure the overall brightness within the frame but will measure it in several specific zones. You have the option to change the weighting of these zones, which will alter the brightness of the subject. Without changing the settings, the camera will default to an "Evaluative", also known as "Matrix", mode where the camera divides the frame into a grid. Each square within the grid is analysed by the camera for levels of light and dark tones equally. The camera will then create an exposure that balances the bright to dark areas within the frame. Evaluative metering mode is not a bad place to start – it can be used for landscape, portrait and macro shooting. If you are photographing a small artefact that is backlit in a lightbox, however, you might find that the "Centre Weighted" or "Spot" metering options are better alternatives. Here, the camera prioritises the light readings at the centre of the frame and the area around the focus point, respectively.

If you are shooting a rotating artefact in a lightbox and one face of the artefact is considerably thinner than the other faces, you might notice that the exposure will change between the larger and thinner faces. If you are shooting a darker specimen with a white background, the exposure will decrease as the object rotates to the thinner side, and conversely, with a lighter specimen with a black background, it will increase as it rotates. Shown in Figure 5.3, there is a significant change in

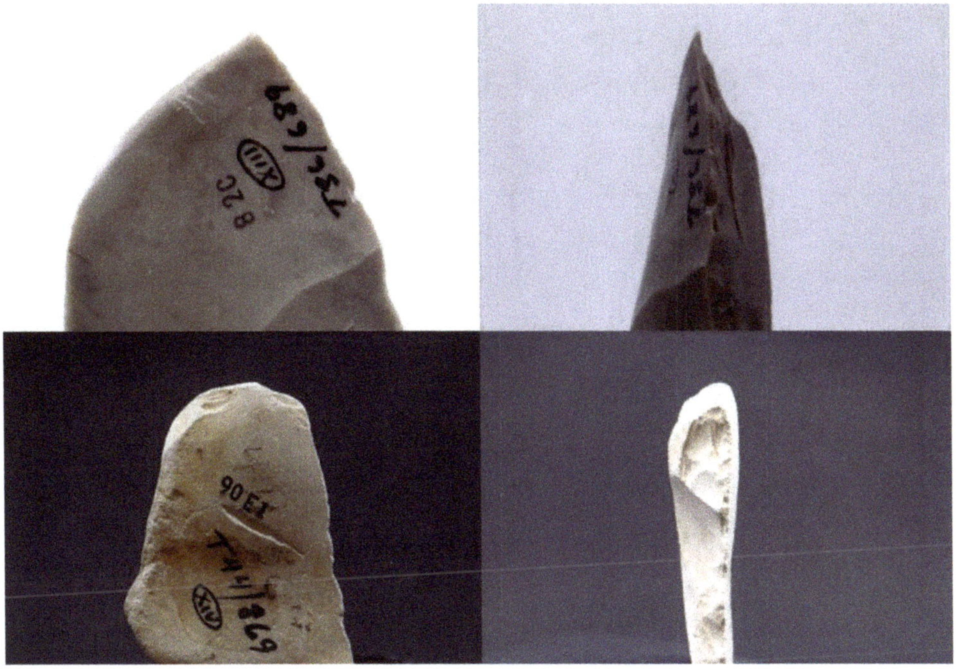

Figure 5.3 Examples of exposure change when a thin specimen rotates on a white (top left and right) and black (bottom left and right) background. Tabun collection, Art Jelinek, Steve Kuhn, University of Arizona, Tucson.

exposure when the object rotates. There is more background for the camera to focus on and therefore it readjusts the brightness levels. This occurs due to the reduced surface area of the subject facing the camera. In the instance of a white background/dark object setup, when the object turns towards the thinner side, the white background suddenly dominates the frame. As such, there is considerably more light being detected by the camera compared to when the artefact had the larger face pointed towards the camera. The camera therefore readjusts to this different reading and brings the exposure down to compensate and balance itself. With a black background, and a light specimen, the darker tones will make the subject lighter to balance out the exposure. This will likely occur when your camera is set to one of the priority modes other than Manual (where the exposure settings are fixed), as the other priority modes allow the settings to freely adjust as the conditions change in the frame (i.e. the artefact rotates). To avoid the exposure changing, either set to Manual or lock the exposure through the Auto Exposure-Lock option (AE-L). This function will fix the exposure and will stop the aperture, shutter speed and ISO from readjusting when the next photograph is being exposed.

5.2.4 Image file format

Digital cameras typically offer the choice of either RAW or JPEG (Joint Photographic Experts Group) image file formats to shoot in. RAW file format captures and stores all data that the camera sensor detects when a photograph is taken; that is, it stores the raw, unprocessed (uncompressed) data – hence its name. RAW images capture a greater dynamic range, a wider spectrum of colours and detail, and are considerably superior to JPEG images. They also allow for greater post-processing flexibility compared to JPEG files and are therefore the better choice if editing is required (see Chapter 6). There are some drawbacks to shooting in RAW, however. As these are large files, they will fill up an SD card faster and consequently will take longer to upload to a computer or the cloud (when transferred wirelessly or by cable) compared to JPEG file formats. It is also crucial to keep in mind that if you are processing your models via Agisoft *Metashape*, *Metashape* cannot process RAW images. They will therefore need to be converted to either JPEG or TIFF files before processing. TIFF is preferable to JPEG as less data is lost in the compression of RAW files to TIFF. Adobe's *Lightroom*, *Photoshop* or *Camera Raw* in the Adobe *Creative Cloud* suite can be used to automate the conversion of images from RAW.

JPEG, on the other hand, compresses the image data when an image is captured and considerable information is lost. The benefit of this is that more images can be stored on the SD card. However, via this compression, the saved data cannot be undone; therefore there is less post-processing flexibility.

Various camera brands, however, offer the choice of different image quality types for both RAW and JPEG file formats. With RAW formats there are typically high-, medium- and low-quality resolution options. With JPEG, there are three choices of size – Large, Medium, Small; then there is the choice of quality (i.e. compression) – Fine and Normal. Fine produces better quality compared to Normal; however, more images can be stored on Normal.

Relating all this information back to photogrammetry processing, selecting the image file format comes down to a couple of considerations. Firstly, time and storage capacity – if you want to capture an object quickly and efficiently and process it in as little time as possible, set the camera to JPEG. Ideally, if you are shooting in JPEG, only shoot in Large, Fine JPEG as you still do not want to compromise on model detail. If you only shoot in RAW you are committing yourself to converting the images at a later date before you can upload them for model processing; however, the images will undeniably be better. Setting the camera to RAW *and* JPEG is a great choice if you want the best of both worlds; that is, you want to process the model straight away but also have the option to edit the images at a later date if you so choose. Whatever file format type you decide to use, it is a good idea to practise checking this setting on the camera before you start your shooting session to ensure that the desired file format is set.

5.3 Tethered shooting

Tethered shooting is a great way to save time when you are shooting for photogrammetry. Tethered shooting is when you connect your camera to a computer or tablet via cable, wi-fi or Bluetooth. Tethering allows you to view the photos on a bigger screen as you take them (which can help with setting exposure), enables organisation of images as you are shooting, and also means you will not fill up the SD card on your camera. Most camera companies and some lightbox manufacturers provide free software that allows for the live-view function and instant wireless transfer of images. Remember, however, if you are shooting in RAW or a high-resolution format, it will take considerable time for images to be transferred as they are large files. The camera may flash as "BUSY" when shooting quickly on a turntable and there will be a time lag in sending over photos; therefore, if you want to upload images instantly it is advisable to send them via cable connection. Simply connect the cable to the computer and select the "Live View" option that the camera software will suggest. It is also possible to shoot from the computer so the camera remains untouched. This is a great option, particularly if you have an electric turntable and if you are using a slower shutter speed. This is possible with the Ortery software and the Orangemonkie Foldio app.

5.4 Video photogrammetry

It is possible to create photogrammetry models from video footage. However, there are two primary issues to contend with. Firstly, image quality is not as good as capturing still photography, due to the reduced resolution of video, so mesh and texture are significantly impacted as a result. Therefore, it is not advisable to take video footage for artefact photogrammetry for archaeological analysis. Secondly, the risk of capturing camera blur in individual frames is significantly increased if the shutter speed is not high enough – image sharpness in photos taken at 25 frames per second will not be as clear as ones taken at 50 frames per second. Similar to the balancing act between the exposure triangle for taking stills, an increased shutter speed will result in a reduction of image brightness. In this case, you will either need to have a shallower depth of field (a lower aperture), increase the ISO, or increase the brightness of your environment.

Despite these issues, there is one clear advantage that video photogrammetry has over photogrammetry from stills and that is speed. An object could be completely captured in less than a minute. This is a considerable benefit when in the field as recording a quick video for a low-quality model could be a great reference tool for later work and research – even using a smartphone photogrammetry app to quickly make a model could be a real help for recording findings in situ and in the surrounding environment. If recording with a digital camera, however, it is important to only take short videos as the longer the recording, the more frames will be extracted from the footage to create the model. It is possible to end up with too many images and consequently waste time processing excessive data, so this is another consideration to take into account. Do not rush through recording the object, however, as setting the turntable on a fast rotation speed or walking too quickly around the object will increase the likelihood of camera blur in the extracted images.

If you are curious to compare video and still model qualities, the method detailed in section 5.6 can be followed for video photogrammetry. The equipment and camera positions are the same, as are the camera settings – the only difference is that the camera is set to video mode. If model quality is a concern, take extra care with the close-up shots when recording. The more detail captured, the greater chance of it being included, so reposition the camera as close as it can focus. Additionally, setting the camera to lock the autofocus can help with stabilising the images and reduce camera blur in your images, particularly if you are walking around the object. This will reduce the likelihood of the lens "hunting" to find a subject to focus on, especially if you are moving over uneven terrain.

The processing side of video photogrammetry includes an additional step where you will need to extract the frames from the video recording. Videos are simply a compilation of individual stills that are played in rapid succession. Depending on the camera's frame per second (FPS) setting and the length of the recording, it is possible to have thousands of images in one batch; therefore, consider how many frames should be extracted to be processed. If you are unsure, start by extracting one FPS, inspect the connectivity between each one and increase if necessary.

Extracting the frames from the video footage is simple to do. In the photogrammetry software Agisoft *Metashape*, you can upload the video directly ("File" – "Import" – "Import Videos") and the software will prompt you for how many frames you want extracted. In *Metashape*, it is referred to as "Frame" step, which you can custom set to every Nth frame or select from the options small, medium and large. It is also possible to extract frames from the modelling software *Blender* and in video editing software such as *VLC Media Player*.

5.5 How many photographs to take

There is no strict rule outlining how many photographs should be taken per camera position (i.e. per round) or per model. The number of photos to take will depend on the size and complexity of the artefact as well as the focal length of the lens and camera sensor size. For detailed, accurate photogrammetry models for archaeological analysis, it is generally recommended that around 75% overlap is maintained. For small, detailed artefacts, particularly for objects with thin edges such as microliths, increasing to around 80% overlap will help ensure images align accurately and the detail is captured in the model. Modelling larger objects, topography or architectural features does not require this amount of overlap and lowering to 70% is perfectly adequate to achieve a decent model.

The number of photographs required to maintain these percentages of overlap will also depend on the lens and sensor size of the camera being used. If a wall is being photographed with a lens that has a shorter focal length, for example between 18–35 mm, more of the wall will be in the frame as the angle of view is larger with this lens type. Therefore, fewer photographs are needed of the wall to ensure complete coverage at 70% overlap. If the focal length is larger, say between 75–100 mm, significantly less surface area of the wall will be featured in the frame as the angle of view is narrower and therefore a lot more images will be required to completely capture the entire feature's surface at 70% overlap. This is why it is important to select a lens that is adequately suited to the object being modelled. Sensor size will also affect the angle of view and therefore the number of images required – cropped sensors have a narrower field of view compared to full-frame and this again will be influenced by the lens being used.

A good starting guide for beginners is to take one shot every 10° so you will have at least 36 photographs per round. If the surface is highly detailed, however, aim for one photograph around every 5°. Just remember the aim in photogrammetry is not to have precise angles between each photograph; the crucial factor is overlap between images. Practise looking through the viewfinder and taking photos as the object is rotated to become familiar with what 75% overlap looks like at different camera angles. As stated above, if a specimen has particularly intricate or complex sections, spend more time capturing these areas with even greater overlap. The more photographs of an area, the more detailed and accurate the model will be – if the images are in focus, well-exposed and sharp.

When thinking about how many photos to take, it is important to remember the fourth golden rule of photogrammetry (listed in 5.8) – to always overshoot rather than undershoot. It is better to have an excess of visual information to build a model than to lack it and create an inaccurate model with holes or a low tie point or mesh face count. Photos can always be removed if there is concern about processing time, your computer's processing capabilities, or storage space. Take note that if you are using an automatic or app-controlled turntable, you are likely going to take considerably more photos than if you are manually rotating the subject or turntable after each shot, or if you have to physically walk around the subject to capture it, so keep this in mind.

5.6 Camera angles and positions for artefact shooting

Once the shooting setup is assembled with the artefact mounted and lights positioned (if you are using them), it is time to position the camera. The process of shooting for photogrammetry involves taking photographs 360° around the specimen at a variety of different angles and heights. This ensures that there is complete coverage of the surface so no holes or mesh inconsistencies will be generated in the digital model. All camera types, from smartphone to mirrorless, can follow this shooting method; the only difference will be the number of camera positions, which depends on the focal length of the lens and the field of view of the camera.

One complete 360° circuit of photographs captured is called for convenience a "round of shots" or a "round" (see Figure 5.4). A "run" is a complete shooting session; that is, all images taken from all the camera positions required.

Regardless of the size or morphology of the artefact, the process of shooting any artefact comes down to a combination of five primary camera positions. The camera positions are high angle, horizontal, close-up, wide and low angle. A high angle camera position is where the camera is physically high and the subject is below the camera; that is, the lens is pointing down. A horizontal position is exactly what it sounds like: the camera is in a horizontal position and the frame and the lens are level. A close-up position is where the lens is physically close to the surface of the subject so it appears larger in the frame and a wide shot is where the camera is positioned away from the subject to fit more of the surface area (if not all) in the frame. A low angle camera position is the opposite of a high angle position – the camera lens is pointing up and the subject is above the lens. This position is useful to capture detail on the undersides of objects that cannot be turned upside down. These positions are not mutually exclusive; that is, you can have a close-up high angle camera position or a wide horizontal shot. Regardless of how the artefact is being photographed – on a turntable or stationary on a mount, in a lightbox, or in an open environment – these camera positions will

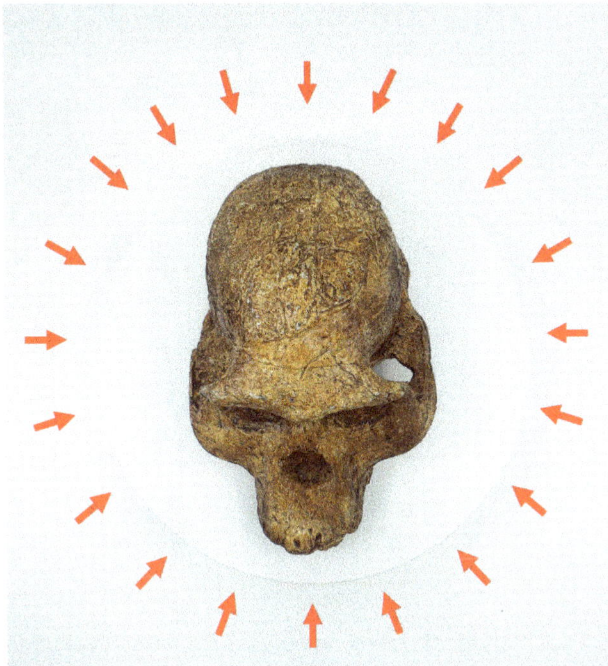

Figure 5.4 A round of photographs captures 360° around the object. The red arrows indicate the positions of the camera. Discipline of Archaeology reference collection, the University of Sydney.

make up the shooting process; the order and number of positions will depend on the subject's morphology and size.

For an object that is being captured in one orientation, the order will follow a combination of these camera positions:

1. high angle
2. close-up horizontal
3. wide horizontal
4. low angle.

This is a standard progression and is illustrated in Figure 5.5. For this particular example, it is possible to conduct an additional round of close-up high angle positions to capture the edges at the top of this lithic specimen (capturing edges is further discussed in 5.6.7). However, it is up to you, the photographer, to decide what positions are necessary to ensure as much information is captured as possible. As mentioned previously, if an artefact is being turned upside down to capture the underside, the object is divided into two hemispheres: the northern and the southern. This is to make the shooting process easier to organise and the model

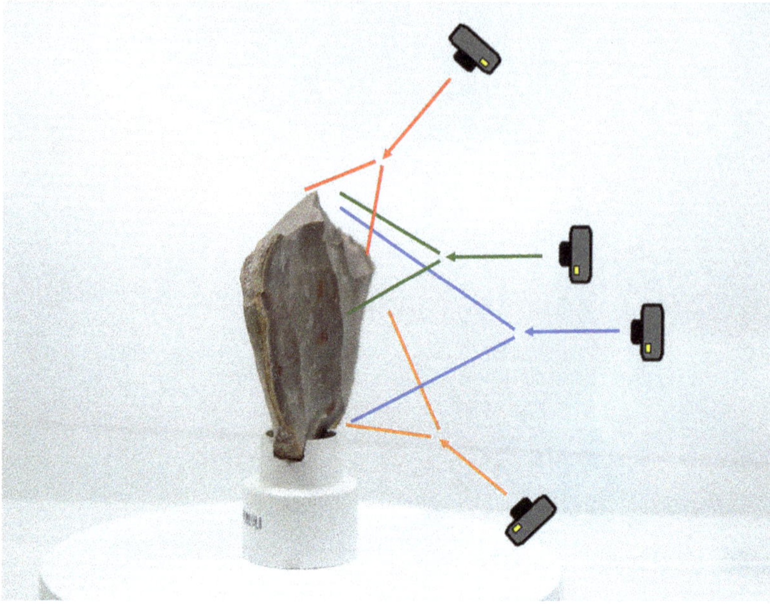

Figure 5.5 Camera position for shooting an object in one orientation; first camera: high angle (red), second camera: close-up horizontal (green), third camera: wide horizontal (blue), fourth camera: low angle (orange). Discipline of Archaeology reference collection, the University of Sydney.

easier to build. If the object needs to be turned on its sides to capture more information, an eastern and western hemisphere can be added as well. For material that has two hemispheres, an example of the order of camera positions can be:

- northern hemisphere – high angle
- northern hemisphere – close-up horizontal
- northern hemisphere – wide horizontal
- close-up connecting (then turn specimen upside down)
- close-up connecting
- southern hemisphere – wide horizontal
- southern hemisphere – close-up horizontal
- southern hemisphere – high angle.

You will notice two additional steps in this method – close-up connecting shots. These are photos that link the northern hemisphere to the southern when it is turned over. More information on close-up connecting shots is provided in 5.6.5.

When a model has finished processing, it is possible to view where the camera was when the photographs were taken. Following the above order of camera positions will produce a model with a similar arrangement of camera locations as shown in Figure 5.6. The order of high angle, close-up and wide horizontal shots will produce a configuration of squares that resembles the planet Saturn. The high angle images can be seen at the top of the inner sphere, the close-up horizontal shots are around the middle, and the wide shots are like the rings of the planet, further out from the inner sphere of shots.

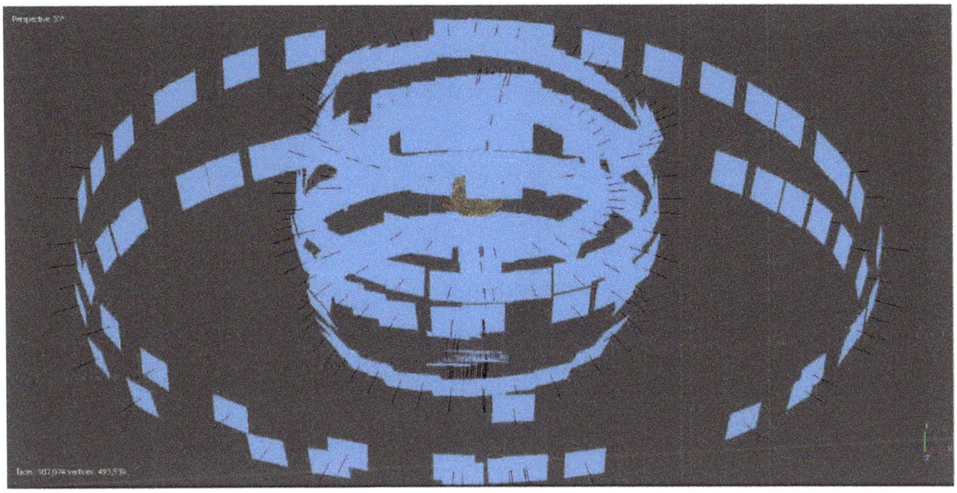

Figure 5.6 The camera positions of each photograph are shown as blue squares in *Metashape*. The high angle and close-up camera positions make the smaller sphere in the centre while the wide shots make up the outer rings.

It is likely that you will need to have multiple rounds of some camera positions at different heights to ensure all of the surface area is photographed. The number of rounds of each camera position will depend on the subject's size, shape and complexity as well as the lens and camera you are using. Large, detailed and complex artefacts may require several rounds of high angle shots at slightly different angles, or several rounds of close-up horizontal shots at various heights. Before shooting, plan the order and number of camera positions for a specific artefact. Tailoring the shooting process for each object will not only minimise the risk of having holes in your model, but also reduces shooting time and processing time. It also means you will have the best chance of producing a highly detailed and accurate model. Organisation and planning are particularly important when preparing to shoot several archaeological objects in one session. Each object may require different shooting methods, so write down a plan for each to reduce the likelihood of holes or other mesh issues developing in the processing stage. Also consider the best orientation for each artefact – is a mount needed or does a different one need to be fashioned? Does the lighting need to be adjusted? Are more light sources required or do the positions need to be changed? All these questions may be intimidating at first, but the more you plan the easier the process will be.

When shooting a fixed object or a site in an open, uncontrolled environment, organising the shooting method and the camera positions is even more crucial. Sun and shadows must be considered as well as the height and angles of the camera if using a monopod. An obstacle-free photography route must also be designed around the site or feature that will allow for the best coverage. It is not a good idea to just start taking photos without considering the order of camera positions and the areas you need to cover. You are risking having holes in the models, having incomplete or warped mesh and you may be increasing the chance of image alignment failure – the first stage of photogrammetry processing. To help build a thorough understanding and foundation of shooting for photogrammetry, several case-study guides have been provided in Chapter 8. These offer some support by explaining what is required when shooting different archaeological artefacts, sites and structures and what the most appropriate shooting methods and camera positions would be.

The primary camera positions used in photogrammetry shooting are discussed in greater detail next so you can further understand what to look for when you are photographing objects in these positions.

5.6.1 High angle shots

For a high angle camera position, the camera is extended up high above the specimen with the lens angled down towards the top section of the subject. This will be the highest position the camera will be in the entire process, so if you are using a tripod, extend the central column to its fullest extent and then adjust the legs to a suitable position. If you are shooting freehand, stand close to the subject and look down over it. Avoid including the mount in the frame if you are using one. If it is difficult to avoid, either move closer to the artefact or angle the camera up slightly so more of the background is in the shot. If the stand or mount is not avoided in the images, it will likely be included in the model and will have to be removed through masking.

Aim to fill the frame with a lot of surface detail. Depending on the specimen's size and shape, you can choose to be very close to the specimen or you can move a bit back to ensure more of the specimen is covered in one frame. For larger, more complex artefacts, it might be necessary to do multiple rounds of high angle shots at different camera heights to ensure all surface detail of the artefact is covered. Figure 5.7 shows four images of the top region of a lithic specimen, the camera moving from top left to right, then bottom left to right.

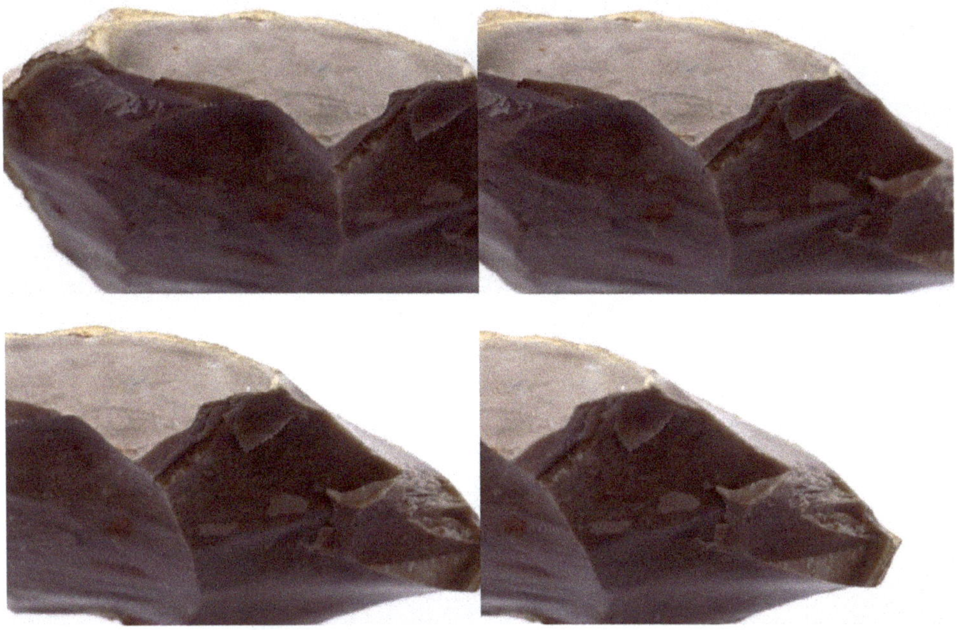

Figure 5.7 Image examples of high angle shots. Discipline of Archaeology reference collection, the University of Sydney.

5.6.2 Connecting shots

Connecting shots are essential between camera positions to visually connect the photographs taken from each camera angle. This is particularly important if the images from the camera positions do not significantly overlap. Connecting shots support the software in identifying how one area of the subject relates to the next and maintain continuity between the images. To take connecting shots, simply capture a few photos as you move the camera from one position to the next. The number of connecting shots will depend on how big the artefact is and the distance between the following camera position from the preceding one. Aim for between two to eight images but ensure there is consistent overlap throughout all the photos. In Figure 5.8, the photographs closely overlap as the camera moves from a high angle position to a horizontal position.

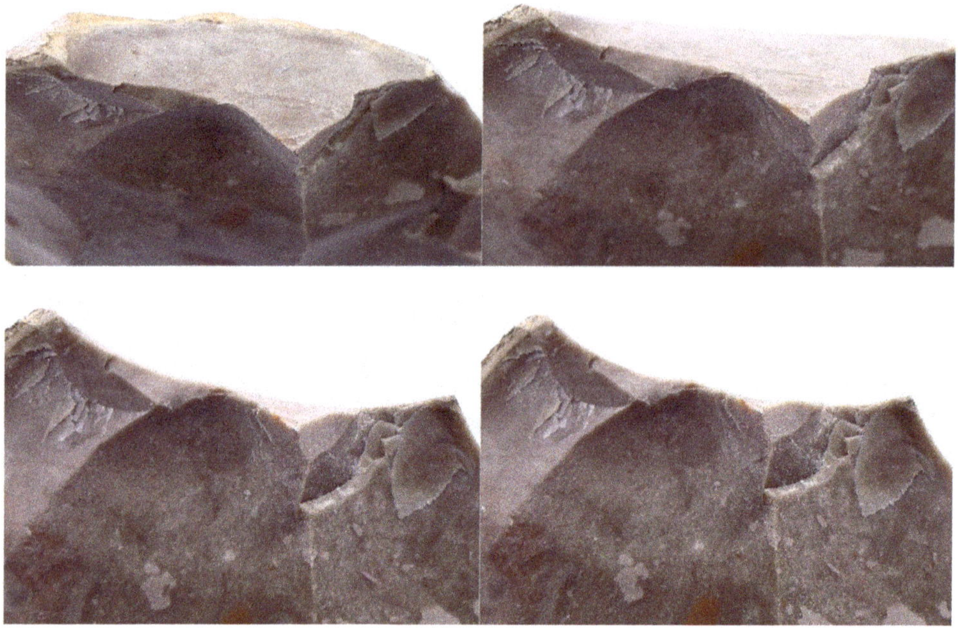

Figure 5.8 Example of connecting shots.

5.6.3 Close-up horizontal shots

The purpose of close-up horizontal shots (Figure 5.9) is to obtain detailed, well-exposed photographs of the object's surfaces and edges. This round of images does not have to be perfectly level; the camera lens just needs to be angled up to a horizontal position to obtain a new perspective of the subject's surface. Make sure that you focus on the complexities and any detail of the surface in this round, particularly the edges of the specimen. If the artefact is thin, this will be the most important round of the entire process, as it will be these photos that connect one face of the subject to the other. In this case, take your time and be sure to have at least 95% overlap between shots. Some examples of thin objects that you will need to increase the amount of overlap between shots will include coins, shells and microliths.

What the archaeological specimen is and how it is being modelled will determine the number of rounds of close-up horizontal shots. For example, if the artefact is long, very detailed and cannot be turned upside down, it would be a good idea to do several rounds of close-up horizontal shots around and down the artefact. If the artefact can be turned upside down, the size of the subject will determine the

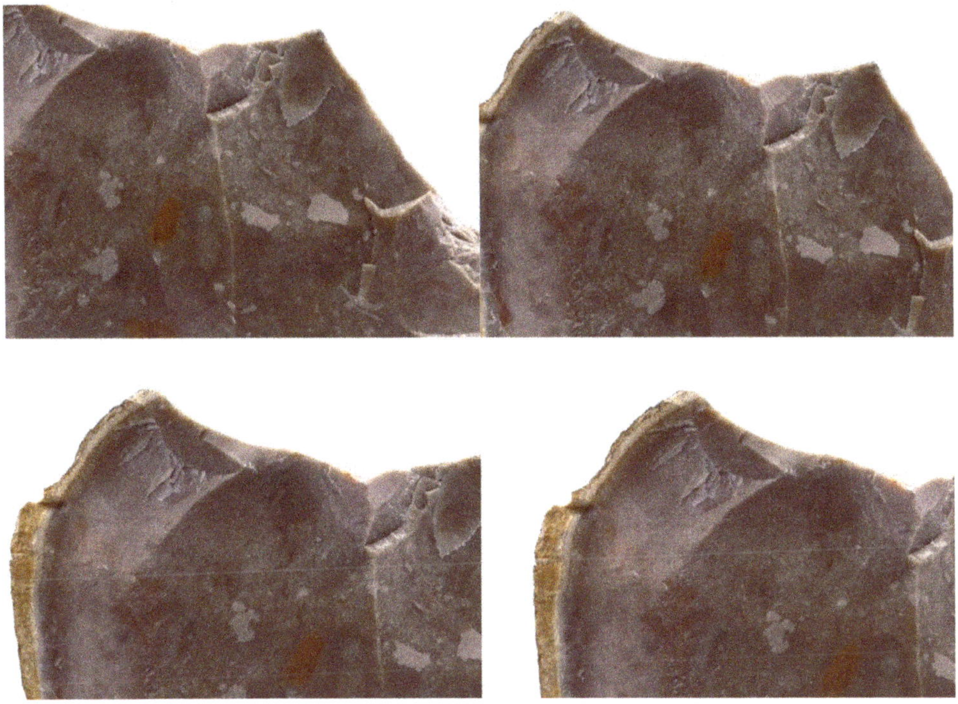

Figure 5.9 Examples of close-up horizontal images.

number of rounds needed to capture all the surface information. If the artefact is roughly between <1–8 cm and a macro lens between 65 and 90 mm is being used, the frame may cover most of the artefact meaning only one round may be required. If, however, the artefact is larger, for example over 20 cm in height, and a macro lens between 65 and 90 mm is being used, multiple rounds of close-up horizontal shots may be needed to completely capture the subject's surface. For larger artefacts, a 35 mm macro lens is much better suited as it is likely only one round of close-up horizontal shots is necessary to completely cover the main body of the artefact.

If the subject is positioned on a mount and both the northern and southern hemispheres are being captured, the close-up shots must not include the mount in any image. The bottom of the frame must end above the mount to avoid it completely. Do not worry that half of the artefact is not captured, as it will be photographed when the artefact is turned upside down. Try to be as close as the lens will allow to the subject's surface to capture as much detail as possible. The number of photographs taken will consequently exceed the number in other rounds due to the camera being closer; however, with more information the quality of the model will improve.

5.6.4 Wide horizontal shots

The next primary camera position is a wide horizontal position. The purpose of these shots is to position the close-up shots within the wider context of the artefact's surface, to identify the boundary edges and overall shape of the artefact. Reposition the camera by moving it back, creating greater distance between the lens and the subject to fit the entire subject in the frame. If a mount is being used, it must still be avoided. It may be necessary to adjust the height of the camera here to ensure the mount is not included in the field of view. Although the camera has been moved further away, do not move so far that there is an unnecessary amount of background in the image – the edges of the subject should be close to the frame's edges. In Figure 5.10, four images are shown in the wide horizontal position. Notice how the top of the lithic specimen reaches the top of the frame; however, the mount is completely avoided.

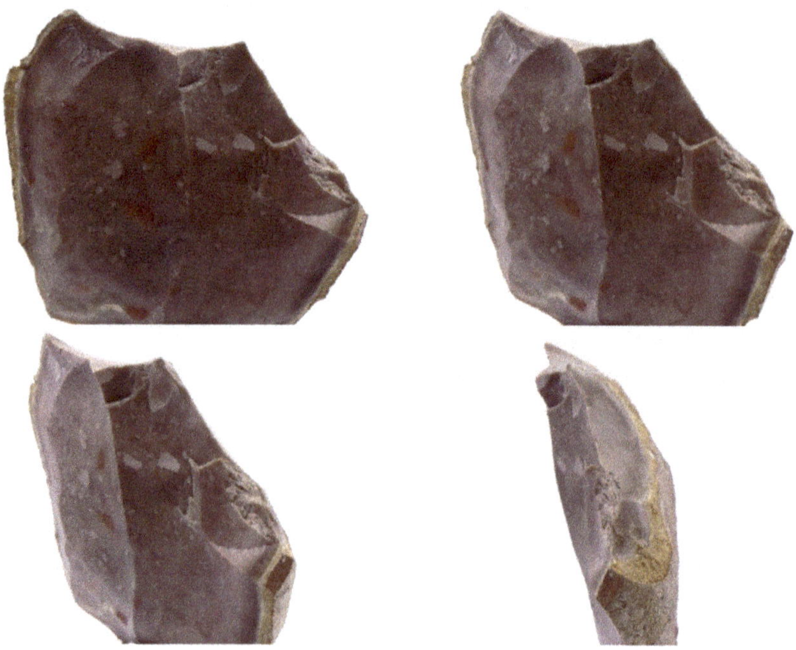

Figure 5.10 Examples of wide horizontal photographs.

5.6.5 Close-up connecting shots

Close-up connecting shots are a very useful way of linking the images of the northern hemisphere of an object to the images of the southern hemisphere. They occur just before and after the object is turned upside down (if the above order is followed, after the first round of wide horizontal shots and before the second round).

The point of the close-up connecting images is to tell the software where the camera is once the object is turned upside down. This is done by moving the camera close to the surface again (taking connecting shots as you move) to a similar position used for the close-up horizontal shots. Find and focus on an obvious feature or detail that is on the surface, around the centre of the artefact. This feature must be at a spot on the specimen that is not obscured by the mount when the object is turned upside down and is still clearly visible. Take a couple of well-exposed photos of the detail, then turn the artefact upside down. The camera may need to be readjusted so that the feature is still in the frame, just upside down. Take another couple of close-up photos of the feature before relocating the camera to the next position, taking connecting photos of the feature as you move.

Close-up connecting images are important for model-building and should not be overlooked. The simple reason is that the close-up horizontal and wide horizontal rounds taken of the northern hemisphere might not overlap enough with the photos taken of the southern hemisphere. The photogrammetry software may struggle to correctly identify how the northern and southern hemispheres relate to each other in three-dimensional space if no clear images connect the two halves. Consequently, the software may fail to achieve 100% alignment and half a model may be produced. Figure 5.11 shows an example of close-up connecting

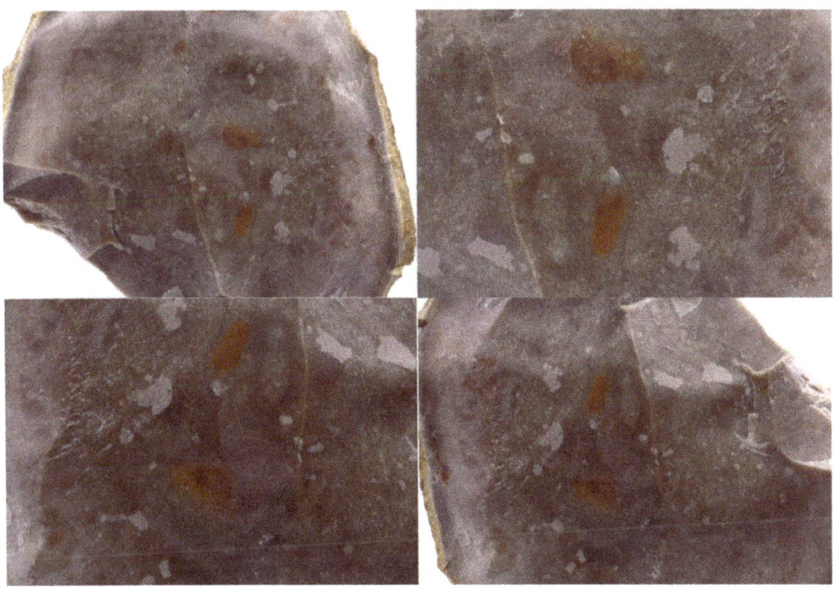

Figure 5.11 Example of close-up connecting images.

shots. The first image shows the camera slightly further back, and most of the lithic's surface is in the frame. The camera is then moved towards the surface and several features can be identified, such as the two orange marks and the fracture line. The third image shows the same three features now upside down as the object has been repositioned so the southern hemisphere is exposed. In the final image, the camera is pulled back to return to the correct position for a round of wide horizontal shots.

5.6.6 Low angle shots

If the artefact cannot be turned upside down, several low angle rounds may be necessary to capture information on the underside of an archaeological object. If shooting in one orientation, this step can follow the wide horizontal position, just remember to connect the shots when moving the camera to the low angle position. If the subject has curves or angular overhangs, there is surface information that high angle shots will miss. This will result in holes or distortions occurring in the mesh or significantly blurred texture. A few low angle rounds should capture this detail to help the software identify the dimensions and contours of the surface. If this is not possible, however, due to the nature of the photography setup or if the object is connected to a stand that inhibits camera access, you may not be able to completely capture all the undersides of the object. In this case, you will have to fill these holes in the processing stage (see 7.10.2).

Positioning the camera for low angle photos involves lowering the height of the camera and moving it back slightly to fill the frame as much as possible. One or several rounds of low angle shots may be necessary to cover the entire object depending on the size and the complexity of the subject's morphology. Between each round, however, take a connecting shot to ensure that each photograph is connected. Figure 5.12 shows some low angle images of the underside of a pottery vessel's lip.

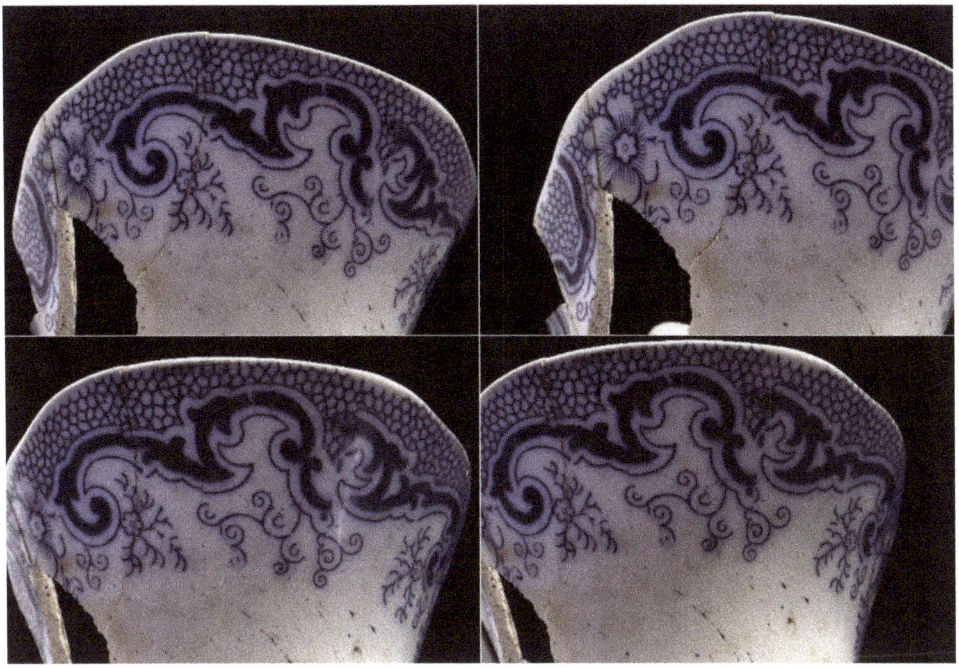

Figure 5.12 Example of low angle images.

5.6.7 Edge and feature shots

Once the entire artefact has been captured using a combination of the above camera positions, a few more rounds may be needed at the end of the shooting stage that focus on fine edges or complex features. More attention is needed at sharp, thin edges and intricate or detailed areas so that the images are aligned and are rendered correctly. Thin or narrow edges of lithic material, shell or bone may not align or mesh correctly if incorrect lighting, lenses or camera positions are used as it can be difficult to successfully capture the physical dimensions of such small surface areas. Additional care must be taken of lighting and the background if the edges are slightly transparent.

If the specimen being modelled does have fine edges or an intricate feature, it may be necessary to reposition the model so the area of interest is in better light and can be captured easily. This is particularly important if the area is in or is casting a shadow. If you do reposition the object, remember to take connecting or close-up connecting shots from the last position so there is a smooth succession of images. The number of photos and camera positions focusing on the region will depend on how much coverage is required and how big or small the object is. For taking edge shots, position the camera as close as possible to the object in a horizontal position, focusing on the edge. Move the camera in an arc-shape from one side of the edge (starting in a close-up horizontal position) to the other by repositioning the camera to a high angle, then back down to a second close-up horizontal position on the other side, shown in Figure 5.13. Once you are on the other side, shift the camera slightly forward along the edge and then proceed to take images back to the other face in an arc-shape. With this motion, the entire length of the edge will be captured and the connecting shots moving over the peak of the edges ensure that the software will stitch them together accurately. Ensure that you have considerable overlap with each image, aiming for around 80% overlap from one image to the next. Incorrect alignment of sharp edges is a very common problem, so adopting this practice will aid in avoiding this.

For capturing intricate features on the face of an object (i.e. not the edge of an object), applying a combination of the positions outlined in this chapter (high angle, close-up horizontal, wide, low angle) but focusing only on the feature, is a good method to ensure the feature area is captured clearly and correctly. Just ensure the area is well-lit before focusing on it. The camera must also be considerably closer to

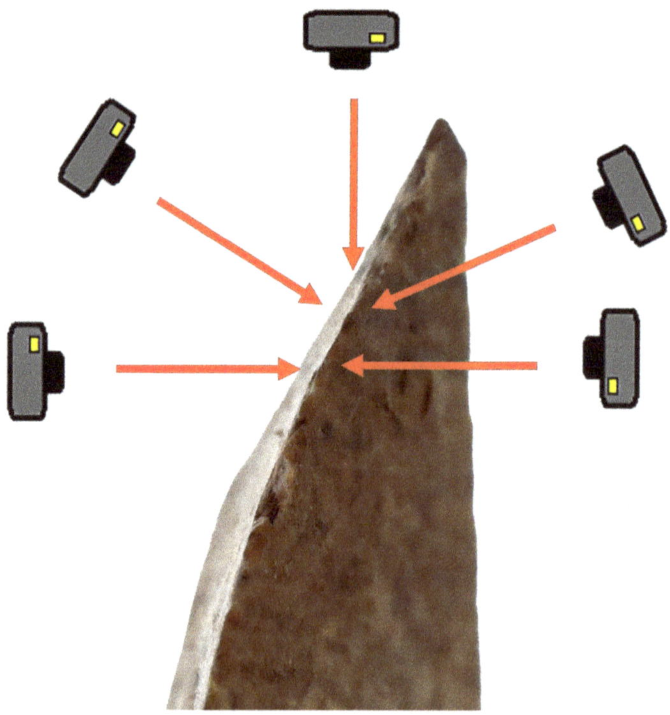

Figure 5.13 Where to position the camera when taking edge and feature shots. Notice how the camera moves over the edges to capture them.

the object. Depending on the clarity of the artefact's features, images may require some editing before you commence processing the model to accentuate the detail in the features (refer to Chapter 6 for image editing techniques). Just remember to be conservative with enhancements to maintain authenticity with the original object. As you will be much closer to the subject to take edge and feature shots, consider taking the camera off the tripod (if one is being used) so you can position the lens closer to the specimen. Additionally, setting the lens to manual focus (identified as "MF", the switch is typically found on the lens or the camera body) will provide you with complete control over the specific areas you want to be in focus. The lens may have trouble focusing when it is so close to the object in autofocus (AF) mode, so using manual focus can help with capturing the necessary images. Manual focus relies on the photographer to adjust the focusing ring on the lens; rotating the dial will change the position of the focal plane. When set to autofocus, the lens' motor will adjust the focus for you depending on the light, the subject's contrast and motion.

If you want to shoot an artefact that has slightly transparent edges, reduce the intensity of the light source (if possible) and move in an arc pattern moving from one face, over the top of the edge to the other face, connecting one side to the other as outlined above in taking edge shots. It is very difficult to model objects that are slightly transparent, so take your time to accurately position the camera and the lights to not have direct reflection or to highlight the edge's transparency. If possible, angle lights away so the edges are darker and turn off any on-camera flashes. Reducing the camera's exposure may also help, but be aware that it can be very time-consuming to generate a model of any objects that have even a slightly transparent or glassy surface.

5.7 Camera lens calibration

Camera lens calibration is essential in close-range photogrammetry modelling as factors such as the lens' focal length and distortion can warp a camera's true parameters. *Metashape*, as well as several other photogrammetry software, automatically calibrates the camera's parameters when aligning the images, meaning you do not have to calibrate the camera before every processing session when using this software. To ensure that the calibration is correct, however, additional steps can be taken before the shooting stage.

An image of a chessboard or a page of systematic dots is needed to calibrate a camera – these can either be on a computer screen or printed on a piece of paper. A chessboard pattern has been included at the end of this manual so that you can calibrate your lens. In *Metashape*, the chessboard can be generated on the screen by heading to "Tools" – "Camera" – "Show Chessboard" (previous versions will have this listed under "Lens"). Zoom in or out of the page by scrolling on your touchpad or mouse wheel so that at least ten squares are shown on each side.

To calibrate your camera lens, position the camera at roughly the same distance away from the page or screen that you were when you photographed the archaeological object or feature. Take at least three photos of the calibration pattern from a range of different angles, such as from the left and right sides, some high angle and some low angle (see Figure 5.14). When shooting the different angles, avoid capturing glare from the page or screen as you need clear images of the squares to calibrate the lens properly. Also, keep the focal length consistent if using a zoom lens for each set of captured angles but fill the frame with the chessboard pattern as much as possible. When finished, simply click the mouse to exit the chessboard view. Upload these images into *Metashape* in a new chunk, and label them "Calibration images" to help you keep track of the photos. Navigate to "Tools" – "Camera Calibration", which will open a new window. For all prime and zoom lenses, ensure that the "Camera Type" option is set to "Frame". If you are using a fish-eye lens, change this option to "Fish-eye" and press "OK". Then head to "Tools" – "Camera" – "Calibrate Camera"

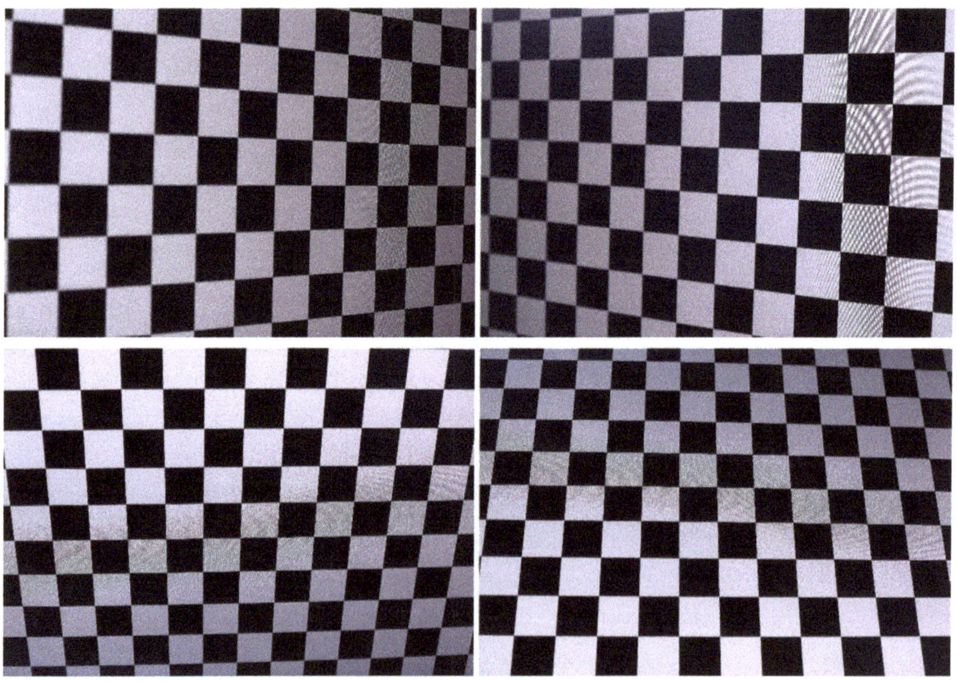

Figure 5.14 Images of the chessboard pattern in *Metashape*. Moving clockwise, the camera was angled from the left, right, at a high angle, then a low angle.

and select all boxes in the window and press "OK". A processing window will appear and, once complete, return to the "Camera Calibration" page under the "Tools" heading and click the "Adjusted" tab. This will show the adjusted parameters of the lens. To ensure that the lens has been calibrated correctly, open one of the chessboard images; there should be dots pinned to each of the corners of the squares. If they are correctly positioned in all the images uploaded, the calibration was a success. If the dots are not positioned well, take a few more calibration images of the chessboard pattern at different angles, upload them to the same chunk in *Metashape*, and recalibrate the lens following the steps above. Once you are satisfied that the coloured dots are positioned correctly, return to the "Camera Calibration" page and save the adjusted parameters to a file by clicking the save icon so that these can be applied to other images that use the same camera and lens. To import a different camera calibration file, click on the neighbouring icon of a folder, which will allow you to open a different calibration file. Once the camera calibration has been loaded and saved to the project, the photographs of the object can be loaded into a new chunk and the workflow to build a model can be run as normal.

5.8 The golden rules for shooting for photogrammetry

1. The first rule to remember when shooting for photogrammetry is to maintain consistent overlap in each photograph. There is considerable debate over the approximate percentage of overlap each image needs, but if you have a complex, small or intricate object such as a microlith or coin, having 80% overlap is a sure-fire way to ensure you have 100% alignment in your photogrammetry model. This might be excessive and many photogrammetrists opt for around 60% overlap, but it is up to the photographer and their judgement. For most objects, both large and small, the general recommendation is that around 75% overlap is maintained as this degree of overlap will ensure the model will successfully align without any holes in the mesh. If you find it difficult to determine what 75% overlap looks like in your images, an easy method to adopt is to look for a feature on the surface of the subject at either the right or left side of the frame (depending which direction you are moving) and aim to capture it in a minimum of six shots as you shoot across the surface. The more overlap you have in the images, the greater number of images that feature will appear in, helping the software to align the shots. There are a number of variables that will affect how many times a feature will be captured, so use this as a general guide when first starting out.

2. The second golden rule is to connect every round, section or area of the subject with photographs; that is, always take "connecting shots". Connecting shots link one focus area to the next through a series of images – there aren't any disconnected images that show unrelated surface area and there is a clear progression of camera angle movement. This is so the software recognises a new section and can work out how it spatially relates to the previous one. This decreases the processing time and increases alignment accuracy. Do not photograph a new area randomly without connecting the two areas with photographs, as the software will struggle to align 100% of the photographs unless the software's settings are changed. When taking connecting shots, you must still abide by the first golden rule – maintain consistent overlap with each photograph. If you are unsure whether you should or should not photograph, a good mantra to remember is "when in doubt, take a shot".

3. The third golden rule to remember is to fill the frame with the *subject* – not the background or the mount. The focus should be the object you want to be made into a photogrammetry model – do not waste space in the frame with anything but the subject. Aim for at least 75% of the frame to be archaeological object to a maximum of 25% background. If there is a chance that the mount could be in the shot, prioritise having more background in the frame than the stand as the background is easier to mask out than a stand.

4. The fourth golden rule is that it is better to overshoot than undershoot when photographing the object. Even if you take an excessive number of images for a small model, photographs can always be removed later. With too few images, the overall quality of the model will be low; there will be a low tie point cloud and polygon face count and holes may occur in the model.

5. The fifth golden rule is to avoid changing the camera's exposure or white balance while shooting. Extreme changes in exposure may result in the software not recognising one image from the next, meaning that these images may likely be ignored by the software in the alignment stage. An example of this may be if a ring flash is being used and there is a delay between a photograph being taken and the flash going off. This can happen if the flash doesn't charge instantly between flashes due to dying batteries. Attempting to merge together images with varying white balances will also not produce aesthetically pleasing models. The software may attempt to combine them but the surface texture will not be accurate or reflect the original object's appearance.

6. The final golden rule for photogrammetry shooting is to not change the focal length of the lens during a shooting session. This means you cannot change lens types or adjust the zoom if you are using a zoom lens once a shooting session has commenced, unless you want to restart from the beginning. The simple reason is that there will be varying distortion in the images for each focal length and it may result in the model having incorrect dimensions. This also means that if you have a setup that includes multiple cameras, every camera must use the same lens type (brand and focal length) and have the same sensor size. Distortions differ between lenses, even across the same focal lengths with different brands, so it is imperative the focal length is consistent in order to create a model with accurate dimensions.

For those who are new to photogrammetry, all this information can be overwhelming, especially if you have never held a camera before. Therefore, the primary steps for setting up a camera and shooting archaeological material have been summarised in a workflow at the end of this book. This can be used as a guide as you progress through the steps, or as a quick reference guide once you are familiar with the process of shooting for photogrammetry.

5.9 Next steps

In this chapter, we outlined the various steps involved to completely capture an object for photogrammetry modelling. There is considerable preparation before the shooting begins, particularly in planning the shooting stage, and organising the images and the metadata. The crucial step of setting up the camera correctly was also covered, as well as choosing the metering mode and the image file format.

The variety of camera positions presented here is necessary to ensure there are no holes in the mesh layer, the morphology is correct and representative of the original object, and that the surface texture is captured correctly and is as accurate as possible. The several "golden rules" are also essential to follow. Ensuring continuous 75% overlap in each image, connecting each shot, and filling the frame with the object to limit negative space are all crucial to generate the best model possible. If there are issues with the images, however, such as imbalanced exposure or white balance, there are ways to rectify them. In the following chapter, we explore how to adjust batch images in image editing software and the importance of including a colour chart in your images to obtain correct colour temperature. We also introduce the concept of focus stacking – a technique that can help with modelling incredibly small objects.

Chapter 6

EDITING YOUR IMAGES

Editing photographs is a great way to improve the final texture of a photogrammetry model or to resurrect photographs that are not at the standard necessary to create a successful photogrammetry model. Issues such as unbalanced exposure, incorrect light temperature or white balance, and even shadows and specular reflection can be corrected very easily with image editing software. Building a photogrammetry model from edited photographs can drastically improve the overall aesthetic and appeal of the model and can even improve alignment success with further enhancements such as brightness, contrast and clarity.

This chapter focuses on the applications within the Adobe *Creative Cloud* suite, specifically the image editing programs *Lightroom* and *Camera Raw* (accessed through *Bridge* or *Photoshop*). Features and detail can be enhanced and colours corrected but, most importantly, these programs allow for batch editing. This means that multiple images can be adjusted simultaneously or edits to one image can be copied and pasted to other images to maintain consistency. This chapter begins with how to adjust the images to improve them for modelling purposes for different outcomes (6.1), how to use colour charts to correct for incorrect colour casts (6.2), and how to focus stack images – a useful trick used in image editing software to help model very small objects (6.3).

Although it may be tempting, do not over-edit your images. Exaggerating features and enhancing the colour may make the model more visually impressive but it will no longer be an accurate representation of the original object. Improving images should only be done when absolutely necessary; that is, if a camera was incorrectly set up. All adjustments should be made cautiously with a record of what settings were tweaked. Correcting the colour of a batch of images, however, is highly recommended. Using a colour checker chart will correct the colours and hues of the images of the object and will ensure that the model's texture is a true representation of the original object.

6.1 Image editing

If you are planning to edit the images you have captured before you process your photogrammetry model, it is recommended to set your camera to RAW file format, or RAW *and* JPEG. RAW images contain more colour information compared to other file formats, therefore producing higher-quality images and greater editing capabilities. If you have not captured your images in RAW, only JPEG, and editing is needed, do not stress as Adobe's *Camera Raw* and *Lightroom* can also be used to adjust JPEG images. Fortunately, *Lightroom* does not degrade the quality of your JPEG images as it is non-destructive software; however, the final product will not contain the same degree of quality that RAW images contain.

If shooting in RAW, keep in mind that RAW images are larger files and will fill up your SD card and storage devices faster. Additionally, *Metashape* cannot process RAW images so any images taken in this file format will have to be converted to a different file format before uploading to *Metashape*. Converting files can be considerably time-consuming so this should also be factored into the processing schedule.

Image editing software offers a range of settings that can be adjusted to improve or enhance your images. Typically, the options include what is shown in Figure 6.1. For improving images for photogrammetry modelling, the settings you may need to adjust include exposure, contrast, highlights, shadows and blacks, with optional settings such as temperature, tint, texture and clarity.

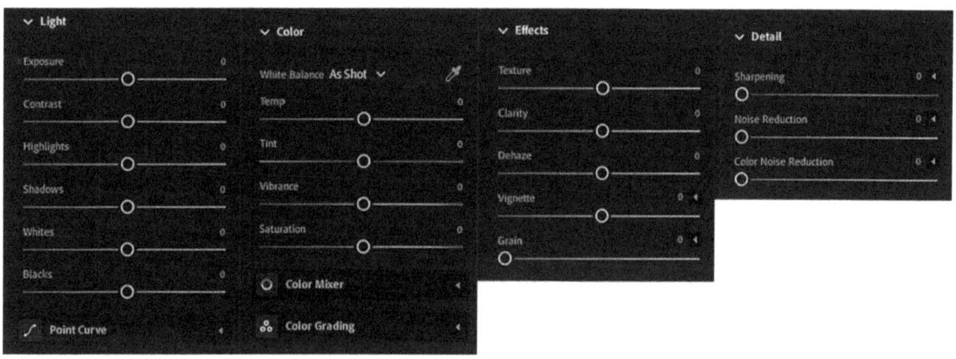

Figure 6.1 The typical settings offered in image editing software to adjust a photograph.

If your images are all too dark or too light, referred to as being underexposed or overexposed respectively, the exposure of the images needs to be corrected. Exposure can sometimes be referred to as "brightness" and balancing it will bring out more of the surficial complexity of the images of the archaeological object you are modelling. Typically, with image editing software, adjustments are made by moving a slider up and down (see Figure 6.1) to adjust a specific quality of an image. For images that are too dark, moving the slider to the right will brighten the image and conversely moving the slider to the left will lower the brightness.

Problems with the white balance of a batch of images should be corrected to a colour rendition chart or greyscale (discussed below in 6.2); however, slight adjustments can be made manually by altering the blue-to-yellow temperature spectrum and the green-to-pink tint spectrum. To remove shadows, two settings need to be corrected. The highlights of the image need to be lowered, while the shadow tool is increased. This may not eliminate the shadows entirely, but it will reduce the severity and it will resurrect the colour and detail of the surface underneath the shadow. If an artefact is highly reflective, reducing the highlights of the images can also reduce areas of localised brightness caused by specular reflection. Saturation and vibrance should be used with caution. Although it may make your images look attractive, excessive use of these two functions may distort the true colours of the original object.

Adjusting a combination of an image's contrast, black tones, texture, clarity and sharpness will accentuate the finer details on the archaeological object's surface and can improve the overall visual quality of the model. Boosting the exposure, texture and clarity tools specifically can help improve a model's alignment accuracy (Figure 6.2). The accentuated detail and definition of the artefact's surface and

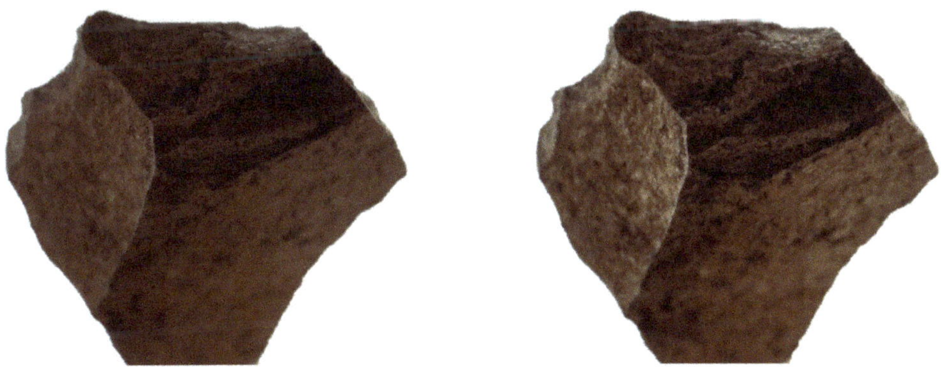

Figure 6.2 Images before and after adjusting the exposure, contrast and texture settings to this high angle photo of a lithic artefact. Discipline of Archaeology reference collection, the University of Sydney.

morphology can provide additional key surface data that the software can identify and use to align images.

Take note: *never* resize or crop images. Photogrammetry software will not be able to position the cameras if images have been geometrically modified. This is why it is crucial to fill the frame with the object being modelled as you cannot crop out any section of the images.

To adjust images using *Lightroom 2024*, create a copy of the images first, labelling it appropriately, and leave the original folder untouched, just in case. Open *Lightroom* and create an "Album" in which to add your images. Select the first image of the batch and make adjustments using the tools in the right-hand panel. Once you are happy with the changes, these can be copied and pasted to the rest of the images by heading to the "Edit" tab – "Copy", or select the "Photo" tab then press "Edit Copy Settings", or select the three dots in the image editing panel – "Copy Edit Settings", or by simply pressing the short-cut key for copy and paste on your keyboard. Select all the images that need to have the same changes applied to them and select the "Edit" tab – "Paste".

To adjust images in *Camera Raw*, Adobe's *Bridge* must be opened first. *Camera Raw* can also be accessed via *Photoshop*; however, it is easier to open multiple images at once in *Camera Raw* via *Bridge*. Once *Bridge* is opened, navigate to the folder containing the images of the object, select all the ones you want to edit, then right-click and select "Open in *Camera Raw*". Once in *Camera Raw*, select all the images you want to adjust and use the tools in the right-hand panel to make the changes. Adjustments will instantly be applied to all the images selected. With this method you are able to see the effects of the adjustments made as you go, allowing you to be more precise with your changes. Once you have finished making adjustments, either press "Done" to save the changes, or press the "Convert and save" icon at the top of the window. This will bring up a new window where you can choose to save the edited images in a new location or as a different file type. If processing in *Metashape*, convert the files to either TIFF or JPEG for processing. TIFF files are preferable to JPEG as less information is lost when RAW files are converted to TIFF compared to JPEG; however, again, as they contain more data they are larger files and will take up more storage space.

6.2 Colour correcting with colour charts

Colour rendition charts, or colour checkers, are charts that contain a grid of 24 coloured squares that are commonly used in photography and film. They are used to adjust a photograph's colour cast so that the images displayed are true to reality.

This is particularly important in photogrammetry; rendered models should exhibit accurate colour casts. There are a number of colour charts on the market, each with its own individual method of use. Additional software is needed to set the colour profiles to the images. Again, Adobe's *Lightroom*, *Photoshop* or *Camera Raw* can be used; however, additional software may accompany the colour rendition chart to calibrate and create colour profiles.

The Calibrite X-Rite *ColorChecker Passport Photo 2* is a great compact and durable colour rendition chart that includes a classic target of the standard 24 colour tiles to correct colour casts, a white balance target to set the white balance and an 18% grey balance target to set exposure and white balance. The calibration software is available online for free. When an image is imported into the software, it can automatically detect the colour targets. Once detected, the software corrects the colour cast, creating a profile that can be saved and applied to other images taken in the same shooting conditions to correct them.

To use this product to colour correct your images, the following method can be applied.

1. After the photography setup has been designed, turn on all the light sources and position the colour chart in the centre of the shooting environment.
2. Make sure that the colour chart is facing straight towards the camera (as shown in Figure 6.3) and not at an angle to ensure the software easily detects the targets.

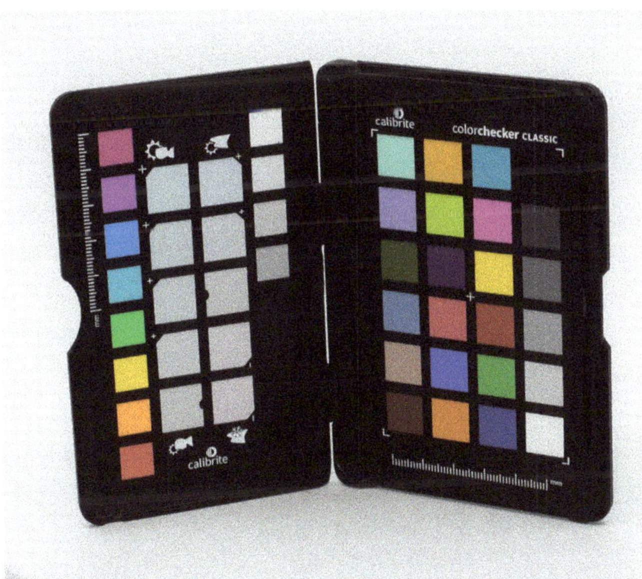

Figure 6.3 The Calibrite X-Rite *ColorChecker Passport Photo 2* is a reliable colour rendition chart for colour correcting images.

3. Set your camera to RAW file format and take a shot of the entire chart, clearly showing all 24 colour tiles in the frame.
4. Continue to take a shot of the info board and then complete the shooting process of the object you want modelled.
5. On a computer, create a master folder in a location that is easily accessible. This is where the original images, the colour corrected images, and the model will be stored. Make two new folders within this folder. Import the RAW images into one folder and label it something such as "ObjectX_Trial1". Label the second folder "ObjectX_Trial1_ColourCorrected".
6. Once you are ready to upload and edit the images, open an image editing software such as *Lightroom* and import all the RAW images – for *Lightroom*, a new folder will need to be created.
7. Select the image of the colour chart and export this image as a DNG file (Export icon – "Custom Settings" – "Image Type" – "DNG") to a new folder in the master folder.
8. Open the *ColorChecker Camera Calibration* software (which is available for free download from Calibrite's website) and drag and drop the converted DNG image. The photo will appear with a grid positioned over the top of each of the coloured squares. If it is slightly askew and not perfectly aligned, there is the option to adjust the borders of the grid.
9. Once happy with the grid's position, click "Create Profile" and the profile will be saved to a location of your choosing – select the master folder.
10. Return to the image editing software (i.e. *Lightroom* in this example) and navigate to the folder of images of your archaeological object. The colour profile needs to be imported to correct the rest of the images.
11. In *Lightroom*, this is done by opening the first image, navigating to the drop-down menu next to the "Profile" setting in the image editing panel, then selecting "Browse all profiles". In this new window, select the three dots at the top and click "Import Profiles" where you can navigate to the colour profile you created and import it. The colour profile will then be added in the list of profiles where it can be selected and applied to that image. Copy the edit settings (outlined in 6.1) then select all the images and paste the profile to them all. This same method can be followed if you are editing in *Camera Raw* as well. The only difference is that to copy and paste the settings, there is no "Edit" tab, so these options are available in the edit panel, under the "More Image Settings" which is shown as three dots or by simply pressing the shortcut key for copy and paste on your

keyboard. Be aware that to use profiles in *Camera Raw* the file may need to be zipped in order to be imported.

12. The images will all be adjusted to the new colour profile then exported as JPGs or TIFFs back to the master folder, into the folder named "ObjectX_Trial1_ColourCorrected" to be used to create the photogrammetry model.

This is a handy method as the same colour profile can be used to adjust the colour casts on all photos that were taken with the same camera under the same conditions. Colour rendition charts include spectrally neutral white targets that can be used for setting the white balance. In *Lightroom* and *Camera Raw*, under the white balance setting, there is a dropper icon that, when clicked onto the white target in the image, will instantly adjust the white balance to match that white coloured tile. In the same way as outlined above, these adjusted settings can be copied and pasted to correct the white balance of the rest of the images in the batch.

6.3 Focus stacking

Focus stacking is the process of obtaining one clear, sharp image that is produced by digitally stacking together several images with varying focal planes. These images are all taken from the same camera position – what is different in each image is the focus plane's position in the image. Due to macro lenses having a short depth of field, focus stacking eliminates the problem of having blurry sections of the object being photographed. Focus stacking is therefore a useful, yet arduous, method to create highly detailed, accurate models of very small or fine artefacts, such as beads or microliths. Photogrammetry modelling of objects of such a small size is typically termed "macro photogrammetry".

To generate one focus stacked image, the photographer will begin by adjusting the lens so the point of focus is directed at the area of the object that is closest to the lens. While taking photos, the photographer slowly adjusts the focusing ring so that the focal plane moves further away and finishes at the furthest point away from the object. For every camera angle and position, this method is repeated, meaning you will likely finish with hundreds to thousands of photos of one object. Each set of images is then collated together using specialised software to produce one sharp image, from foreground to background. As fine adjustments are made to the camera's point of focus, a steady tripod and a camera rail are essential.

It can be incredibly time-consuming to collate several images to create one single decent image (especially if you are processing hundreds of photos!); therefore, cameras are now offering an in-built focus stacking option, making this process considerably easier and very useful in close-range photogrammetry. Panasonic, Sony and Nikon have models that have this function, as do the majority of all the mirrorless EOS R series of Canon cameras (although Canon refer to it as focus bracketing).

If the camera being used does not have this function, there are software programs available that can focus stack images, although take note this will be a slower process. Adobe's *Photoshop* and *Lightroom* offer the option to focus stack images; however, programs such as *Helicon Remote* and *Helicon Focus* are better alternatives. *Helicon Remote*, for example, is operated while the camera is tethered to a computer or laptop. When using the "Live View" function, the software will determine the number of images required per camera position when the closest and furthest depths of field are set. This number is based on the aperture of the camera and the focal length of the lens. The camera must be set to autofocus, and it is recommended that the camera is also set to Manual priority as this will allow you to adjust the exposure. Once the images are taken, the software will focus stack the images which can then be saved into another folder for processing into a model.

6.4 Next steps

In this chapter, we looked at the necessary settings to adjust to improve images in Adobe's *Lightroom* and *Camera Raw*, how to correct the colour casts of photographs using a colour checker chart, and what focus stacking is. Now that we have the images, the next step is to process the photographs in photogrammetry software to create a model. In this manual, the guide to processing models uses Agisoft *Metashape* using a Windows PC. *Metashape* is one of the most commonly used software for creating photogrammetry models of cultural material. The following chapter explores the steps to generate a model in *Metashape* along with some handy tips and tricks on how to navigate the software, and edit and improve the quality of your models.

Chapter 7

MODELLING IN *METASHAPE*

7.1 Agisoft *Metashape*

Agisoft *Metashape*, previously known as Agisoft *Photoscan*, is currently one of the most utilised software for professional photogrammetry modelling. As such, a guide to processing 3D models in *Metashape* is provided in this chapter with instructions on how to conduct all the necessary actions to create a textured model.

There are currently two editions of *Metashape*: the Professional Edition and the Standard Edition. The standard workflow for both editions is the same; however, the Professional Edition has considerably more capabilities compared to the Standard Edition. Therefore, the functions unavailable in the Standard Edition will be noted.

The instructions here are based on Version 2.1.0 of *Metashape* released in December 2023. Users operating earlier versions should note that certain settings and tools will look slightly different to what is presented here. As *Metashape* frequently releases software updates, it is also likely that changes to the interface layout, available settings, tools or terminology may occur in future updates; therefore, there may be future inconsistencies with what is presented in this guide.

7.2 How is a model made?

As we have already established, photogrammetry is the process of turning 2D photographs into digital 3D models. By taking a series of overlapping photographs of an object or landscape from a range of different angles, photogrammetry software "stitches" these images together to produce a digital replica. How the software determines the three-dimensionality of the object is by using the positions of the camera when it takes the photographs to generate the X, Y and Z coordinates of the pixels within each image. This process is called "structure from motion" (SfM).

The processes and algorithms employed to create a photogrammetry model vary between photogrammetry software. The method presented here in Agisoft *Metashape* uses four primary stages to build a textured model. Until the update to Version 2.0.0, these steps were named the sparse point cloud, dense point cloud, mesh and texture. In the update, however, several changes occurred including the terminology of some processing jobs. The four primary steps are now identified as the tie point cloud, point cloud, mesh and texture (see Figure 7.1) and are discussed in greater detail below.

In this chapter, the stages of building a photogrammetry model in *Metashape* have been broken down into the respective processing jobs with explanations of the terminology and important settings. A summary of these settings looks at how they affect the final model and, when pertinent, the processing time. After each stage is discussed, a variety of editing tools are presented that can be used to clean up or improve the model. Editing the model after each of the primary four jobs has finished processing is a very helpful way of improving the quality and accuracy of the final model.

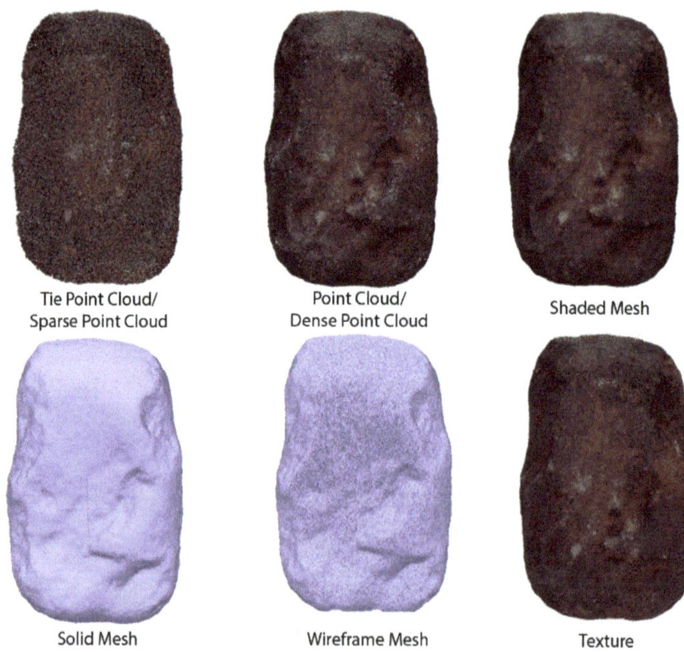

Figure 7.1 Evolution of a model from sparse point cloud to a textured model. Private collection, Colin Hornshaw.

Beyond the model-building stages, an assortment of other important and useful tools *Metashape* offers is also presented. Instructions on how to scale a model to obtain its real-life measurements and volume, how to mask models following a variety of different methods, and how to fill holes and smooth mesh are provided. More advanced tools such as importing new images to an existing model and merging two models accurately are also covered. A brief introduction to adding ground control points to topographical models and how to create orthomosaics are included towards the end of this chapter, as well as instructions on how to design and export video fly-throughs for presenting your models.

7.2.1 The tie point cloud (sparse point cloud)

The first stage of building a photogrammetry model is aligning the images to create a tie point cloud, previously referred to as the sparse point cloud in earlier versions of *Metashape*. The tie point cloud is created after the photogrammetry software goes through each uploaded photograph to identify key points. Key points are features in the images that the software deems important, usually a point of high contrast or interesting texture. Photogrammetry software commonly employs an algorithm called Scale-Invariant Feature Transform (SIFT) to identify these key points. Key points are used to determine the positions and orientations of the cameras in three-dimensional space to build the tie point cloud. Key points are not to be confused with tie points; tie points are matches in key points (also known as SIFT points) that occur in two or more images, representing the same key location. Once the software has identified all the key and tie points in the images supplied, a model will be produced that will resemble the subject but made of tiny dots. Depending on the number of images uploaded, the resolution of the photographs and the alignment job settings, the number of points could range from a few thousand to a few hundred million. These dots can be edited to improve the alignment success and aesthetic of the final model; how to do this is discussed later in this chapter in 7.6.

In this stage the depth maps are also generated. Depth maps are two-dimensional images that show the distances the surface of the subject is from the camera. Distance is indicated through a spectrum from red through to dark blue – the closer the subject is to the lens, the redder the region is coloured on the subject (see Figure 7.2). Depth maps are the basis to creating the point cloud (dense point cloud) and, in *Metashape*, can be reconstructed at each processing stage.

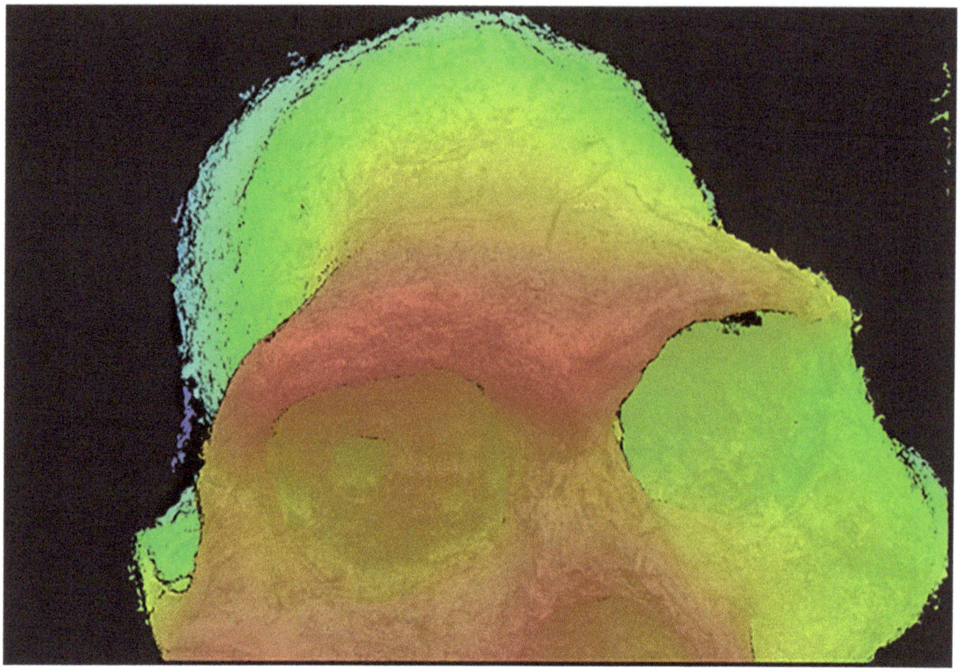

Figure 7.2 Depth map of a replica *Africanus* skull. The areas close to the lens are redder while those that are far away are blue.

7.2.2 The point cloud (dense point cloud)

After the tie point cloud, the point cloud can be produced. The point cloud is a more informative three-dimensional cloud model of points and is configured based on the estimated camera locations and the image pixels. In some software the point cloud does not necessarily need to be built to produce the final model; however, it is useful for editing purposes in *Metashape*, particularly when modelling small objects.

7.2.3 The mesh

The next step in the photogrammetry building process is to create the surface of the model, known as the mesh. Simply put, the mesh layer consists of triangle faces or "polygons" formed from three connected points, based on information obtained by either the tie point cloud or the point cloud. The more faces in the model, the more detail captured in the surface mesh. The mesh model provides a useful visualisation of the success or failure of a model. The mesh can be viewed with the captured colours from the images, displayed as a single colour, as a wireframe – which means the triangle faces have no infill colour and only the borders of the triangles are shown – by the elevation values of the mesh vertices, or the confidence values of the vertices (red as low confidence, violet as high confidence).

7.2.4 The texture

After building the mesh surface layer, the final step to produce a basic photogrammetry model is to render the texture of the object. Here, the stitched photographs are wrapped over the mesh to provide the photo-realistic finish to the model.

These four main steps are the building blocks for producing a textured photogrammetry model; however, there are several subsequent processing tools available to explore that can be employed for analysis or observational purposes, such as building a tiled model, a DEM (digital elevation model) or an orthomosaic (a high-resolution 2D image made from orthophotos).

7.3 Import photos

The first step in making your 3D model is to open a new file in *Metashape* and import the photos needed to create the 3D model. This can be accomplished by clicking "Workflow" – "Add Photos" or by simply clicking the second icon under the "Workspace" pane, which, when you hover the mouse over it, will read "Add Photos".

This will open a new file explorer window where you can navigate to the folder of photographs you want to process and import them into the project. If you cannot see the imported photos or have accidentally deleted the "Photos" pane, head to the "View" tab in the main header and click on "Photos". The pane will open, and you can relocate it around the interface to a different spot of your choosing by clicking and dragging the header. If you want to integrate a pane into the interface so it is not floating, click and drag the pane to either the top or bottom margin of the model interface. A grey bar will appear, and you can release the mouse and it should realign into the interface.

Once the images are imported and presented on the screen, look through the images to ensure they are in order, are all there, and are of decent quality. If you notice some images that you do not want to be included in the model (such as images of an information board), you can select these photos and disable them by clicking the "Disable Images" icon in the "Photos" toolbar (which looks like a circle with a dash through it) or you can delete the images entirely from the batch by clicking the "Remove Cameras" icon, which is distinguished by an "X" symbol.

If you want to run multiple models within the same saved file, click the "Add Chunk" icon, which is the first button under the "Workspace" pane. This icon looks like a chessboard with a plus sign on it. This will open another model "chunk" where you can add photos to build another model. If you want to run the same model with a variety of different settings, this is a helpful way to keep all the models together in one place.

7.3.1 Image estimation quality

Once you have uploaded the photographs, it is recommended that the photographs are assessed for their quality. Again, if the "Photos" pane is not open already, click "View" – "Photos" for it to appear. Right-click on one of the photos in this window and click "Estimate Image Quality" – "All Cameras". This will initiate a scan of the quality of the photographs in this chunk. To see the estimated value of the images, click the drop-down arrow in the "Change View" icon in the "Photos" ribbon and select "Details", which will produce the list. The image value is under the heading "Quality". The higher the number is, the better the quality of the image. Although it is not the ultimate test of image quality, what this analysis does is look for image sharpness through pixel contrast and image blur. The less contrast in the images and the less the subject is in focus, the lower the resulting value. *Metashape* (see "User Manual: Professional Edition, Version 2.1.0", Agisoft, 2024) recommends that all images that have a value less than 0.5 should be disabled; however, this is not mandatory for producing decent models.

7.4 Batch process

In *Metashape*, you have to run several jobs to produce a fully textured model. To build a standard textured model, the order is as follows: "Align Photos", "Build Point Cloud", "Build Model" and "Build Texture". The "Build Point Cloud" job is optional but aligning the photos and building the mesh (generated via the "Build Model" job) is necessary for a textured model. These jobs can be run one at a time by clicking the "Workflow" tab and selecting the job from the list. A better option, however, is to run a batch process. This allows you to set up the order of the jobs and what specific chunks the jobs should be applied to. To access the batch processing window, head to the "Workflow" tab, scroll to the bottom of the list and press "Batch Process". Here you can add jobs, save the batch process settings list, and import an existing saved batch process. The four main jobs and their associated settings are listed below. Remember that once you have added all the jobs to the batch process, you must select “Save project after each step” to ensure you do not lose any progress, then press “OK” to run the batch process.

7.5 Align photos

The first stage of model processing is to align the photos. Here, the camera positions and orientations are determined, and the tie point cloud (or sparse point cloud) is produced. Camera position is estimated on image data alone and this is why having consistently overlapping images is so important when shooting for photogrammetry.

In this dialogue box, you have the option of setting the alignment accuracy, any preselection tools, the key and tie point limits and whether a mask should be used in making the model (see Figure 7.3). When this stage has been completed, you can view the model product by clicking on the icon of the four dots in the main ribbon labelled “Tie Points – Colors”. Sections 7.5.1–7.5.10 will take you through the properties of this window.

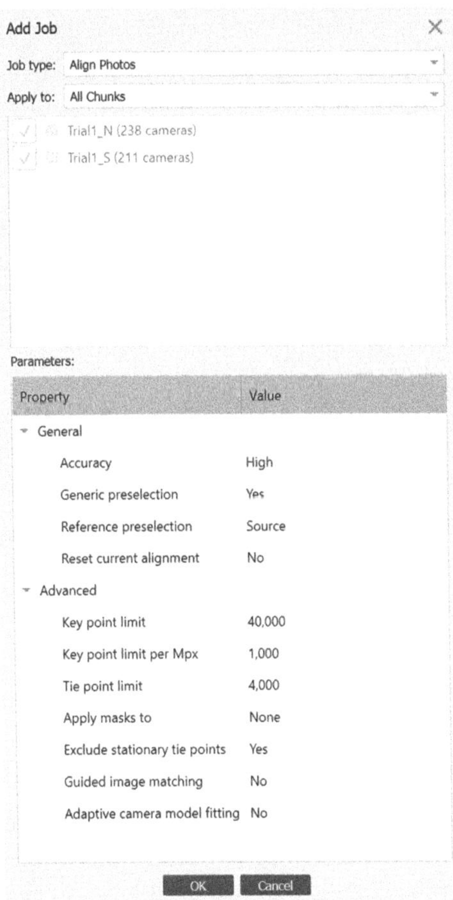

Figure 7.3 The “Align Photos” window where settings can be adjusted to build the tie point cloud.

7.5.1 Accuracy

The primary concern in the alignment stage is the accuracy setting of the alignment of images. The options are Highest, High, Medium, Low and Lowest. Be mindful of your choice here as the overall quality of the model will depend on what you select. Remember, the higher the accuracy setting, the longer the processing will take. This is important to consider if you want to process thousands of photos in one batch as this will take considerable time.

The difference between the accuracy settings is simply the higher the setting, the deeper the software will analyse the images for features and, as such, will produce more accurate estimates of the camera positions. Low accuracy settings will produce coordinates that are not as accurate; however, this option will produce a tie point cloud in less time. How the software does this is by upscaling and downscaling the resolution of the images. At High accuracy, the images are untouched, and the software will analyse the images at the resolution size of the original image. At Medium, however, the software divides the resolution of the image, or downscales the image, by a factor of 4 (divided by 2 on each side). This means an image that is, for example, 8 pixels by 6 pixels, is downscaled to 4 pixels by 3 pixels. At the Low setting, it is downgraded again by another factor of 4 and then by a further 4 in the Lowest accuracy setting. A lot of information is therefore lost as the pixel count (resolution) decreases in the image. This means the software will find fewer features in the images and will reduce the number of tie points in the tie point cloud. In the Highest setting, however, *Metashape* upscales the image and increases the resolution by a factor of 4. Therefore, *Metashape* only recommends the Highest setting for very sharp, high-resolution images.

7.5.2 "Generic Preselection" and "Reference Preselection"

Clicking "Yes" to "Generic Preselection" is very helpful for faster processing as this tells the software that images have consistent overlap and, instead of matching individual images to each other, it will match image pairs. The pairs are selected using a low setting first, while in "Reference Preselection", these pairs are selected on the measured camera positions if camera coordinates have been input.

7.5.3 Reset current alignment

If the "Reset current alignment" is set to "Yes", the process of matching tie and key points is started from the beginning. If you want to add more images to a model to improve or add to the existing model, make sure you turn this option to "No" otherwise all existing matched points will be discarded. When adding images to an existing model, you must also tick the "Keep key points" option that is under the "Advanced" tab in the "Preferences" window ("Tools" tab – "Preferences" – "Advanced").

7.5.4 Key point limit

The default setting for the key point limit is 40,000. This means that a limit of 40,000 feature key points will be obtained from every image when producing the tie point cloud. This default value is a good setting and is recommended by Agisoft; however, it can be increased if desired, and if no limit is wanted, can be changed to zero.

7.5.5 Key point limit per Mpx

This tool aids the "Guided image matching", another setting available in the "Align Photos" job. If the "Guided image matching" is changed to "Yes", *Metashape* will use the value (default setting of 1,000) of the "Key point limit per Mpx" (megapixel) multiplied by the image's size in megapixels, to determine the number of key points detected in each image. For further details on this function, see the information on "Guided image matching" at 7.5.9.

7.5.6 Tie point limit

This is the maximum number of tie point matches *Metashape* will make for every image. The default setting for the tie point limit is 4,000; however, *Metashape* recommends a value of 10,000 ("User Manual: Professional Edition, Version 2.1.0", Agisoft, 2024). Like the "Key point limit", this means that the upper limit of matching points is 4,000 per image; however, a higher value can be set or, if no filtering is desired, the setting can be changed to zero. Having no upper limit to the key and tie points, however, will produce a large dot point cloud with a greater percentage of unreliable or misaligned points. Unreliable dot points can be filtered out from the model by using the "Gradual Selection" tool, which is outlined in 7.6.1. Alternatively, if a model is produced with excessive dot points, they can be thinned by going to "Tools" – "Tie Points" – "Thin Point Cloud", and a new limit can be input and then rerun. If your tie point limit is too low, however, some areas of the object being modelled may be overlooked and therefore missed in the point cloud, consequently impacting the quality of the final rendered model.

7.5.7 Apply masks to

If you have any masked images and want to run a model with these masks included in the alignment stage, change the drop-down menu next to "Apply masks to" from "None" to either "Key points" or "Tie points". There is a difference between these two options. When set to "Key points", the software will ignore all masked areas of the images from being analysed for key features to create the tie point cloud. This is a good option if all images have been masked. When set to "Tie points", the software will instead ignore the tie points in the masked areas *and* the corresponding tie points in other images from the alignment procedure. That is, if a section has been masked in one image, the software will ignore all the connecting tie points that are detected in the other images, even if they have not been masked. This setting can be very powerful as it only requires a few images to mask unwanted features. It is particularly convenient when shooting an object on a turntable with a seamless background; only a few masked images are needed to mask it.

If you are planning on processing this way, it is recommended that you create at least one mask per camera position. This is to ensure that the entire background is identified and excluded from the model. Masking by tie points saves time, as it can be an arduous task if done manually. More information about masking is discussed later in 7.14.

7.5.8 Exclude stationary points

This is a very useful feature that should be enabled if you are shooting on a turntable with a stationary camera. This setting will ignore all tie points that are consistently detected in the same location in several images; that is, the background of a lightbox, even if no masking has been coordinated.

7.5.9 Guided image matching

Enabling the "Guided image matching" setting increases the number of key points *Metashape* will detect in each image without seriously impacting the processing time. The amount of additional key points is determined by multiplying the "Key point limit per Mpx" setting by the size of the image in megapixels. The software will analyse and match a small percentage of these points and use this information to match the rest of the points. This setting is ideal for high-resolution cameras and satellite imagery, and *Metashape* states it is particularly useful for photography of areas of vegetation.

7.5.10 Adaptive camera model fitting

This option is useful for datasets that have either strong or weak camera geometry. Camera geometry is the real-life positioning and orientation of the camera when it is capturing images. This setting enables the reliability estimates of the camera parameters to be selected and applied in the adjustment of other alignment parameters. If turned off, *Metashape* will only adjust the fixed set of camera parameters, which are focal length (f), principal point position (cx, cy), the radial distortion coefficients (k1, k2, k3) and the tangential distortion coefficients (p1, p2). See 7.6.2 for further details about these parameters.

7.6 Editing the tie point cloud

Once the "Align Photos" job is complete, a tie point cloud is created. To navigate around the tie point cloud to see it from different views, click the icon of a mouse in the main ribbon labelled "Navigation". A transparent sphere will appear in the middle of the screen with three coloured rings: blue, red and green. The screen can then be clicked and dragged around to change the perspective. For a more precise shift in perspective in either the x, y or z axes, click on one of the corresponding coloured rings to highlight it and then move the mouse and the model will rotate only along this axis.

It is important to check how many photos are successfully aligned after the tie point cloud has run. This information is shown in the "Workspace" window in the drop-down menu under "Images" (note that previous versions of *Metashape* referred to photographs as "Cameras"). Ideally, 100% of the images have aligned. If you have not achieved perfect alignment, there are ways to improve the alignment of the photos, outlined in 7.6.2, to avoid having to rerun the entire alignment stage. If the camera alignment is off and an incorrect model has been produced, you can reset the camera positions by highlighting and right-clicking on one or several images that have incorrectly aligned and then selecting "Reset Camera Alignment". This will remove those cameras from the model. You can then optimise the images ("Tools" – "Optimize Cameras") and realign those cameras by selecting them, right-clicking and choosing "Align Selected Cameras".

To view what images matched with other images, either click "Tools" – "Tie Points" – "View Matches" or navigate to the "Photos" dialogue box, right-click on an image, and click "View Matches". A new window will open showing a list of the images that the particular image matched with.

7.6.1 Gradual selection

The "Gradual Selection" tool should be run after the alignment job has finished to ensure the tie point cloud comprises the most accurate tie points. This tool allows you to filter and remove points in the tie point cloud that are unreliable within certain criteria. By selecting "Model" – "Gradual Selection", *Metashape* will present a window that has a drop-down menu of filters. The options are "Reprojection error", "Reconstruction uncertainty", "Image count" and "Projection accuracy". These filters are largely self-explanatory: each point contains a level of error, uncertainty, accuracy, and an associated number of photographs used to create each tie point. When one of these filters is selected, the slider can be used to adjust the strength of the filtering tool. Sliding to the right increases the sensitivity the software has to the respective filter, meaning more points will be selected, and sliding to the left reduces it. Moving the slider to the end will select 100% of the tie points. *Metashape* informs you how many points are being selected of the total number of tie points in the model at the bottom left corner of the central "Model" window. Filtering between 5–20% of the points (percentage dependent on the tie point cloud size) from each of the "Reprojection error", "Reconstruction uncertainty" and "Projection accuracy" filters and deleting them will produce a model with higher accuracy as the remaining points contain lower error, lower uncertainty and higher accuracy and are therefore more reliable building blocks for the mesh. After each of these filters has been applied, it is recommended to optimise the alignment of the images by heading to "Tools" – "Optimize Cameras", which is further discussed below.

7.6.2 Optimise alignment

Optimising the image alignment readjusts the point coordinates and the camera positions to minimise the reprojection error and reference misalignment error. As some camera position errors can occur during the alignment stage, this is a useful tool to readjust any misaligned coordinates. To optimise the alignment of your images, navigate to "Tools"– "Optimize Cameras", or select "Optimize Alignment" via the "Batch Processing" tool, under "Miscellaneous" in the job type selection.

The specific properties that can be optimised are outlined below:

- f = focal length of the camera measured in pixels
- cx, cy = principal point coordinates of the lens optical axis interception with the sensor plane, measured in pixels
- b1, b2 = affinity and skew transformation coefficients
- k1, k2, k3, k4 = radial distortion coefficients
- p1, p2 = tangential distortion coefficients.

When the optimising camera alignment function is selected, three additional options can be enabled. These are "Adaptive camera model fitting", "Estimate tie point covariance" and "Fit additional corrections". The "Adaptive camera model fitting" adjusts the camera's orientations, similar to the option available in the alignment stage under the same name. The second function, "Estimate tie point covariance", can be enabled if an analysis of the model requires a calculation of the covariance matrix for the set of adjustments. This will then indicate the level of uncertainty of the processed model. The calculated standard deviation values of coordinates can be viewed in the Reference window under "View Variance" and also visually represented by heading to "Model" – "View Mode" – "Tie Point – Variance" or in the drop-down menu under the "Tie Points" icon in the main ribbon.

Every time the tie point cloud is edited (i.e. if dot points are deleted, the tie point cloud is thinned using the "Gradual Selection" tool, or if new images are added to the model), the "Optimize Alignment" option should be run. This will reassess the alignment properties and adjust them if necessary. This tool can also be found both in the "Batch Process" job list and under the "Tools" tab.

The last option, "Fit additional corrections", permits further camera calibration corrections that will allow for compensation of lens distortion. If you have a wide or ultra-wide camera (mostly concerning drones), this is particularly useful as you will have greater radial distortion in these images. Turning this setting on will aid in improving accuracy, particularly if you do not have any ground control points.

7.6.3 Improving image alignment

There is a useful method of improving alignment in *Metashape* if the software has failed to align the model accurately. The "Gradual Selection" tool under the "Model" tab can be used to resurrect any misaligned or missing images in the model instead of reshooting the object.

To do this, open the model in the tie point cloud view and clean up any outlier points that are not part of the main conglomeration by using the "Free-Form" selection tool (found in the drop-down menu of the "Rectangle Selection" icon). Open the "Gradual Selection" tool and select the "Reprojection error" criterion from the drop-down list. A slider will appear which, when dragged to the right, will systematically select more points in the model that have high reprojection error. The more the slider is adjusted to the right, the more the software is sensitive to error. To improve the alignment of a model, adjust the slider so that approximately 10% of the points are selected. Press "OK" then delete them. Run an optimisation of the model ("Tools" – "Optimize Cameras"). Repeat this process of selecting points, deleting and reoptimising the model, with the "Reconstruction uncertainty" and "Projection accuracy" criteria. With larger tie point clouds, it is possible to repeat the process twice for each criterion. Once these steps have been completed, open the "Photos" pane. Select the last icon on the ribbon labelled "Change View" and click on the "Details" option. The entire batch of images will be displayed with their properties. Organise the photos by alignment success by clicking the "Aligned" heading so that the images that were not aligned are listed first. Select all the images that do not have a tick under the "Aligned" heading, right-click, and select "Align Selected Cameras". Hopefully, all the selected images have aligned to the model correctly. If not, repeat this process but increase the threshold of selected points in the "Gradual Selection" tool. If there are images that have been incorrectly aligned in the model, either select the images in the "Photos" pane and right-click the "Reset Camera Alignment" or select the points in the model and delete them. Once satisfied with the alignment of the images, run another optimisation and continue with the rest of the model-building process.

7.6.4 Resizing the bounding box

After the tie point cloud is produced, it is good practice to confirm the borders of the bounding box. The bounding box is the faint transparent box that the model is situated within. It is important to note that whatever is outside the bounding box will *not* be modelled in the following jobs after the tie point cloud. Therefore, if there are any points outside the bounding box, you will have to readjust the size of the bounding box so they can be modelled. To adjust the size or position of the bounding box, simply click on the drop-down arrow of the "Move Region" icon in the main ribbon. This will open a menu of different functions. To adjust the size of the box, click "Resize Region" and drag the corners so that they are at a suitable dimension to contain the model. As you are resizing the box, change your perspective of the model (look from the top, side and front) to ensure the entire model is within it. There is also the option to rotate and move the box under this same tool. Take note that the "X" featured on one of the box's faces should be on the face underneath the model.

7.7 Build point cloud

The next step in building a photogrammetry model is generating the point cloud (again, previously named the dense point cloud). Although it is not essential to generate a point cloud to create a mesh layer, having a point cloud provides the user with greater opportunities to edit the model.

Remember to ensure that the entire model is within the bounding box before running the point cloud. As outlined in 7.6.4, the bounding box is the transparent box that contains the model. If the bounding box does not encompass the entire tie point cloud, all points outside the box will be ignored in the following processing stages. Once the entire model is within the bounding box, you can then proceed to build the point cloud.

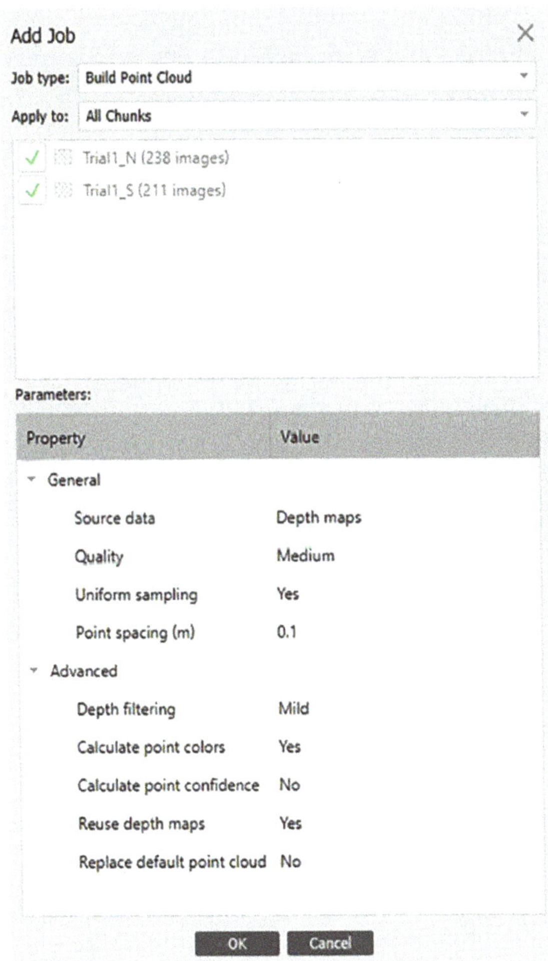

Figure 7.4
Settings to build the point cloud.

7.7.1 Source data

There are several options offered as the source data to build the point cloud. The options are depth maps, model or tiled model. Depth maps is ideal if you only have the tie point cloud created, and is the default option. Model is available once you have generated the mesh, meaning that it is possible to run the mesh before the point cloud is created. However, for editing and accuracy, creating the point cloud first is recommended; therefore, leaving this setting at depth maps is the recommended choice.

7.7.2 Quality

The first reconstruction parameter in the point cloud job is setting the quality of the point cloud. The higher the level chosen, the better the quality of the detail and the accuracy of the geometry. Remember that a higher quality setting will increase the processing time. This setting is analysed in a comparable way to the alignment accuracy in the "Align Photo" job, where each step down in quality downscales the image quality by a factor of 4. In this case, however, the "Ultra High" option analyses the original photo.

7.7.3 Uniform sampling

When enabled, this setting allows for uniform point sampling.

7.7.4 Point spacing (m)

It is possible to set your own point spacing value in the point cloud, which can reduce the number of points generated. The default setting is 0.1, which is suitable to produce a model.

7.7.5 Depth filtering

The level of depth filtering will impact the appearance of the point cloud and later the complexity of the mesh. If you are shooting an object that has significantly rough or morphologically complex surface detail that has been photographed accurately, a depth filtering level of "Mild" is suitable. Mild depth filtering will identify the important finer details and indicates to the software that these small features are not point outliers but essential detail to the model. Photos that are not good quality – that is, they are blurry, contain a bit of noise or are unfocused – can produce more outlier points, so it is important if an artefact does have a complex surface to set the camera correctly and take well-exposed images.

If the artefact does not have small important details on the surface, or some issues with photo quality have been noticed, reduce the filtering mode to either the "Moderate" or "Aggressive" settings. These settings will produce a smoother point cloud. Any small detail here will be assumed to be a point outlier of the depth map and ignored during processing. If you are unsure, opt for the "Moderate" choice or play around with the different options to see which is most suitable for your particular project. The depth map filter can be disabled completely; however, this will produce a very noisy model, so it is not advised.

7.7.6 Calculate point colours

The "Calculate point colors" function enables the point cloud to exhibit the colours of the object being modelled. If colour is not needed, it can be turned off and will reduce processing time considerably. If it is turned off, a single-coloured point cloud will be produced, and consequently you will not be able to use the helpful editing tool "Select Points by Color".

7.7.7 Calculate point confidence

If "Calculate point confidence" is set to "Yes", the number of depth maps used to produce each point cloud point is calculated and recorded by *Metashape*, giving each point a confidence rating that will be within a range from low to high. By enabling this function, you will be able to use the useful "Filter by Confidence" tool, which will allow you to decimate large point clouds.

7.7.8 Reuse depth maps

If there is a depth map already in the chunk and you want to reuse it, check the "Reuse depth maps"; otherwise, marking it as "No" will recreate a depth map.

7.7.9 Replace default point cloud

If this option is enabled to "Yes", the default point cloud will be replaced when processed.

7.8 Editing the point cloud

Editing the point cloud can be the fastest method of cleaning smaller models as it is the final stage where the model is made up of dot points and it contains more information than the previous tie point cloud model. Editing the point cloud will also, most importantly, improve the quality of the mesh – if the mesh is being made from the point cloud. The user has greater control over cleaning and fixing problems with the model. The most common problems include: the background appearing in the model; fragments of isolated mesh or "artefacts" suspended around the main model; or the mesh surface having an incorrectly dappled surface.

There are several options provided in *Metashape* to clean the point cloud. The simplest option is to use the "Free-Form" selection tool to select areas of the model that are not wanted (such as the background or mount) and delete them. This allows the user to be very precise in the selection of what points should be deleted. This is very useful for cleaning up sharp edges of artefacts, such as stone tools. Conversely, the sections that *are* wanted can be selected and everything else can be deleted by pressing the "Crop Selection" tool, circled in Figure 7.5.

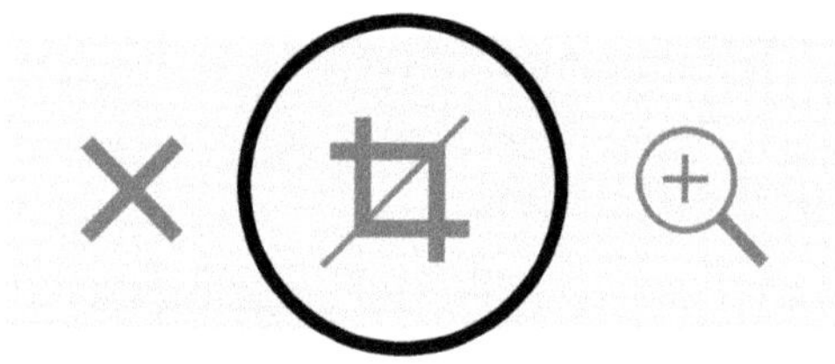

Figure 7.5 The "Crop Selection" tool (circled) deletes everything that is not selected.

Other options to edit the point cloud are via the "Select Points by Color" and "Select Points by Masks" functions, both found under "Tools" – "Point Cloud". These are two useful and powerful tools that can aid in removing unwanted floating point cloud points, captured background, mounts or other features that have been included in the model.

If the point cloud has excessive issues, streams of points shooting away from the main conglomeration of points, or the model appears "furry" due to a haze of points scattered around the surface, these issues may not be able to be solved by the cleaning methods outlined below. In this case, return to the tie point cloud view and filter out incorrect points through the "Gradual Selection" tool found under "Model" (see 7.6.1). Deleting excess tie points by adjusting the threshold of the "Reprojection error", "Reconstruction uncertainty" and "Projection accuracy" options will create a cleaner tie point cloud, which will consequently produce a cleaner point cloud.

7.8.1 Filtering the point cloud

The number of point cloud points can be decimated to a lower number if the cloud appears too congested, which possibly creates a mottled appearance on the model's surface. Selecting "Tools" – "Point Cloud" – "Filter Point Cloud" will open a new window where you can specify the spacing between point cloud points. This will remove points that are within the spacing specified by the user.

Another useful option is to filter the point cloud by confidence level. As stated in 7.7.6, if the "Calculate point confidence" function is enabled, *Metashape* will assess each point cloud point and record the number of depth maps used to generate the point and allocate it a confidence value. These confidence values can then be used in filtering the point cloud. "Filter by Confidence" is located under "Tools" – "Point Cloud" and once selected will open a window that will allow you to set a confidence range, with a default minimum value of 0 and a maximum of 255. Increasing the minimum setting will restrict the number of depth maps used for each point. The maximum value is 255 – meaning this is the highest confidence value a point can have. Playing around with different minimum values will produce a more accurate point cloud as this tool will eliminate all points that have a lower confidence value.

A crowded point cloud with excessive points may slow down processing and also cause the production of the mesh to fail. It is possible to receive error messages such as "Bad allocation" or "Index overflow". In these cases, filtering the point cloud is recommended to allow the model to finish processing. Alternatively, the number of points in the tie point cloud can be reduced in preparation to creating a thinner point cloud through the "Gradual Selection" tool (outlined in 7.6.1).

7.8.2 Editing via the colour selection tool

If there is an additional feature that has been included in the model that is entirely one colour, such as the backdrop sheet or the mount, it is possible to delete its point cloud via the colour selection tool. To use this tool, it is vital that you confirm that the subject of the model does not contain any similar hues of the feature you want to delete, as this editing tool will also select points of the same colour in the subject's point cloud. This is one of the reasons why having a contrasting background to the object is important.

To edit the point cloud via the colour selection tool:

1. Open the point cloud view of the model, go to "Tools" – "Point Cloud" – "Select Points by Color".
2. Click "Select …" and then either choose one of the provided default colours that most closely matches the point cloud you wish to delete in the palette provided or click "Pick Screen Color", which will then allow you to click on a point of the unwanted point cloud to select its colour, then press "OK".
3. The colour tolerance can be adjusted by moving the slider to the right, increasing the colour range from the one selected, then press "OK".
4. Click the "X" button in the main ribbon or press delete to erase these points.

These steps can be repeated with various tolerances or colour selections until the background is entirely cleaned from the model subject. If there are still areas that cannot easily be removed from the model as they are too similar to the subject's surface colour, another method is to select and delete these areas through masking the images.

7.8.3 Editing via masked images

This option allows the user to select areas of the point cloud that need to be deleted by using masked images. If no images have been masked, or you are not familiar with the method, there are a few options for masking images outlined in 7.14. To select and delete point cloud points using masked images, the steps are as follows:

1. In point cloud mode, go to "Tools" – "Point Cloud" – "Select Points by Mask".
2. Select the image or images that contain masks of the areas you want removed from the model. The "edge softness" can be adjusted and once satisfied, press "OK".
3. The sections that are masked in the images will then appear selected in the model and can be deleted.

After selecting the points, confirm that no points within the main model are highlighted before pressing delete otherwise these points will also be deleted. This process, like the colour selection tool, can be repeated multiple times until all the unwanted points are removed.

7.9 Build model

7.9.1 Source data

The mesh model can be built by using source data from the tie points, the point cloud, depth maps and laser scans, laser scans alone, or a DEM. For close-range object photogrammetry, mesh quality is best sourced from the point cloud compared to the tie points or the depth maps; however, the processing time will be longer. The depth maps setting will take less time and can be used if a point cloud was

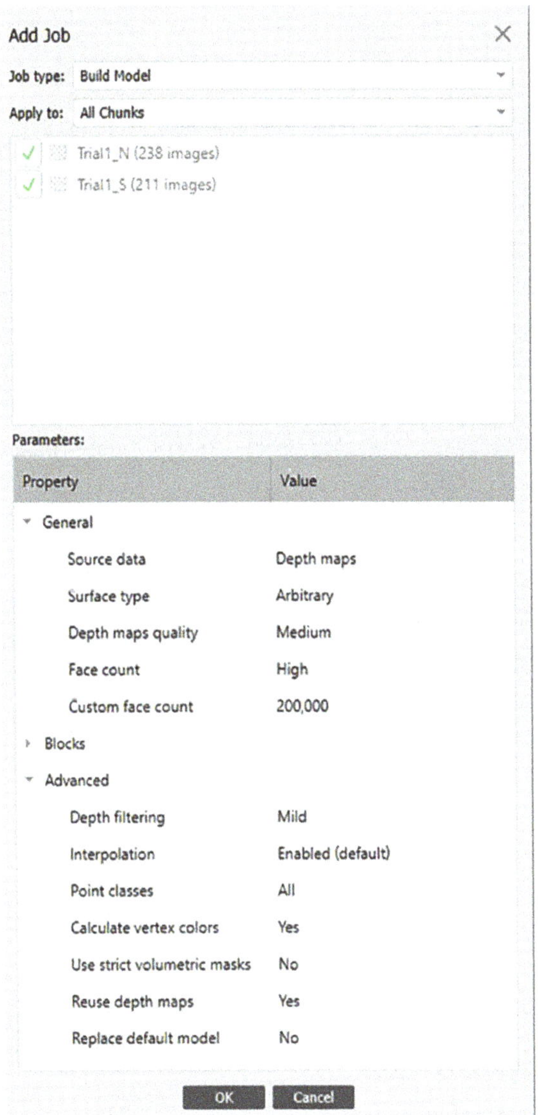

Figure 7.6 Settings to process the mesh layer.

not built in the modelling process. The fastest option is the tie point cloud setting, although the quality is not as good compared to the other two options. Take note, if you have edited the point cloud and want those adjustments included in the mesh, it is essential that the source data is set to the point cloud as any edits will be lost and not considered if the source data is set to another option.

7.9.2 Surface type

The "Arbitrary" option for the "Surface type" can be used for any type of modelling project; however, it is a better option for closed models, such as archaeological artefacts. The difference between the "Arbitrary" option and the "Height field" surface type option is that the "Arbitrary" option uses more memory. "Height field" should be chosen for modelling large flat areas, such as aerial photogrammetry. This option consumes less memory and therefore is beneficial for larger projects.

7.9.3 Depth maps quality

This setting will determine the quality of depth map reconstruction, but only if source data was set to depth maps. The higher the setting ("Ultra High" and "High"), the better the detail and geometric accuracy; however, the longer the processing will take. The quality of the depth maps follows the same parameters as the quality of photo alignment accuracy in the "Alignment" job. The difference here, however, is that the "Ultra High" depth map quality setting looks at the original untouched images, while each following quality setting downscales that image by a factor of 4.

7.9.4 Face count and Custom face count

The "Face count" setting allows you to choose the upper limit of polygons for the mesh. The higher the setting, the higher the number of faces. If "Source data" is set to point cloud, the reconstruction of the mesh polygons is calculated from the number of points in the point cloud. The ratio for a "High" setting is 1/5, 1/15 for a "Medium" setting and 1/45 for a "Low" setting. If you want to input the upper limit of the polygon face count, you can set a value in the "Custom face count" setting.

7.9.5 Blocks

The "Blocks" settings are designed for building large-scale photogrammetry models (i.e. landscapes) and therefore do not need to be considered in our process of creating models of archaeological objects.

7.9.6 Depth filtering

This function can be adjusted if the source data is set to depth maps. "Mild" has the least filtering effect, followed by the "Moderate" setting and then the "Aggressive" setting which has the most. "Aggressive" is suitable if the surface is quite rough or if there are random mesh artefacts scattered around the main model; however, this will cause finer mesh details to be eliminated from the model. For models with fine features, "Mild" is recommended so these areas are preserved in the mesh.

7.9.7 Interpolation

Disabling interpolation will result in *Metashape* creating a reconstruction that only uses the points in the point cloud to create the mesh and therefore generates accurate reconstructions. When interpolation is enabled, however, *Metashape* interpolates a specific radius of surface area around each point to make the reconstruction. Enabling will result in fewer holes being generated in the mesh later, therefore if disabled, it is more likely that the user will need to manually fill these holes at a later stage. If the "Extrapolated" setting is chosen, *Metashape* will reconstruct a solid model with no holes, as it extrapolates further into these missing sections. Although useful, this must be used with caution as *Metashape* may simply generate large additional sections of mesh geometry.

7.9.8 Point classes

This setting is only available to point cloud-based reconstruction as this mode allows the user to choose the type of point cloud used to build the mesh.

7.9.9 Calculate vertex colours

This setting will enable the mesh to reflect the colours of the modelled object. This will result in the processing time being longer. If set to "No", the processing time will be shorter, but the mesh model will be a monochrome colour.

7.9.10 Use strict volumetric masks

Strict volumetric masking will eliminate any masked space from the model from at least one masked image. If the background of an image is merging into the model, mask at least one image and run the mesh with this setting enabled and it will prevent the background from being included in the model. As its name suggests, however, it is *very* strict and may mask important features if masking is not done correctly, and can only be used if the source data of the mesh is set to "Depth maps".

7.9.11 Reuse depth maps

This setting should be checked if you want to reuse the same depth maps from the chunk. Take note, however – it can only be selected if the "Source data" was set to "Depth maps".

7.9.12 Replace default model

If enabled, the default mesh model will be replaced.

7.10 Editing the mesh

7.10.1 Remove floating mesh

If a mesh model has been generated with small fragments of suspended mesh "artefacts" floating around the model, instead of manually selecting each artefact and deleting it, there is a tool available in *Metashape* that makes removing them simple. The steps are as follows:

1. Under any of the mesh or texture views ("Model" – "Textured", "Shaded", "Solid", "Wireframe", "Elevation" or "Confidence"), navigate to "Model", "Gradual Selection", then in the drop-down box, select "Connected component size".
2. Increase the tolerance dial as high as is necessary to select everything other than the main model. If the dial is pushed to 100%, everything, including the main subject, will be selected.
3. After setting the tolerance level, press "OK". All the suspended fragments of mesh will be selected and can then be deleted by either pressing the delete button on the keyboard or by the "X" icon in the main ribbon.

It is good practice to run this process after every model has been produced, just to ensure that no hidden artefacts that cannot be easily seen are floating around the model.

7.10.2 Closing holes

If there are insignificant holes in a model that need to be filled, there is a very quick method to fill them that does not require reshooting the object. In the mesh or texture view, head to "Tools" – "Model" – "Close Holes". A window will appear where you can adjust the threshold of hole size that will be selected and filled. Once this has been set, all the holes in the object will be highlighted pink.

The holes will not contain the correct texture and will be a single colour, so to rectify this, run the texture job, outlined in 7.11, to apply a seamless texture to the entire object, including the filled holes.

In the mesh view, a hole will be created if a portion of a model is selected and deleted; therefore, running this process can improve the appearance if editing is conducted through the selection tool.

7.10.3 Smoothing the mesh

Occasionally, surface mesh can be generated incorrectly and exhibit a dappled or rippled appearance. This could be due to incorrect lighting, the object having a shiny or reflective surface, the photos were not taken correctly or there was incomplete coverage.

Sometimes this is unavoidable simply due to the object's material type, but there are some ways of reducing the appearance of this effect after the model has been generated and that is to smooth it out. To do this:

1. Go to "Tools" – "Model" – "Smooth Mesh".
2. In the new window, set the smoothing strength. A figure between 1 and 10,000 can be input. It is not advisable to start at a high number but to gradually increase the level from a smaller figure, such as 5 or 10, until you are satisfied with the mesh. Press "OK".
3. Assess the new mesh in either the solid, wireframe or confidence modes in the mesh view.

As this method reconfigures the mesh surface, it should not be used excessively if the intention is to replicate an artefact for analysis. This process is better suited for models that are only designed for presentation purposes.

7.11 Build texture

Processing the texture is the final step in creating a basic close-range photogrammetry model. This job involves positioning and wrapping the original photographs over the mesh model, thereby producing more detail and photo-accuracy than the simple shaded mesh model.

Before running the texture job, another step may be necessary if the lighting conditions changed during the shooting period. The "Calibrate Colors" option, under the "Tools" menu, may need to be applied to adjust the white balance and brightness of the entire photo collection to even out variations in lighting. This is suitable for artefacts or topographical features that were photographed in

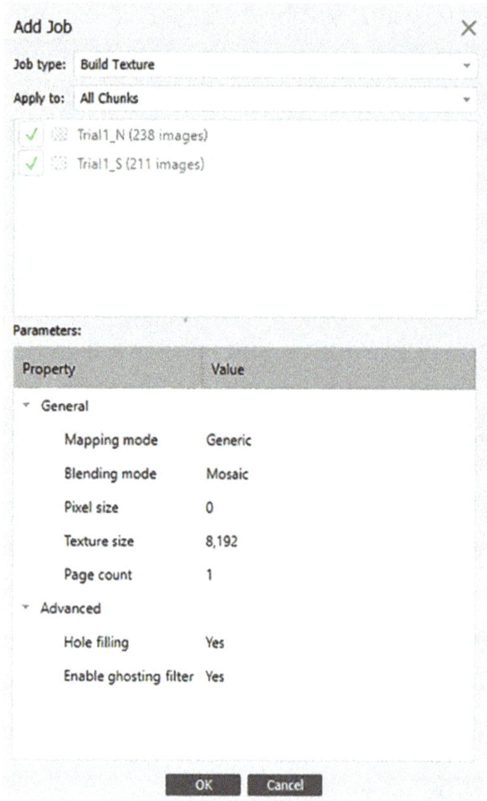

Figure 7.7
The settings to build the texture.

an uncontrolled environment over a period of a day or several days. Take note, however, that for large projects this will take a considerable amount of time.

When adjusting the lighting settings, there are two options for source data to calibrate the colours, either from the tie points or the model. The tie point option is the faster of the two yet will produce a less accurate estimation compared to the model option. If the white balance also needs to be adjusted, tick the "Calibrate white balance" box to adjust the colour temperature of the images.

7.11.1 Mapping mode

Texture mapping is the process of determining how the model texture will appear in the texture atlas. Selecting the most appropriate option will improve the clarity and quality of the texture and depends on the shape or type of model created.

When building the texture, several options can be chosen for the mapping mode. The choices are "Generic" (the default setting), "Adaptive orthophoto", "Orthophoto", "Spherical" and "Keep UV". The "Generic" setting is not a bad option as the software makes no assumptions regarding the type of model and will attempt to make a uniform texture. With both the "Adaptive orthophoto" and the "Orthophoto" options, the texture produced is compact. With the "Adaptive orthophoto" option, the surfaces are divided into horizontal and vertical sections where the horizontal areas are textured using the orthographic projection and the vertical are produced separately. The "Orthophoto" option generates texture entirely through orthographic projection meaning that the quality of the texture in vertical sections is affected. The "Spherical" option, unsurprisingly, is best suited for spherical models. The last option, "Keep UV", maintains the same texture parametrisation to construct the texture atlas. This option also allows the user to select different resolutions for the texture atlas.

7.11.2 Blending mode

Blending mode is how the software decides the best way to combine colour from different photos to generate the final texture. The default option, "Mosaic", blends low-frequency components that feature in overlapping images so there is no "seamline" in the texture showing a division of image, while it will select one image to use for high-frequency components, typically a good image that has high resolution. The other options are "Average", "Max Intensity", "Min Intensity" and "Disabled". Simply put, the "Average" option takes the weighted average of each photo's pixels, "Max Intensity" chooses the photo that contains the maximum intensity of the associated pixel and, similarly, the "Min Intensity" option chooses the image with the least intensity. "Disabled" is similar to the "Mosaic" option, in that the choice of image is based on the image quality.

7.11.3 Pixel size

This value is automatically configured if left at the default setting of 0, however the pixel size can be specified (in metres) if necessary, to improve the texture.

7.11.4 Texture size

The texture size is the size of the texture atlas (in pixels); the default setting is 8,192.

7.11.5 Page count

Page count is the number of files the texture information will be exported to.

7.11.6 Hole filling

The "Hole filling" option's default is "Yes", and it is recommended that this function remains activated to avoid complicated holes in the mesh.

7.11.7 Enable ghosting filter

This option filters out any "ghosting effect" that may appear on the texture caused by moving objects caught in the frame that was unable to be digitally reconstructed. It is advised that this option is set to "Yes" on the off-chance that this occurred during the shooting session.

7.12 Build tiled model

After you have finished building a model, running the "Build Tiled Model" job will produce a surface layer with a photo-realistic finish similar to the texture surface. Depending on the source data, and its quality, tiled surfaces can produce models of greater detail and resolution compared to the texture surface. Tiled models can be created from the point cloud, the mesh (listed under "Model"), the depth maps, depth maps and laser scans or just laser scans. For small models of objects, selecting the mesh source will generate a tiled surface with sharper detail – if the mesh layer itself is of good quality. For larger models, such as a landscape or large architectural structures, running this job from the depth maps or point cloud is a better choice as processing will take less time. There is one downside to building a tiled model, however – you cannot edit the tiled model. Therefore, you must ensure that the stages preceding the generation of the tiled model – specifically the source data – are edited to a standard you are satisfied with, then run the tiled job.

7.13 Scaling a model in *Metashape*

Scaling is the process of inputting known, real-world dimensions into a photogrammetry model, enabling *Metashape* software to calculate the dimensions of the entire model, including surface area and volume. By so doing, any region or section of the photogrammetry model can then be measured for analytical or research purposes.

There are several ways to scale a photogrammetry model in *Metashape*. The first two methods (7.13.1 and 7.13.2) involve positioning coded *Metashape* targets or non-coded ground control point (GCP) targets in the shooting area so they are generated as part of the model. Through this method, the software can detect the targets, and measurements can be input directly into the model. Coded targets will have an associated number that *Metashape* identifies, while non-coded targets will be identified by the order in which they were detected. The next suggested scaling method (7.13.3) requires a scale bar to be part of the model. Points are manually positioned along the scale at known intervals and the distances are input into the software. 7.13.4 is similar to the previous method; however, measurements are taken from 2D images of the scale bar that is adjacent to the subject. The final suggested method (7.13.5) is to input measurements directly onto the model after measuring the real-life object using calipers. After the model has been scaled, it is possible to obtain the area and volume, outlined in 7.13.6. Take note that there is no function to scale models in *Metashape* Standard Edition; it is only available in *Metashape* Professional Edition.

To print coded targets of a specific radius size in *Metashape*, follow the steps outlined in 7.21.10. When detecting markers, "circular" refers to circular-shaped targets while "cross" will identify GCP targets and, if large enough, black and white scale bars. This means that if you are using scale bars that are large enough to be detected by *Metashape* in your shooting environment, the method outlined in 7.13.2 can be used.

7.13.1 Scaling from a model using a coded target

Measurements can be obtained from models that include one or several coded *Metashape* targets by following this method:

1. Position the targets around the subject in locations that can be seen clearly, and are close to the object but do not cover it.
2. Go through the shooting workflow and include several rounds of wide, high angle shots so both the subject and the targets are captured in the same images.
3. Run the model to at least the mesh job without importing any masks so the entire shooting environment is generated.
4. Open in either the mesh or texture views.
5. Head to "Tools" – "Markers" – "Detect Markers" and select "Circular 12-bit" (if these are the ones used). Adjust the tolerance if necessary.
6. Select one of the targets and zoom into its central point. Right-click on the outer edge of the inner back circle of the target and select "Add marker" (see Figure 7.8).
7. Open the "Reference" window, next to the "Workspace" pane, and under the heading "Markers" you should see the target marker points and the new point that you recently created.
8. Using the "Control" key on your keyboard, select both the target marker number that you chose *and* the corresponding point marker that you input on the central circle. Right-click and select "Create scale bar".

9. This new scale bar will appear in the below pane, under the heading "Scale Bars".
10. Double-click on the space under "Distance (m)" and input the measurement (in metres) between the two markers. If you printed the targets from *Metashape*, this distance will be the value you set for the centre point radius when creating the targets.
11. Repeat this process at least three times – it is recommended to have a minimum of four scaled areas to increase the accuracy.
12. Once finished, press the "Update Transform" icon at the top of the "Reference" pane.
13. To obtain new measurements from the model, select two areas on the subject and input markers. Create a scale bar from these two new markers then press the "View Estimated" icon in the "Reference" pane. This will give you the estimated distance, with the associated error. If the error reading is high, increase the number of scaled sections and delete those scale bars with high error readings.

An example of where this method is used is in Case study 8.8, where a coin is modelled with the targets positioned on a polystyrene cube to help with the alignment of images.

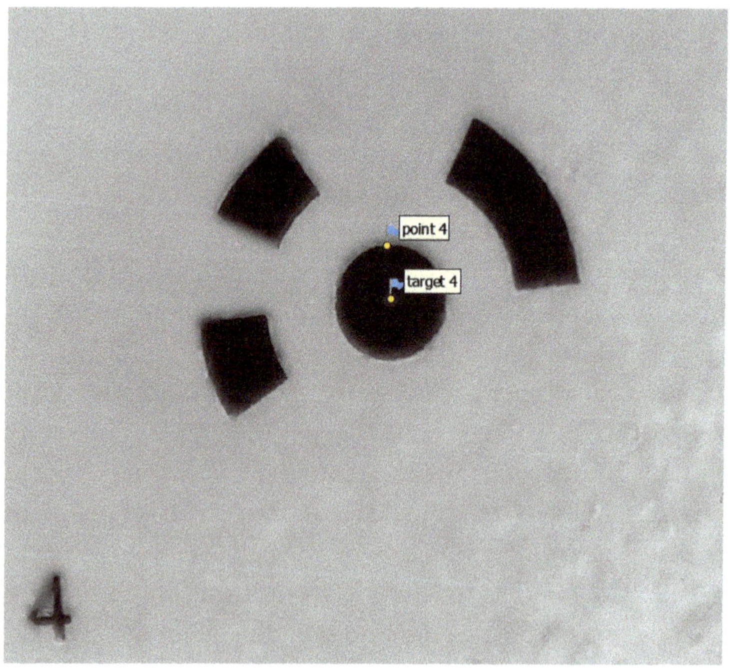

Figure 7.8 Coded target showing the target number and new marker point.

7.13.2 Scaling from the model using a GCP target

Measurements can be obtained from models that include one or several non-coded GCP or laser scan targets; however, the dimensions from the central point to the edge must be known. Large black and white scale bars can also be detected by *Metashape* with this method. The following steps are similar to the above:

1. Position the GCPs around the subject in positions where they can be clearly seen but do not obstruct the object.
2. Go through the shooting workflow and include several rounds of wide, high angle shots so both the subject and the targets are captured in the same images.
3. Run the model to at least the mesh job without importing any masks so the entire shooting environment is generated.
4. Open in either the mesh or texture views.
5. Head to "Tools" – "Markers" – "Detect Markers" and select "Cross (non-coded)". Adjust the tolerance if necessary. Typically, the tolerance will have to be lowered so other points are not detected.
6. Markers should appear in the centre of the targets, at the intersection of the black and white squares or triangles.
7. Select one of the targets and zoom into the central point where the marker is. Right-click on the outer edge and select "Add marker".
8. Open the "Reference" window, next to the "Workspace" pane, and under the heading "Markers" you should see the target markers and the new point that you recently added.
9. Using the "Control" key on your keyboard, select both the target marker number that you chose *and* the corresponding point marker that you input on its edge. Right-click and select "Create scale bar".
10. These new scale bars will appear under the next pane, under the heading "Scale Bars".
11. Double-click on the space under "Distance (m)" and input the distance between the central marker and the edge of the GCP (in metres).
12. Repeat this process at least three times – it is recommended to have a minimum of four scaled areas to increase the accuracy.
13. Once finished, press the "Update Transform" icon at the top of the "Reference" pane.
14. To obtain new measurements from the model, select two areas on the subject and input markers. Create a scale bar from these two new markers then press the "View Estimated" icon in the "Reference" pane. This will give

you the estimated distance, with the associated error. If the error reading is high, increase the number of scaled sections and delete those scale bars with high error readings.

7.13.3 Scaling from a scale bar

Measuring from a scale bar is also possible if it has been included in the model. The method is similar to the above options; however, with this process *Metashape* does not detect the scale bar.

1. Position the scale bar in front of the subject so that it can be clearly seen but not covering the subject.
2. Go through the shooting workflow and include several rounds of wide, high angle shots that capture both the subject and the scale bar in the same images.
3. Run the model to at least the mesh job without importing any masks so the entire shooting environment is generated.
4. Open in either the mesh or texture views.
5. Zoom into the scale bar so it is large on the screen. Right-click on one of the ruler markings (ideally at the centimetre marking), and select "Add marker". Move along to the following ruler marking (that is a clearly measurable distance away), right-click again and select "Add marker".
6. Open the "Reference" window, next to the "Workspace" pane, and under the heading "Markers" you should see the two points that you added.
7. Using the "Control" key, select these two markers you input on the scale bar, right-click and select "Create scale bar".
8. This new scale bar will appear in the next pane, under the heading "Scale Bars".
9. Double-click on the space under "Distance (m)" and input the measurement (in metres) between the two markers.
10. Repeat this process at least three times – it is recommended to have a minimum of four scaled areas to increase the accuracy.
11. Once finished, press the "Update Transform" icon at the top of the "Reference" pane.
12. To obtain new measurements from the model, select two areas on the subject and input markers. Create a scale bar from these two new markers then press the "View Estimated" icon in the "Reference" pane. This will give you the estimated distance, with the associated error. If the error reading is high, increase the number of scaled sections and delete those scale bars with high error readings.

7.13.4 Scaling from images

Scaling a model from an image follows a slightly different process compared to scaling from the model. It requires images of a scale bar (targets are also fine) to be included in the batch of images used to build the model and is as follows:

1. In the shooting stage, position the scale bar (or printed targets) in front of the object, and take at least four photographs of the object and the scale bar together that are in focus, well-lit, and with the camera level and facing directly at the object (i.e. the camera is not at an angle). Then continue with the shooting process as usual, again making sure to include the scale bar in the images where possible.
2. Import the images to *Metashape* ensuring that you included the images of the scale bar and run the entire model-building process to the texture job.
3. If the scale bar does not appear consistently enough in the batch of images imported to make the model, *Metashape* may not align it correctly, or at all, in the model. If the images of the scale bar have aligned, there will be a tick above the image in the "Photos" pane, and if so, you can skip to step 8. If there is no tick, these images will need to be manually aligned.
4. To manually align these images, follow the marker-based method: open the first image of the scale bar and find four distinctive points of interest on the *object* and add markers to them (right-click – "Add marker"). It is important these four features are identifiable in other images of the object.
5. Open the second image that includes the scale bar and input these same markers (right-click – "Place marker").
6. Find two correctly aligned images that clearly show these four distinct points. Place the same markers in the same corresponding locations on both images (right-click – "Place marker").
7. Return to the two scale bar images and select both. Right-click and select "Align Selected Cameras". This will align these images to the model.
8. With the two images of the scale bar aligned to the model, double-click on the first image of the scale bar and zoom into an area that clearly shows where the ruler markings are.
9. Right-click on the beginning of the ruler marker and add a marker (right-click – "Add marker"). Move to the next ruler marking and add another marker. Continue adding markers until you have between four and six markers spaced at measurable distances along the ruler.
10. When finished, open the second image of the scale bar. Input the same markers in the same exact locations that you put in the first image (right-click – "Place marker").

11. Open the "References" pane and select two of these marker points on the ruler under the heading "Markers". Right-click and select "Create scale bar".
12. In the pane below, the newly created scale bar will appear under the header "Scale Bars". Double-click on the space under the heading "Dimensions (m)" and input the known distance of those two markers into this cell (remember to convert the measurement to metres).
13. Repeat this process so you have at least three scale bars listed under the "Reference" pane. With four markers you can have at least three scaled sections. The more scaled sections, the higher the accuracy will be.
14. Press the "Update Transform" icon in the "Reference" pane to update the measurements.
15. New measurements of unknown distances can now be created on the model. Follow the same steps as above: add two markers to the model and create a scale bar once they appear in the "Reference" pane. Select "View Estimated" in the "Reference" pane which will show the estimated distance in the "Scale Bars" pane.

If an error message appears saying "Not enough reference data", this means that you have only input one image with scaled sections – not two – or the scale bar images have not aligned to the model. Once two images with the scaled sections with the same markers are included in the model, the rest of the model can be scaled.

7.13.5 Scaling from the object

Another method is to measure identifiable points on the object, such as text, a distinct pattern or markings, with calipers and scale the corresponding points on the photogrammetry model (see Figure 7.9). This method ideally should be done after the model has been processed so that you can input the markers onto the textured model as you physically measure the points with the calipers. Using the same method as above, right-click on the points where the caliper jaws are on the object and select "Add marker". Ensure you have a minimum of three scaled sections to increase the accuracy of the model's measurements. Once you have finished, press the "Update Transform" icon on the "Reference" pane and then you can proceed to create measurements from the model.

If the markers do not appear on the model, press the icon of the flag in the main ribbon labelled "Show Markers".

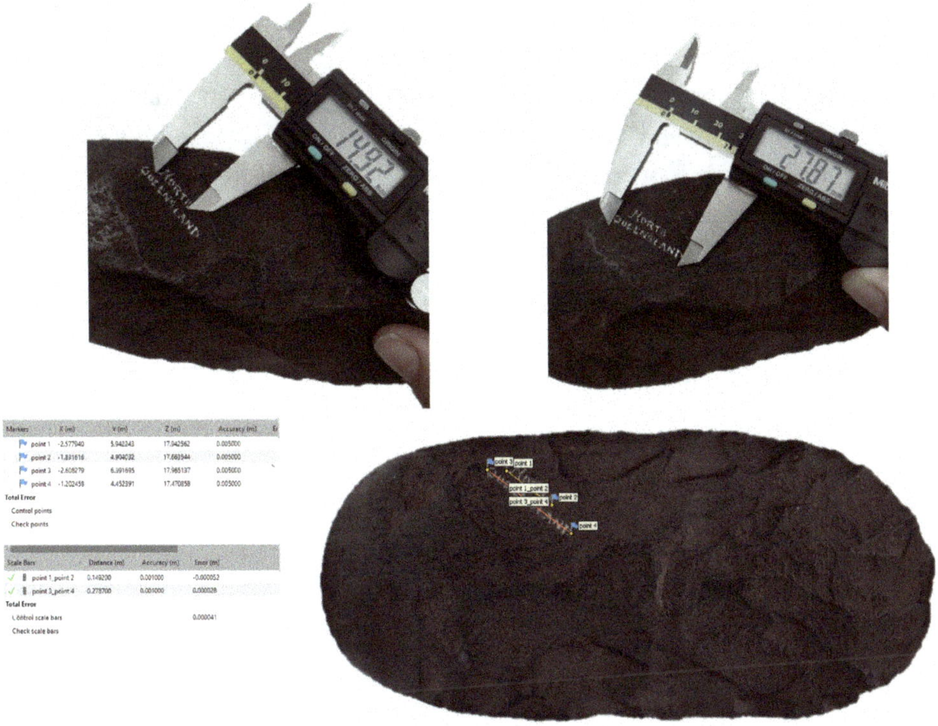

Figure 7.9 Scaled section of a model. In this example, text written on the specimen was used to scale the model. Private collection, Colin Hornshaw.

7.13.6 Measure area and volume

Once a model has been accurately scaled, you can obtain the surface area and volume of the object. Navigate to "Tools" – "Model" – "Measure Area and Volume". This will open a window showing (in metres) the area and volume. As the measuring functions are not available in the Standard Edition, this function is also not available for users of the Standard Edition.

7.14 Masking in *Metashape*

Masking is where part of an image is hidden from detection by the photogrammetry software. Any area that has been masked is excluded from analysis throughout the entire processing procedure, meaning that it will not be included in estimating the camera's locations, or in the alignment stage, nor will it be included in the render. What is left is the subject of the image, which can be then stitched together to create a model free of the masked features. This is very useful to prevent the background, a mount or turntable from featuring in any models.

There are several ways in which one image or a batch of images can be masked. The methods outlined here are primarily performed through *Metashape* software. These include masking from tie and key points, from the background, and creating a mask via a 3D model. Another method included here covers how to create an automated masking process in the image editing software Adobe *Photoshop*, where the software identifies the background of an entire folder of images and sequentially masks the images. These can then be imported into *Metashape* as a mask file which can then be applied to the images.

7.14.1 Masking from tie and key points

Once images have been masked, *Metashape* needs to be instructed to apply these masks when building the model. This is done in the first stage of the process, the alignment job, under the option "Apply masks to". There are two choices the masked images can be applied to in the drop-down menu: "Key Points" and "Tie Points". The main difference between these two options is simple. Masking by key points means that all the key points (i.e. not the tie points) found within these masked areas will be ignored by the software. There is no connection between one image and the next; therefore, this is a good option when every single image has been masked.

The mask by tie points option is slightly different. If one image has its background masked, the tie points associated with the masked key points within the background will mask the corresponding key points in all other images that are linked by the same tie points; that is, all images that share the same tie points will be masked if one image has some percentage of its key points masked. To ensure this process works efficiently, however, it is best to mask at least one image from each camera position using one of the steps listed below. Using the mask by tie points method is best suited for photos taken in a lightbox and that have a seamless monochrome background. If a busier background is present in the images, more images will need to be masked to ensure the masking is effective.

7.14.2 Manually masking images

Manually masking images is simple to do yet can be time-consuming. Knowing how to do it is helpful, however, for running a tie point mask when creating a model, or to improve incorrect auto-generated masks. Open the "Photos" pane and double-click on the image you want to mask so that it appears in the main window. Navigate to the main ribbon and select the icon of a rectangle labelled "Rectangle Selection". Click the drop-down menu to see the range of options which include “Rectangle Selection”, “Intelligent Scissors”, “Intelligent Paint”, “Magic Wand” and “Magic Wand Settings”.

The fastest option to mask an image manually is via “Magic Wand” where you simply double-click on the background for the software to detect the subject. The tolerance can be increased in the “Magic Wand Settings” selection as well. Once the area has been selected, right-click and choose “Add Selection” to mask (or Control + Shift + A). If you want to add more sections after the initial double-click, hold the “Control” key then click on the other areas that need to be masked.

The “Intelligent Scissors” option is slower; however, it will provide the most masking accuracy as it allows the user to select the specific boundary of the area that needs to be masked. Clicking on a suitable location to begin the mask, a line will connect the mouse to this point. Clicking along the subject’s outline will continue this line, plotting the area that will be masked. By holding the “Control” key down, this line will conform to the boundary of the subject as you move around it, making very precise adjustments to the mask boundary. Plot points around the subject specifically and connect the last and first points by clicking the “Escape” key. This will then highlight the subject; however, to reverse the selected area, right-click in the image and choose “Inverse Selection” so the selected area will change to the areas that are not highlighted – that is, the areas to be masked. From here you can then right-click “Add Selection” so the background is masked.

The “Intelligent Paint” option allows the user to select small sections of the image when the mouse is clicked and dragged over an image. This tool only selects small areas of the image when applied, and is therefore better suited for masking particularly small sections of the photograph. Once selected they can be masked out. The “Rectangle Selection” option is the least flexible and only selects areas of the image in a rectangular shape.

7.14.3 Masking from the background

With this technique, a mask of the background is generated, saved as a separate file, and then applied to the images before processing. The process involves the following steps:

1. Take a photo before or after the shooting session of the entire photography setup, with the lights on and any additional features such as the mount or turntable that are used when the subject is being photographed.
2. Upload this image along with the other images of the subject to *Metashape* and before running the model, open the image of the background.

3. Using the rectangle selection tool, select the entire image of the background and mask it.
4. From here, export that masked image (right-click on the image – "Masks" – "Export Masks"), rename the file (note: if the image is not saved as a PNG file, be sure to change the file type to match the image's file type), and save it in a new folder within the master folder where the rest of the images are, and label it "Masks".
5. Go back to the batch of photos and on a new image, right-click and select "Mask" – "Import Masks", and on the drop-down menu choose "From Background".
6. Change the file template name to the mask's name, increase the tolerance dial, and select the option to apply to all images.
7. Navigate to the "Mask" folder and select it. *Metashape* will go through each image and apply a mask to the background of each. The option to apply masks to key points in the alignment stage can then be applied.

Note: it is possible to create a background mask from an image that has the object with only the background masked. The issue with this process, however, is that there will be an area behind the subject that is unmasked that could be included in the model.

7.14.4 Batch image masking using *Photoshop*

Masking an entire folder of images is laborious, and if the image is blurry or the subject is complex, it can take a long time. Batch processing in Adobe's *Photoshop* is an easy and fast way to mask the background of multiple photos. There are several ways to create masks in *Photoshop*, one of which is outlined here:

1. Duplicate the folder that contains the images that need to be masked and identify the folder as "Masked images" or something similar so it is not confused with the other original folder.
2. Open *Photoshop* and load the first image of the mask folder.
3. Open the "Actions" menu ("Windows" – "Actions"), and create a new action by selecting the "+" icon at the bottom of the panel.
4. Name the action "Mask" and press record.
5. Click on "Select" in the top tab then "Subject" and the entire subject should be selected.
6. Go back to "Select" and choose the "Inverse" option which will invert the selection to the background.

7. Press delete, save the file, and then stop the recording process in the "Action" window by pressing the square stop icon.
8. To make this a batch process to edit the entire folder of images, go to "File", "Automate", then "Batch".
9. Change the "Action" option to "Mask" in the drop-down list and under "Source" click "Folder" and choose the mask folder and press "OK".

Photoshop will then go through each of the images, select the subject and mask out the background. This folder can then be imported into *Metashape* by opening the "Photos" pane, right-clicking an image, selecting "Masks", and choosing "Method" – "From File". Choose "Replacement" as the "Operation" and apply to all images for the entire batch to be masked. Navigate to the mask folder and load it into *Metashape*. The masks will be applied to all the images. It is a good idea to go through the masks to ensure they are correct and fix up those that have been incorrectly masked. Once satisfied with the outcome, you can continue to process the model with the mask by key points function turned on.

7.14.5 Mask from model

It is possible to mask the background of a batch of images from a completed mesh model in *Metashape*. This is a good alternative if the shooting environment had a complicated background that needs to be masked out, or if you are building a larger model by merging two chunks together (outlined in 7.14.6). With this method, the user can control what areas are masked areas by editing the point cloud and mesh of the model:

1. Run a batch process from the alignment job to the point cloud job on all low settings (to speed up the process) without masking any of the images.
2. Remove all traces of the background and other areas you want masked in the point cloud view using the selection tool or colour selection tool (outlined in 7.8).
3. Proceed to run the mesh job ("Build Model").
4. Once complete, right-click on one of the photographs under the "Photos" pane and select "Masks" – "Import Masks". Under "Method", select "From Model" in the drop-down menu and change the "Apply to" setting to "All images". A mask will be generated from everything that was deleted from the model and applied to the photos.

The masked images can be saved by right-clicking on an image and selecting "Masks" – "Export Masks". Fill out the filename and save it to a folder labelled "masks" where the model and images are located. To import these masked images to another *Metashape* file with the same images, simply right-click on an image in the "Photos" pane and select "Masks" – "Import Masks" – "From File". Navigate to the "masks" folder and press "OK".

Note: you do not have to save the mask files to use them if you just want to apply the masks in the same *Metashape* file. Simply rerun the same chunk with the masks applied to key points (and with higher accuracy and quality settings) or duplicate the chunk and run the copy with the new masks applied to the key points. Just remember to set "Reset current alignment" to "Yes" to rerun the alignment job otherwise the same tie point cloud will be used.

7.14.6 Building a model from two masked hemispheres

The "mask from model" method outlined in 7.14.5 is a helpful tool that can be used to successfully build small or complicated models that are not correctly aligning. The first step requires the northern and southern hemispheres of the object to be captured and loaded into *Metashape* into two separate chunks and labelled by their orientation (e.g. "Trial1_N" and "Trial1_S"). Without masking any images, process these chunks on a low alignment setting starting from the alignment stage and running to the mesh stage. Edit the model in either the point cloud and/or mesh model views to remove all traces of background, turntable or stand from the model, following the methods outlined in 7.8 and 7.10. Once the model is edited and the mesh model has been processed, run a mask for both these models with the mask settings changed to "From Model". This job will mask the images in both batches.

Once complete, move the entire contents of one batch to the other by selecting all the photos, right-clicking, choosing "Move Images" and selecting the other chunk so all images are now in the same chunk. (If you want to keep the original images and associated models, duplicate the two original chunks and collate the copies together.) Once you have a chunk of all the masked images, run a batch process on the new chunk from the beginning, but change the "Apply masks to" setting to "Key points" in the alignment stage. What will be produced is a complete, clean model without any background or stand featured in the model. If the alignment of the photos fails, rerunning the alignment job but with the "Generic Preselection" setting turned off may improve the accuracy of the alignment.

This process is a very useful way to model small objects such as coins. An example of this method with a coin is supplied in Chapter 8.

7.15 Adding new images to an existing model

There may be an occasion in which additional photos need to be added to an existing model. This could be for several reasons such as filling a hole in the mesh, adding another section to the model, or simply improving the mesh or texture quality. Fortunately, there are methods to build a model instead of starting from scratch, by adding the images to the tie point cloud, or adding new images via a marker-based approach.

7.15.1 Adding images to a tie point cloud

If you have additional images that you want to add to a pre-existing tie point cloud, the simplest method requires that the "Keep key points" function was turned on before the original model was generated. This is found under "Tools" – "Preferences" – "Advanced"; tick the box next to "Keep key points". Select the chunk that you want to add images to and press the "Add Photos" icon under "Workspace" (or head to "Workflow" – "Add Photos") and select the new images to import them. The tie point cloud will need to be rerun with the new images, so return to the "Align Photos" job but change the "Reset alignment" option to "No"; otherwise, the existing tie point cloud will be wiped. Run the alignment job and the new images will be added to the existing tie point cloud if there is sufficient overlap with the existing images and they are of consistent camera settings, lighting conditions and camera lens focal length.

7.15.2 Adding new images via a marker-based approach

If an area of a model has not been correctly modelled or the texture appears blurry, it might be necessary to improve the model by adding additional images of that specific section to the existing model. This can be achieved by following a marker-based approach. After adding the new photos to an existing batch, select two images from the original batch that share the same features as the new set of images, and strategically place four markers on the first image by right-clicking and selecting "Add marker". Place these same markers in the second image by right-clicking on the same locations and selecting "Place marker" and choosing the corresponding marker in the first image (Figure 7.10). You will notice that flags will appear in the images that show these marked locations.

In the new batch of images, find an image that displays the areas where the four markers were placed, right-click on the points and re-enter the same marker points that were input in the first two images from the drop-down list under

"Place marker". Continue this method with the rest of the new images, adding in new marker points as the others go out of frame. Once all the images have been marked, select the new images, right-click and select "Align Selected Cameras". *Metashape* will then run through the new images and position them based on the markers and include them in the tie point cloud.

Remember, if an image has been positioned incorrectly in the tie point cloud, it can be removed and realigned by selecting the "Reset Camera Alignment" and then the "Align Selected Camera" options. Although the marker-based approach is only available to Professional Edition users, it is still faster to follow the first method outlined in 7.15.1 to add in images.

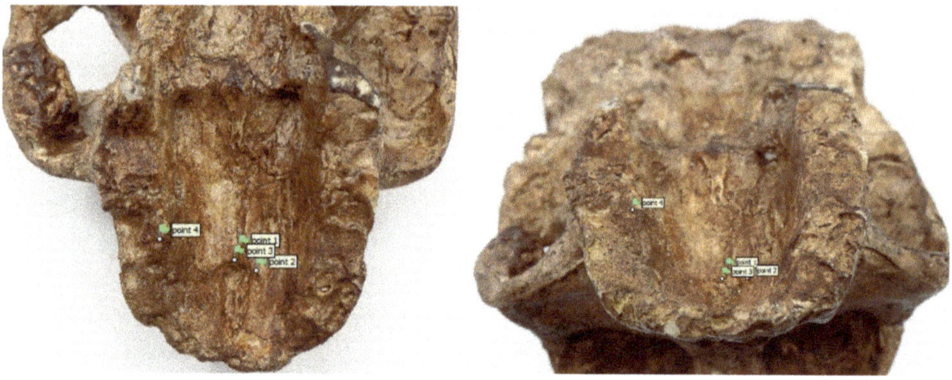

Figure 7.10 Two images with different camera orientations with the same markers positioned on both images.

7.16 Merging two models

It is possible to merge two or more models to create a larger photogrammetry model in *Metashape*. This is a useful tool when making large models of a terrestrial archaeological feature or site. Occasionally it might be necessary to separate a batch of images into smaller groups to run them as separate smaller chunks, and merge them at a later stage. Doing so can significantly decrease the processing time and improve alignment success.

To achieve a successful, seamless merge of two models there must be considerable overlap of the same features that appear in both models. The software must be able to clearly recognise the shared sections so it can reposition the models together correctly and create a seamless connection of the mesh. Having around 30% overlap will be enough for the software to align and merge the chunks correctly.

In *Metashape*, there are several ways in which merging two or more chunks can be achieved, with two basic ways outlined here. When using either method, have the two separate chunks fully processed and ready to merge. If they are in completely separate files, it is possible to move a chunk from one file to another by heading to "File" – "Append" and selecting the chunks you want copied and pasted into the file you are working on. Once the two chunks are in the same saved file, select "Workflow" – "Align Chunks". A window will open which will list all the available model chunks with a tick next to them. Keep the models you want to merge ticked and untick any that you do not want to be aligned. You will notice that one of the models (the one that is currently showing in the interface) is bold. This means that this is the primary model that all other model chunks will align to. It is recommended that the largest model be the primary model as it is the one with the most surface information. To change the primary model, simply double-click on a different chunk to change it. Keep the method of alignment as "Point based" and the other settings as default (unless you want to adjust them). Once the chunks are ticked and the primary model is chosen, press "OK". After the software has finished processing, return to the "Workflow" pane and select "Merge Chunks". This will produce a new chunk in the "Workspace" window that will have the smaller chunks merged into a new whole model. If there is a noticeable line where the two models merged due to different lighting conditions or altered camera settings, editing the point cloud and rerunning the mesh and texture may diminish the intensity of the join.

A second method is a marker-based approach; however, this option is only available for users with the Professional Edition. Open the photos of one of the chunks and double-click on an image that shows an area that overlaps with the other model. Position at least four markers (right-click – "Place Marker" – "New Marker") on identifiable features that can be recognised in the other model. These markers do not need to be positioned from the same image, but you will notice that once you create a few markers, they will start to appear in the other photos. After at least four markers have been positioned, go through the rest of the photos to verify whether they have been correctly positioned. They can be dragged to a better location by clicking the marker and moving it if they are not in the right place. It is also possible to input a specific marker in an image by selecting it under the "Place Marker" tool.

Once markers have been properly allocated in this batch of images, switch to the other model and repeat the same process with these images, ensuring that the markers go in the exact same location and in the same order – it is crucial that the markers in this model have the same location as the corresponding markers in the other model to correctly align. When you have finished, head to "Workflow" – "Align Chunks" and tick the chunks you want to align, and make the primary model bold. Change the method of alignment to "Marker-based" under the "General" heading and press "OK". Once *Metashape* has finished processing, return to the "Workflow" pane and select "Merge Chunks". Here you can select whether you want the point cloud, tie points, entire models, and markers merged. At a minimum, merge the point clouds. Like the first method outlined, it is recommended to edit the merged point clouds and rerun the mesh and texture to reduce any obvious seams in the mesh. Press "OK" once you have selected what to merge, and a new chunk will be produced under the "Workspace" pane of the two models merged together. If the model did not perfectly align, create a few more markers in the two original separate chunks to help *Metashape* configure the correct dimensions of where the two chunks connect.

If problems persist when attempting to merge two models of an archaeological object, follow the steps outlined in 7.14.6, building a model from two masked hemispheres, as this might be a preferable method to create a seamless model.

7.17 Exporting files from *Metashape*

To send photogrammetry models from *Metashape* to other software to be edited, exhibited or printed, the models will have to be exported as a different file format first. To do this, click "File", go down to "Export", then select "Export Model". This will take you to a file to save the exports. Underneath the filename window, there is the option to save the model in a variety of formats. The most commonly used export file formats are Wavefront OBJ (.obj), STL model (.stl), Filmbox (.fdx) and 3D studio (.3ds), which are also able to be compressed to zip files for easy transfer.

If a model's file size is too large and it needs to be reduced so it can be uploaded or electronically transferred, one option is to decimate the mesh. By decimating the mesh, the polygons are larger and less accurate therefore containing less information and making the file size smaller. Even reducing the mesh faces by 10% can significantly reduce the size of the file. To do this, head to "Tools" – "Mesh" – "Decimate". The texture of the model will be lost after the mesh has been decimated, so remember to rerun the texture before exporting the model.

7.18 Build DEMs and orthomosaics

Beyond a textured model, *Metashape* allows for the creation of DEMs and orthomosaics. DEMs are used for topography or submerged landscapes to help with research concerning elevation or bathymetry and mapping. DEMs can be produced either from the tie point cloud, point cloud or mesh, although the most accurate results are produced from the point cloud. To build a DEM, the model needs to be georeferenced with geotagged images or contain a local coordinate system. Distance, area and volume measurements can be determined, and contour lines can also be input in the DEM. Like the rest of the model-building process, the job to build a DEM is listed under "Batch Processing" in the drop-down menu of the jobs.

Like DEMs, orthomosaics are also very useful when creating photogrammetry models of topography and bathymetry. An orthomosaic is a high-resolution aerial image that has been constructed from stitching together orthophotos. Orthophotos are "orthorectified"; that is, the scale, distortions and camera tilt in the imagery have been corrected so the distances and measurements are consistent. This means that true distances can be obtained from orthomosaics – a very useful tool when using photogrammetry models of terrestrial features.

In *Metashape* Professional, you can reconstruct an orthomosaic from a variety of different projection planes including the current view of the model that is showing in the interface, from markers positioned on the model, and from different axes. Access these options and more via "Workflow" – "Build Orthomosaic", not through the "Batch Process" option as it provides fewer settings. Building orthomosaics, like building DEMs, is not offered in the Standard Edition software.

7.19 Adding ground control points (GCPs)

Adding GCPs or GPS coordinates to a *Metashape* model is a straightforward task. All that is needed is for the GCP names, their respective coordinates and altitude to be clearly organised in either a text or Excel file and saved as a .csv file. Firstly, align the images of the model with alignment accuracy set to high or highest. Once complete, navigate to the "Reference" pane and select the first icon on the ribbon of a folder labelled "Import Reference". This will open a file explorer window where you can find and open the file that contains the coordinates of the GCPs.

A window titled "Import CSV" will open (see Figure 7.11) where you can adjust how the GCPs will be imported. It is crucial that you select the right coordinate system that was used when taking the GCPs, otherwise the points will appear incorrectly on the model. Under "Delimiter", select the appropriate option that reconfigures the data neatly into the table shown. Following this, ensure that the Label, Latitude, Longitude and Altitude, and if available the Yaw, Pitch and Roll records, have been correctly identified by column label in the corresponding

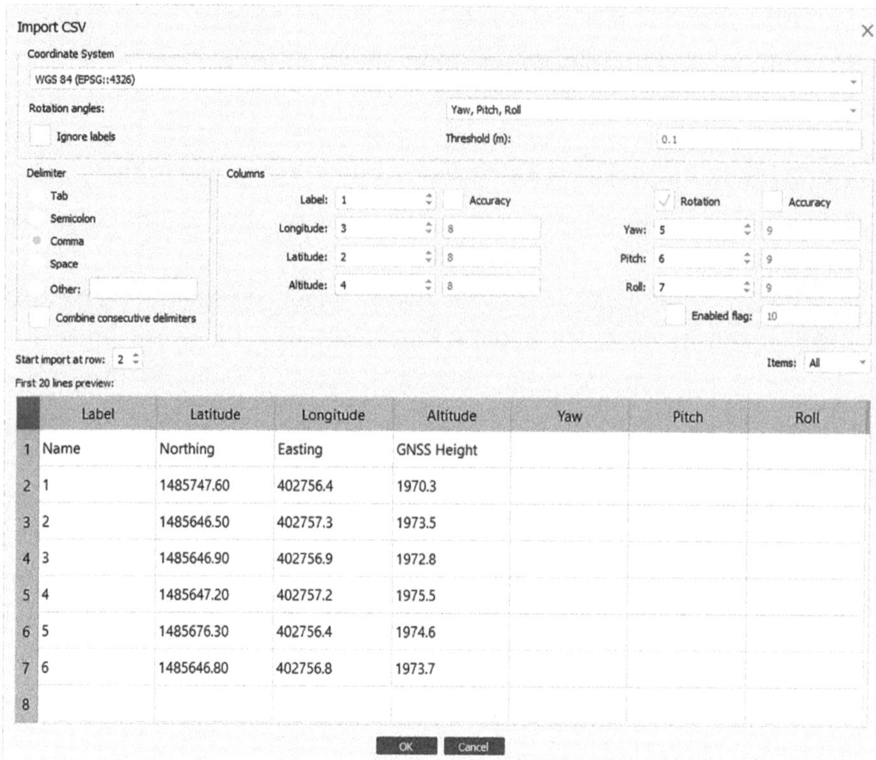

Figure 7.11 The interface when importing ground control points into a model.

settings and adjust if necessary. If you have headings in the spreadsheet, adjust the import to start at row 2 where it says "Start import from row".

When you press "OK", the labelled GCPs will appear under the "Reference" pane. It is possible that an alert will appear stating that a match for a certain marker could not be found and asking whether a new marker should be created. If this box does appear, select "Yes to all" so they are included in the model.

In the "Reference" pane, the GCPs will be listed with the corresponding "Eastings", "Northings" and "Altitude" under the heading "Markers". Click on the first marker and select "Filter photos by marker"; this will open all the images containing this GCP marker. Ensure that the marker is on the GCP in the image, and if not click and drag so it is positioned on it. For each GCP, position the marker accurately in at least six images to consolidate its location and press the refresh button in the ribbon to update the coordinates and error. This process needs to be repeated for all GCP markers that have been imported. To further improve the camera positions and the accuracy of the data, run the "Optimize Cameras" tool under the "Tools" tab before continuing to process the rest of the model.

7.20 Creating a fly-through

Creating a fly-through, also known as creating a camera track, is easily achieved in *Metashape*. Fly-throughs are a great way to exhibit a model in a presentation or on social media and can be exported and circulated at a significantly lower file size compared to photogrammetry models.

There are two methods to create a fly-through in *Metashape*; the first is using the preset camera tracks supplied by *Metashape* (which are based on the dimensions and position of the bounding box) and the second way is to create the camera tracks manually.

The following steps outline how to generate a preset fly-through:

1. Select the "View" tab in the main ribbon and click "Animation". This will open a new window with a series of icons in the ribbon.
2. Click on the first icon labelled "Create".
3. Depending on the orientation of the model, you can choose to configure the camera tracks horizontally or vertically. These positions are based on the dimensions and position of the bounding box so it might be necessary to resize and rotate the bounding box (outlined in 7.6.4) to correctly configure the preset camera tracks.
4. Set the keyframe count – this is the number of camera track positions around the model – and press "OK".
5. The camera positions will appear in the "Animation" panel and the fly-through can be viewed by pressing the "Play" icon.

To manually position the camera tracks for a video fly-through, the following steps can be followed:

1. Orient the model to a position that is suitable to begin the fly-through video.
2. Press the icon of the plus sign labelled "Append"; this will create a camera track position based on this view, and an associated record will be made in the "Animation" window of the x, y and z coordinates.
3. Rotate, zoom in and out, around or through the model in small increments, pressing the "Append" button as you move to set the camera tracks for the fly-through. Ensure to capture interesting features and include a wide view of the whole model; and it is also a good idea to end where you began to create a loop of the circuit if necessary. To have a smooth fly-through, have smaller gaps between track locations.
4. Press play to view the fly-through one complete time. To make any adjustments, the camera tracks can be deleted; however, take note you are only able to add in new camera tracks to the end of the list.

The time spent at each camera track can be changed by adjusting the percentage figure under the heading "Speed". Once you are satisfied with the fly-through, the camera tracks can be saved by pressing the "Save" button. Similarly, previously made camera tracks can be imported by selecting the "Load" icon. To export a video fly-through, press the "Capture" icon in the "Animation" toolbar ribbon that looks like a floppy disk. This will bring up a new window where you can adjust the resolution, compression format, and frame rate parameters. Once exported, the fly-through can be opened and viewed in video software. Further settings can be adjusted under the "Settings" icon. Here you can adjust the duration (in seconds), the field of view (in degrees), enable smooth camera tracking and looping the camera track.

7.21 Tips and tricks when using *Metashape*

There are many tricks, functions and methods to improve photogrammetry model-making in *Metashape* that both new and seasoned users may not know about. As such, a collection of useful tips has been listed here to help with model-building and to address certain issues that may arise.

7.21.1 Graphics card

Ensure that the graphics card (GPU) is switched on in *Metashape*. If the GPU is not activated, processing will be run by the Central Processing Unit (CPU). To check whether the GPU is turned on, click on "Tools" in the main ribbon, then go down to "Preferences" and then "GPU" tab. Tick the graphics card listed in the window and press "OK".

7.21.2 Point cloud is not essential

In *Metashape*, it is not essential to run the point cloud to build the mesh. When running the mesh, simply change "Source data" from "Point cloud" to "Depth maps + Laser scans", "Tie points", or "DEM" if creating a topographical model. Note that this will affect the quality of the final product and your ability to edit the model. While this may be time-efficient for large-scale topographical models or structures, it may not be the best choice for small-scale close-range photogrammetry modelling as irregularities or holes can occur in the mesh. Additionally, the easiest and most effective way of cleaning and editing a model is in the point cloud. The primary benefit of skipping this step is that a significant amount of time will be saved processing the model.

7.21.3 The visible selection tool

There is a tool available that allows you to only select visible mesh or point cloud data, ignoring any mesh or point cloud data behind this layer, and that is using the "Visible Selection" tool, under the tab heading "Model". This is a useful tool if you want to select and delete surface information on one side of a model but want to leave the other side as is. If activated, the "Visible Selection" tool will have a tick next to it.

7.21.4 How to increase the size of a small model

There are a few reasons why a model may appear tiny when generated in *Metashape*'s interface. One explanation may be due to outlier tie points produced a great distance away from the main model, potentially off-screen. As a result, *Metashape* makes the model smaller so these outlier tie points are not as far away from the model. What can also happen is when you scroll into the model, it quickly shoots off-screen. In this case, right-click on the model and select "Centre model", positioning the model in the centre of the screen. Then click on the tie point cloud view button in the main ribbon, select the entire model using the free-form selection tool and then click the "Crop Selection" icon in the main ribbon which will delete everything that has not been selected.

Another reason why a model may appear small in the *Metashape* interface may be due to it being incorrectly scaled. This can be adjusted by going to the "Reference" panel and inputting the correct dimensions of measured areas. The scale bar metric is in metres so be aware when inputting the measurements that the decimal point is in the right place. Remember, the "Reference" pane is not offered in the Standard Edition.

There is the option to easily increase or decrease the size of the model by selecting the "Scale Object" option under the "Move Object" icon in the main ribbon. Simply click on the model and drag the mouse to resize the object. *Metashape* will show an orange line with the magnification the model has been adjusted to next to it.

7.21.5 Centring the model

If you find that the model is very small, will not stay in the middle of the screen and scrolling into the model pushes it quickly off-screen, right-click the model and hit "Centre View". This will stabilise and centre the model, allowing you to move and zoom into the model smoothly.

7.21.6 Photograph pathways

Be careful to not move or rename images once a model has started processing, otherwise the software will lose the pathway to the stored image files and fail to run. If you do decide to move images, it is possible to find and reset the image pathway. All that needs to be done is to right-click an image and select "Change pathways". This will take you to a dialogue box where you can search for the new location of the image file.

If a failure alert keeps occurring while a model is being processed, it might be due to the software losing track of the image pathway, even if you have not moved any images. The failure alert will read "Error: Can't open file: The system cannot find the path specified". To check to see if the software has lost the pathway, simply right-click on an image and select "Check pathway", and the software will either not find any missing images or will list those that it cannot find. If it cannot find the images, simply select the "Change pathways" option and redirect the pathway back to the images folder. Once the image pathways are relocated, the processing should continue as normal.

7.21.7 Repositioning a model

It is possible a generated model will be positioned in a random location and orientation if no coordinates are imported into *Metashape*. To reposition a model, first turn on the grid view so you can see where the x axis is, to position the model. Head to "Model" – "Show/Hide Items" – "Show Grid". Zoom out to see where the model has been generated in relation to the grid. Select the "Move Object" icon in the main ribbon and select "Move Object" in the drop-down menu. A blue, red and green figure showing the x, y and z axes respectively will appear in the centre of the model and these axes can be selected and dragged to reposition the model. Try and position the model in the centre of the grid, marked "X". Alternating between the "Move Object" view and the "Navigation" tool (the icon of a mouse) will help in centring the model properly. Select the "Rotate Object" tool in the drop-down menu if the model needs to be levelled and the "Scale Object" to resize.

Repositioning the model should be conducted after the model has finished processing and is necessary if models are to be exported and before making video fly-throughs.

7.21.8 Show/Hide items

By selecting the "Model" tab, then navigating down to "Show/Hide Items", you can change what you see in the "Model" view pane. The options include the camera positions ("Show Cameras"), a grid ("Show Grid"), model information in the corners of the pane ("Show Info"), or the trackball ("Show Trackball"). The trackball can also be shown/hidden by pressing the space bar on your keyboard, once a function has been clicked in the main ribbon.

7.21.9 Using the Console pane

If a job was unsuccessful, *Metashape* will indicate this by showing an exclamation point next to the failed job and will say "Failed" (see Figure 7.12). The fastest way to determine the cause of the issue is to look in the "Console" pane. The "Console" pane exhibits all the information of the model-building process, including Python scripts and error messages. To open the "Console" pane, click on "View" and select "Console". The error warning will be listed in red and will tell you the problem.

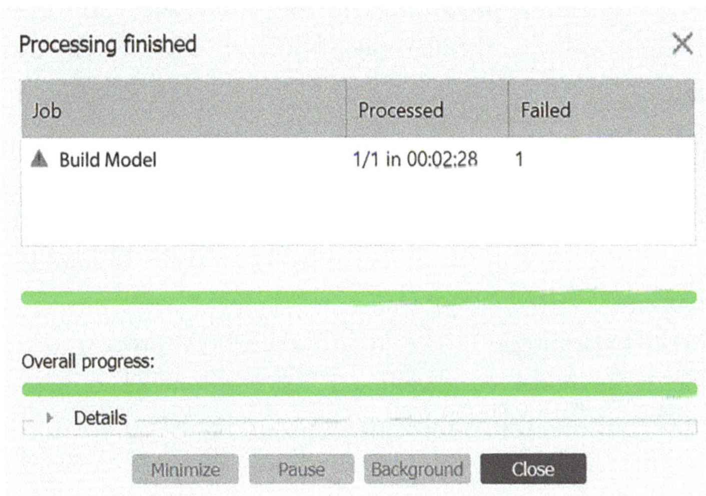

Figure 7.12 An error in the mesh job detected by *Metashape*.

7.21.10 Printing targets

Targets are an incredibly useful way of improving image alignment and scaling an object. To access targets to print from *Metashape*, simply head to "Tools" – "Markers" – "Print Markers" and input the ideal size of the centre point radius in millimetres (mm). It is possible to adjust the number of targets printed per page, the font size and the marker type before the targets are generated. This will depend on the size of the object being modelled – the larger the area being photographed, the larger the targets should be. Save the files as pdf (it is good practice to label the file with the radius size you have chosen) and print them out. Targets can then be cut out and positioned around an object or feature or attached to a mount. Take note: the saved document of targets consists of multiple pages, so confirm how many pages of targets you need before you print.

Targets with central radiuses of 5 mm and 10 mm have been included at the end of this manual, which can be cut out and used for your own photogrammetry modelling.

7.21.11 Cloud processing

To process models on the cloud, head to "Tools" – "Preferences" – "Enable Cloud Processing". Type in the associated email address to the licence and password, then press "Apply". When you run a job or a batch process, a window will appear prompting whether you want to schedule processing on the cloud; click "OK". The model will begin cloud processing and, once complete, you will get an email notification. The project can then be opened in your *Metashape* for further editing or processing.

7.21.12 Shortcut keys

On your keyboard, there are several shortcut keys that can be used. They include:

1. pressing the "1" orients the model to the front view; "Control" and "1" to the bottom
2. repeatedly pressing the "2" key rotates the object down
3. "3" orients the model to the right and "Control" and "3" orients it to the left
4. repeatedly pressing "4" rotates the model to the left
5. pressing the "5" key changes the view from "Perspective 30°" to "Orthographic" view
6. repeatedly pressing "6" rotates the model to the right
7. "7" reorients the model back to the top view and "Control" and "7" to the bottom view
8. repeatedly pressing the "8" key rotates the model up
9. "9" switches the model into "Stereoview"
10. the "0" key resets the view
11. pressing the "space" bar will switch between the navigation "ball" mode and the previously selected tool

12. to zoom in, press the "Control", the "Shift" and the "+" keys (on some machines just the "Control" and "+" keys are necessary)
13. to zoom out, press the "Control" key and the "-" key
14. double-clicking on a section of the model will reorient it so the clicked area will move to the centre of the screen.

7.22 Next steps

This chapter explored how to process a model in the photogrammetry software Agisoft *Metashape*, a reliable and user-friendly program that is commonly used in modelling archaeological material. Now that you have an understanding of the shooting and processing stages of photogrammetry, we can look at a range of photogrammetry case studies suited for archaeologists. In the following chapter, 11 case studies are presented of particular objects and features chosen to reflect the types of material that an archaeologist may have to model in their career. In this chapter, a guide to capturing each case study is presented, with the camera settings and the photography kit outlined for each case. The model settings, products and associated metadata are also presented so you can see what type of results are to be expected. The case studies range in objects of different sizes, shapes and material types, such as long, thin bones, rounded clay vessels, coins, and small artefacts like microliths. Three examples of larger features that an archaeologist may encounter have also been included, for example, an excavation pit. This chapter is to help build on your understanding of photogrammetry and demonstrate the type of shooting setup, camera settings, camera positions and model settings that can be used for a range of different jobs.

Chapter 8

CASE STUDIES

The capturing and processing of workflows will vary depending on the size, shape and colour of the subject being modelled, as well as its environment. Tall, thin objects may require multiple rounds of horizontal close-up shots down their body, while a rounded object may need several high angle rounds of shots to capture the curvature of its morphology. A small bead may need a 90 mm lens to accurately capture the detail, whereas a large stone structure may need a wide angle lens. To provide you with some understanding of how to capture a range of different object types and features, a collection of 11 case studies is presented in this chapter. These case studies have been specifically chosen to cover a range of different sizes, shapes and material types that an archaeologist might work with, to exhibit how each can be successfully modelled. The case studies start easier and progressively tackle harder material types (e.g. a black, metal object and a small coin).

The 11 case studies are:

8.1 A mid-sized artefact capturing the northern and southern hemispheres
8.2 An object in one orientation
8.3 A small artefact without targets (microlith)
8.4 A round object (an aryballos)
8.5 A long, thin artefact (bone fragment)
8.6 A triangular prism (lithic specimen)
8.7 A black, metal object shot in a semi-open environment (head of Dionysus)
8.8 A coin (tetradrachm)
8.9 An excavation pit
8.10 A terrestrial feature
8.11 A walled structure with corners

Although large-scale topographical photogrammetry is not the focus of this manual, three case studies have been included at the end of this chapter (8.9, 8.10 and 8.11) that describe some methods for photographing excavation pits, terrestrial features and walled structures as this is useful information for any archaeologist exploring photogrammetry.

For each case study, a step-by-step guide of the shooting method is provided, outlining what camera positions were required for each object (with image examples) and how the object was oriented for each round. A list of all the equipment used and a summary of the camera settings are also supplied for each case study. A brief outline of the processing settings applied to build the photogrammetry models in Agisoft *Metashape* Professional is also presented. The final model products for each case study are presented with the associated tie point and mesh face metadata and overall alignment success.

Case studies 8.1–7 and 8.11 were processed on Dell computers with Intel i7-7800X CPU @ 3.50 GHz 64 GB RAM, and NVIDIA GeForce GTX 1080 GPU. For case studies 8.8–10, a Dell workstation was used with an Intel Xeon W-2275 CPU @ 3.30 GHz, 192 GB RAM, and a NVIDIA GeForce RTX 3090 graphics card.

8.1 A mid-sized artefact capturing the northern and southern hemispheres

Artefacts measuring between 15 and 30 cm are ideal for beginner photogrammetrists. Objects around this size are relatively easier to model as they are likely to be portable and can be moved into a controlled photography setup, are not so big that they cannot be photographed on a turntable and can be photographed using a greater range of focal lengths compared to smaller archaeological artefacts. They are also not so small that additional aids such as targets or marker-based alignments need to be used for accurate image alignment, nor are they so big that creating holes in the mesh is a concern.

For this case study, a resin replica of an *Australopithecus africanus* skull, the shooting method was tailored specifically to accurately capture its rounded shape and the complexity of its underside.

The order of camera positions used for this case study was as follows:

1. A high angle round of the northern hemisphere to capture information at the top area of the subject.
2. A second high angle round at a lower height to capture the surface information on the curved edges.

3. A close-up high angle round to capture the important detail on the skull's face.
4. A round of wide shots for the overall morphology of the subject's northern hemisphere with the camera positioned further away from the subject.
5. A series of close-up connecting shots of a small section of the object with the camera close to the surface.
6. The object was turned upside down for a round of close-up connecting shots of the same location previously photographed in step 5.
7. A round of wide shots to capture the overall shape of the southern hemisphere
8. A high angle round to capture the complex curvature underneath the skull.
9. A round of close-up high angle images to cover the complex morphology of the southern hemisphere.
10. A high angle round focusing on the entire top region of the southern hemisphere.

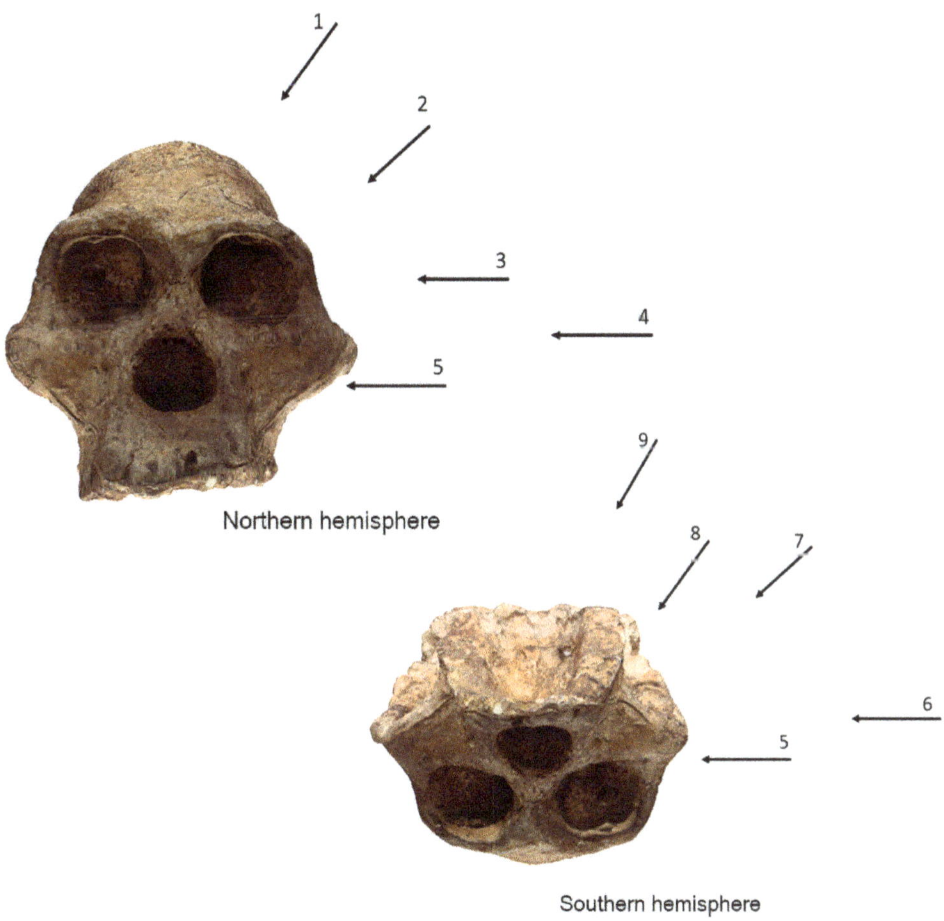

Figure 8.1 The camera positions to capture the northern and southern hemispheres of the *Australopithecus africanus* resin skull.

Equipment used:

- Canon 80D DSLR APS-C camera body
- Canon 35 mm f/2.8 macro lens
- Foldio lightbox with all LED lights turned on with additional attachable lights
- White background sheet
- Foldio 360 app-controlled turntable set to 3x speed
- Manfrotto studio tripod
- Kiwi camera rail
- PVC mount
- Scale bar

Camera settings:

- Manual priority
- Aperture: f/13
- Shutter speed: 1/100
- ISO: 800
- Large, Fine JPEG file format

Here is the step-by-step guide to the method taken to capture this mid-sized object:

1. After positioning the subject in the centre of the turntable and turning all the lights on, a few clear shots were captured of the scale bar in front of the skull so the model could be scaled later. The tripod was then extended to its maximum height and then the camera attached, pointing down to capture the top area of the resin skull. The camera was close enough that the frame was filled with the subject, capturing the edges of the skull. This camera position was in preparation for a round of high angle shots.

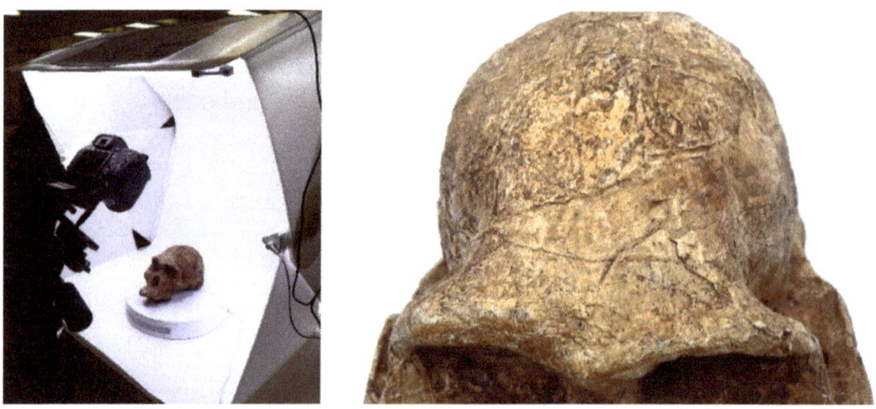

Figure 8.2 The camera's position for the first round of high angle shots of the resin skull and the first image taken from that round.

2. The skull's globular shape meant that another round of high angle shots was necessary to correctly capture its curvature, particularly around the brow ridge, so the camera was lowered slightly and the lens lifted to include more of the skull's face in the angle of view. Angular or complex subjects benefit from having images taken from multiple camera positions to improve alignment and reconstruction accuracy.

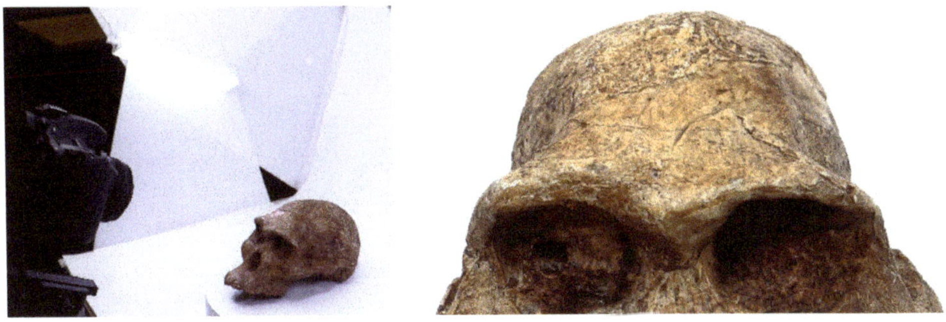

Figure 8.3 The camera's position for the second round of high angle shots and the first image from that round.

3. The third camera position was for close-up horizontal images. The camera was lowered and moved closer to the resin skull with the lens tilted up slightly to be parallel to the ground. As you can see in Figure 8.4, only the face was in the frame. These close-up images were crucial in the photography process as there was a lot of complex surface morphology in the skull's face that needed to be captured. Notice that the camera was not in a horizontal position but still slightly high angled. This was to match the slope of the skull's face. It is important to analyse the object being modelled and decide whether a high angle or horizontal camera position will capture the best detail.

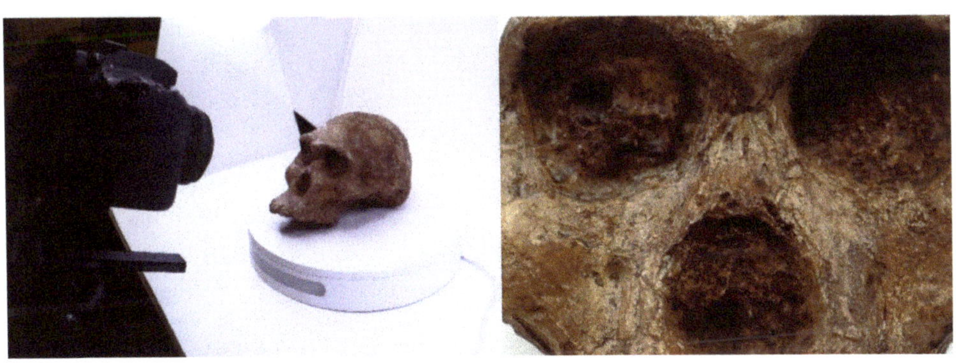

Figure 8.4 The camera's position for a round of close-up shots and the first image from that round.

4. The fourth camera position captured wide horizontal images (Figure 8.5). This was to photograph the entire morphology of the skull's northern hemisphere. The camera was moved back from the subject, lowered slightly and the lens tilted up. It was important to avoid the bottom of the skull in these shots as there was a lot of shadow on the turntable, which the software would have included in the model.

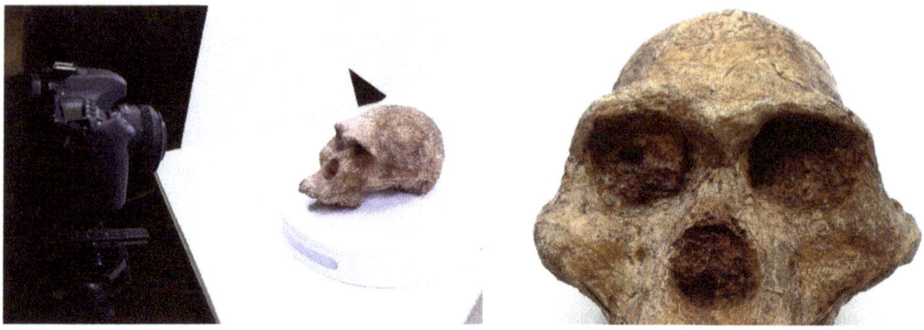

Figure 8.5 The camera's position for the round of wide horizontal shots and an image example from that round. Notice the turntable is not included in the image.

5. Before rotating the skull and taking pictures of the southern hemisphere, a few close-up connecting shots were taken. The camera was moved towards the skull again and a specific spot on the skull's face was chosen for the camera to focus on. Four shots were taken before the skull was repositioned upside down on a mount, where a further four shots were captured of the same spot on the skull's face.

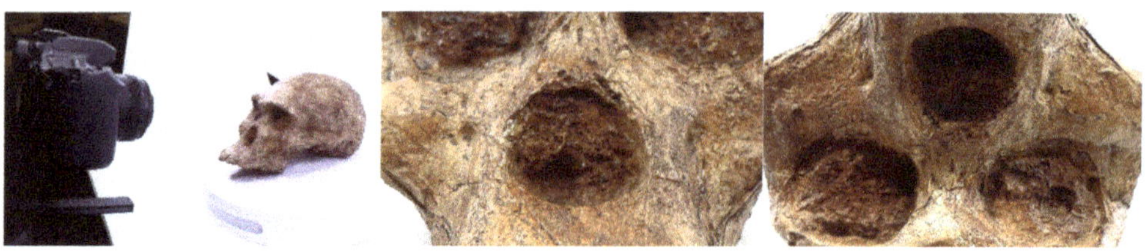

Figure 8.6 The camera's position to take several close-up connecting shots of both the northern and southern hemispheres. The following images are examples of the close-up connecting images in both orientations.

6. The camera was then repositioned to do a round of wide horizontal shots of the underside of the skull. Again, it was important to avoid the bottom of the skull's southern hemisphere. Due to the shape of this case study, the lights that were previously positioned on either side were moved in front of the subject to illuminate the face. If the lights were not repositioned, a shadow would have been cast over the front. It is important to be aware of how the light and shadows may change when the subject is repositioned.

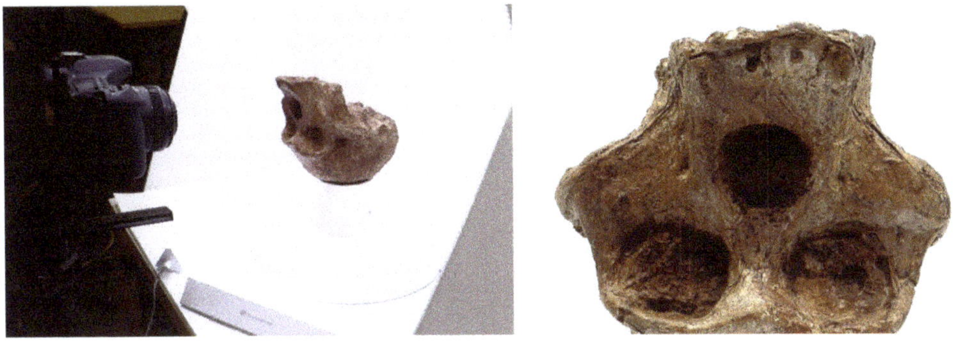

Figure 8.7 The camera's position for the round of wide horizontal images with an image example from this round. Notice the lights were moved to the front of the turntable.

7. Depending on the complexity of the shape of the subject, a round of close-up or high angle shots could be taken next. In this case study, the shape is complex, so a high angle round was performed first to capture the sides of the subject. The lights were repositioned back to the sides of the lightbox to illuminate the sides of the skull.

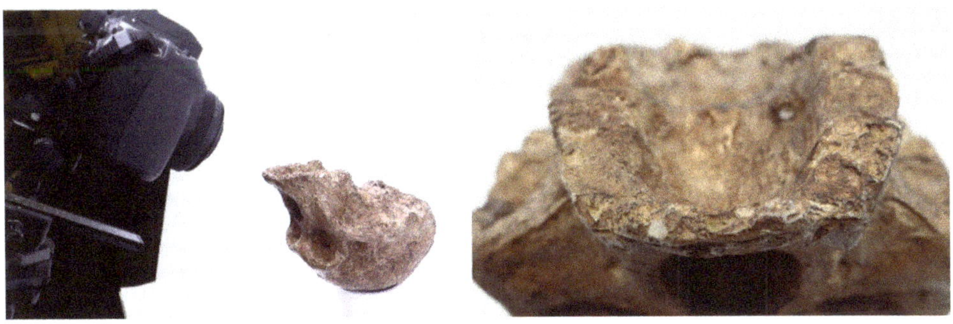

Figure 8.8 The camera's position for the round of high angle images and the first image from that round.

8. As there was a lot of detail on the underside of the resin skull, a round of close-up images was taken to capture the complex morphology of the underside of the skull. The camera was repositioned closer to the skull but was still at a high angle.

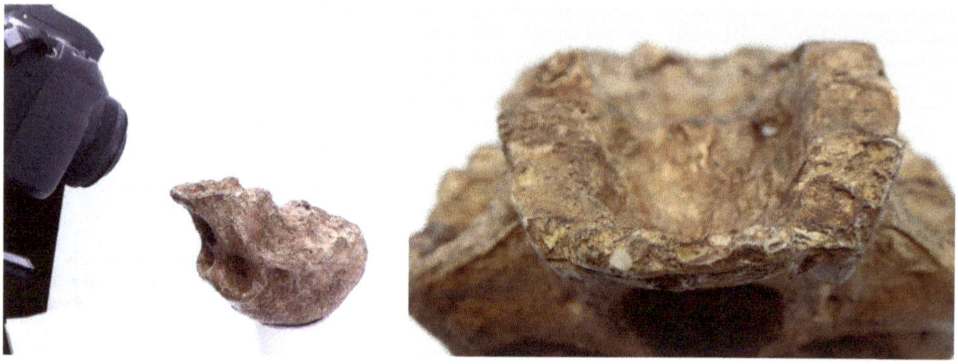

Figure 8.9 The camera's position for the close-up shots and an image example.

9. The final camera position was a second round of high angle images to capture the entire top area of the southern hemisphere. The tripod was extended to its fullest length and moved back slightly with the lens pointed down, so the entire frame contained the skull's underside.

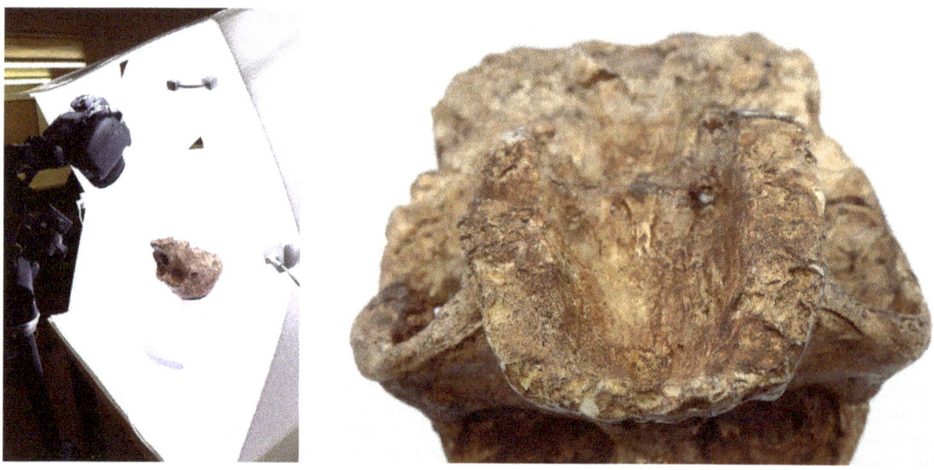

Figure 8.10 The camera's position for the second round of high angle shots and the first image from this round.

8.1.1 Model product

The model (Figure 8.11) was processed through Agisoft's *Metashape* Professional Edition using 436 images taken in Large, Fine JPEG file format. All the images were processed in one batch (as the turntable was avoided) and there was enough overlap between the two hemispheres to process in one batch. Using the high-accuracy alignment setting, 100% of the images aligned. "Generic Preselection" was turned on due to the photos containing sufficient overlap. The key point limit was changed to 100,000 and tie points to 10,000 with no masking used as the lightbox was a seamless white background and the turntable was avoided. The point cloud quality was set to high with mild depth filtering, and high settings for the depth map quality and mesh face count. The model had a total of 3,554,682 dot points (which were later reduced through editing) and a total of 11,418,305 mesh faces.

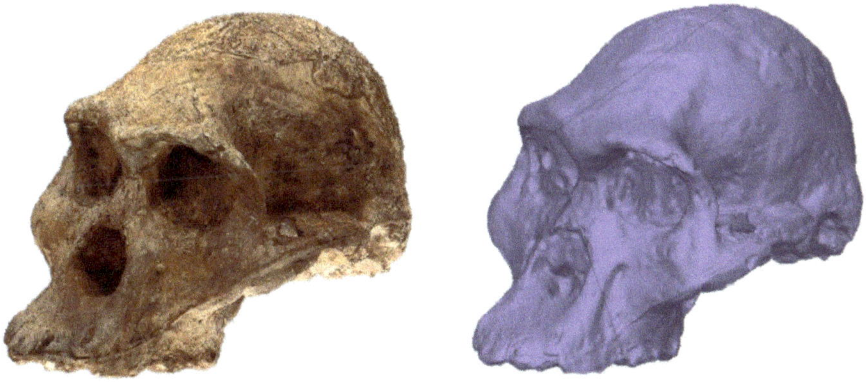

Figure 8.11 The photogrammetry model of the *Australopithecus africanus* skull replica created from 436 images following the above steps shown in the textured and mesh views.

8.2 An object in one orientation

Photographing an object in one orientation uses the same camera positions (high angle, horizontal and wide) with an additional step at the end of the process. Photographs taken from a low angle position ensure that all surfaces are captured if the subject cannot be turned upside down. The main concern in shooting objects in one orientation is that any surface information hiding under overhangs or surface projections of curved or angular objects is missed. Without taking low angle images these areas will not be captured and the photogrammetry model produced will likely have holes or distortions in the mesh layer, which is why this step of the shooting process is so important.

The example used here of a stone statue of the head of the Buddha had a metal stand attached to it and was also too heavy and fragile to be turned upside down. As such, it had to be photographed in one orientation with the following camera positions (see Figure 8.12):

1. High angle
2. High angle
3. Close-up horizontal
4. Close-up horizontal
5. Close-up horizontal
6. Close-up horizontal
7. Low angle
8. Wide

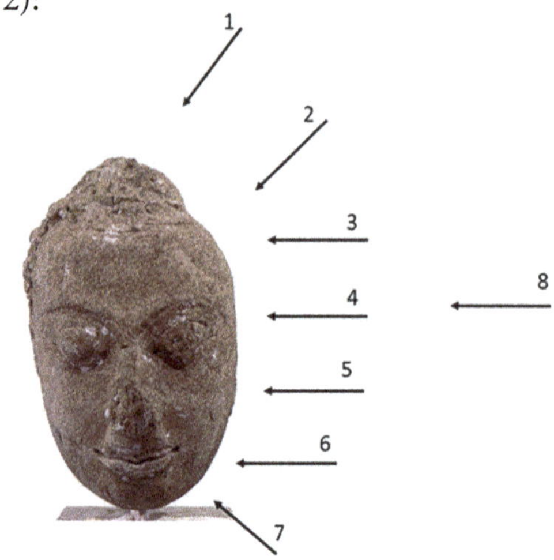

Figure 8.12 The camera positions for capturing an object in one orientation. UA2012.1241, University Art Collection, Chau Chak Wing Museum, the University of Sydney.

Equipment used:

- Canon 80D DSLR APS-C camera body
- Canon 35 mm f/2.8 macro lens
- Foldio lightbox with all LED lights turned on with additional lights on either side
- White background sheet
- Foldio 360 app-controlled turntable set to 3x speed with backlight on
- Scale bar

This case study was photographed freehand as several positions were more easily reached without a tripod due to the size of the subject and the dimensions of the lightbox.

The camera settings were:

- Manual priority
- Aperture: f/11
- Shutter speed: 1/125
- ISO: 1250
- Large, Fine JPEG file format

1. For the first round of high angle shots, the camera was positioned high above the statue with the lens pointing down to capture the entire crown of the statue's head. The camera was rotated into a vertical orientation (i.e. portrait style) to capture more of the subject and less of the background.
2. A second round of high angle shots was required as the crown and forehead of the statue were considerably rounded and tall. Again, the camera was in a vertical position to capture more of the surface area.
3. The first of the four rounds of close-up horizontal images was then taken with the camera lowered and levelled. This round focused on the upper region of the statue, covering the forehead and the eyes. The camera was repositioned into a horizontal, or landscape, orientation.
4. The camera was lowered again for the second round of close-up shots focusing on the eyes and nose of the statue; again, the camera was in a landscape orientation.
5. The third round of close-up horizontal images focused on the nose and the mouth.
6. The fourth and final round of close-up horizontal images focused on the mouth and chin of the statue and included a little bit of the stand.
7. The next round of images was taken in the low angle camera position. The camera was repositioned to a vertical orientation and the photographer kneeled under the lightbox and moved the lens close to the statue while keeping everything in focus. As the sculpture is supported by a metal stand, only one round of low angle shots was able to be conducted as the stand restricted access underneath the sculpture. The low angle shots captured the surface detail under the chin, ears and hair.

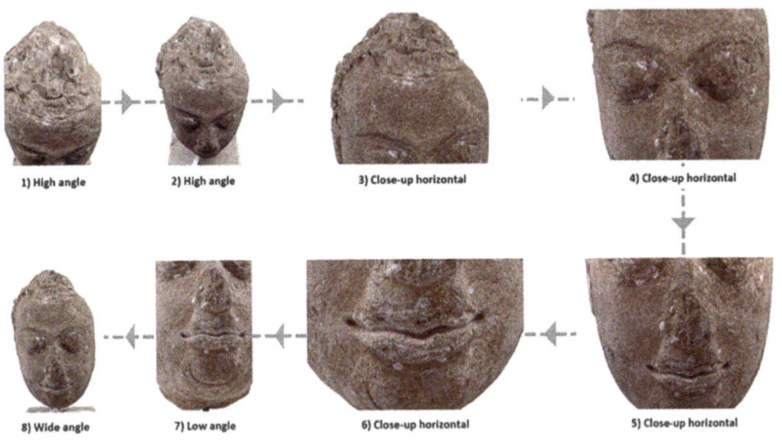

Figure 8.13 The first images taken from each camera position for photographing an object in one orientation.

8. The final round of shots were wide angle, and this required the camera to be moved slightly back from the subject so the entire statue was in the frame to ensure the full outline of the statue was captured. This was to consolidate all the data captured and reduced the likelihood of excessive masking in the processing stage.

8.2.1 Model product

This model was processed in one chunk from 295 Large, Fine JPEG images. As the object was photographed in one orientation, only three images needed to be masked (one image each from the high, low and wide angle camera positions) of the background to ensure the corners of the lightbox were not modelled. The alignment accuracy was set to high and the tie and key point limits were set to 100,000 and 10,000, respectively. Masking was from tie points, depth filtering was set to moderate and depth maps and mesh quality were set to high. The model produced a total of 1,760,007 tie points and 8,816,380 mesh faces with 100% alignment success.

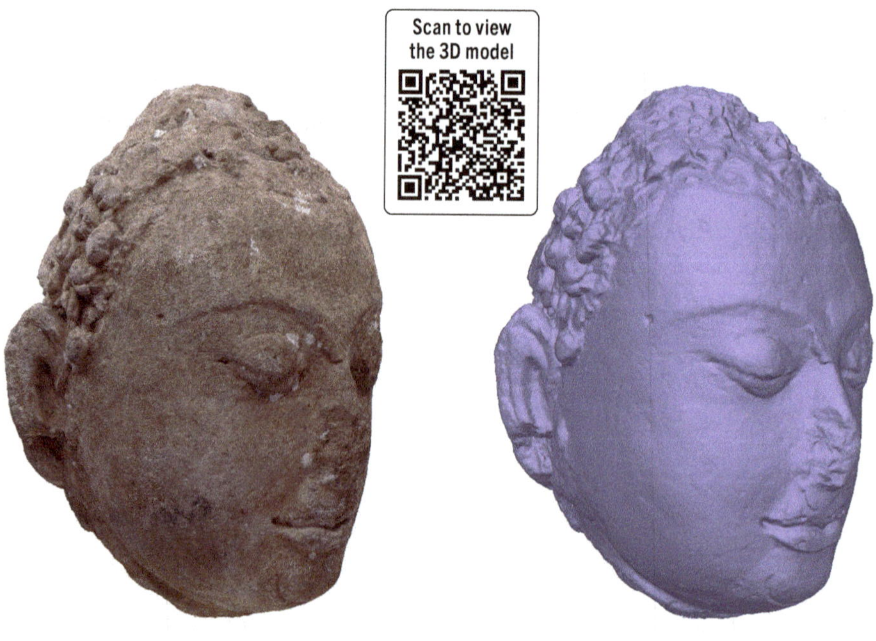

Figure 8.14 Final model product of a stone head of the Buddha photographed in one orientation. The underside can be seen to have been modelled correctly. UA2012.1241, University Art Collection, Chau Chak Wing Museum, the University of Sydney.

8.3 A small artefact without targets (microlith)

The method outlined here is tailored for modelling small objects that are less than 3 cm long without the help of targets. This shooting process is well suited for objects that have relatively thicker edges such as microliths, beads or pottery sherds. For modelling thin objects with targets, see the method outlined in 8.8.

When modelling objects that are very small, the main concern is that one face will not align correctly with the other. Increasing the percentage to at least 80% overlap is essential, particularly around the edges, so that the software identifies the surface features and morphology and aligns them successfully. Smaller objects are a lot trickier to model successfully compared to larger ones as there is less surface area to work with, so do not be disheartened if it takes a few trials to successfully build the photogrammetry model.

For this case study, a microlith, a wire stand was required to hold and stabilise the microlith in a vertical position as it rotated when the northern and southern hemispheres were being captured. Wire stands also provide height, which not only makes positioning the camera easier but also makes it easier to avoid the stand in the photos. You will notice the introduction of two new terms here as well – the eastern and western hemispheres. These are the sides of the microlith that will also be captured individually when it is positioned flat on the turntable.

The order of rounds and artefact position was as follows (see Figure 8.15):

- Northern hemisphere:
  1. High angle
  2. Close-up horizontal
- Eastern hemisphere:
  3. High angle
  4. Close-up horizontal
- Western hemisphere:
  5. Close-up horizontal
  6. High angle
- Southern hemisphere:
  7. Close-up horizontal
  8. High angle

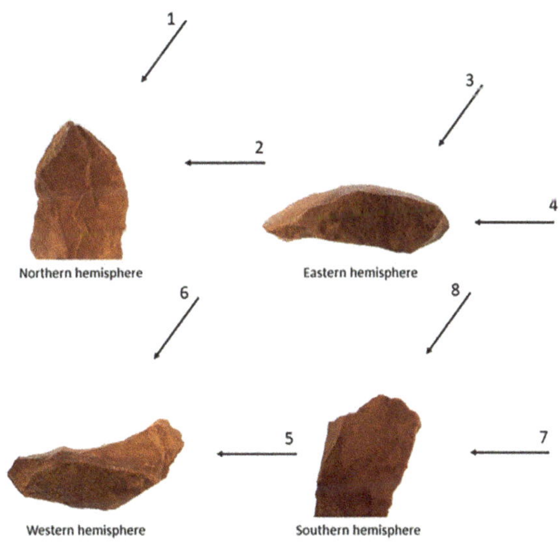

Figure 8.15 The camera positions and object orientations to capture the microlith.

The equipment used:

- Canon 80D DSLR APS-C camera body
- Tamron 90 mm f/2.8 macro lens
- Ortery PhotoBench 80 with temperature set to 5600 K (Figure 8.16)
- Manfrotto studio tripod
- Kiwi camera rail
- Wire stand
- Scale bar

The camera settings were:

- Manual priority
- Aperture: f/14
- Shutter speed: 1/125
- ISO: 1600
- RAW (converted to TIFF for processing) and Large, Fine JPEG file format

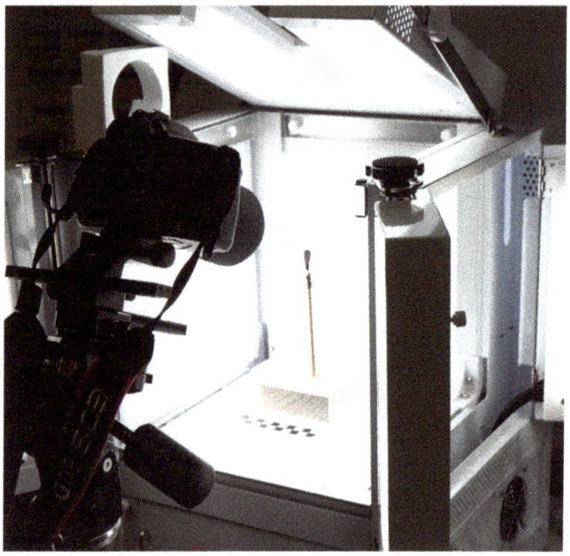

Figure 8.16 The photography setup in the Ortery PhotoBench 80. The microlith can be seen on the wire stand.

A detailed outline of the steps taken is as follows (Figure 8.17):

1. The artefact was positioned vertically on the wire stand with the camera focused on the entire northern hemisphere for a round of high angle shots. The wire stand was avoided at all times and it was ensured that each image captured the outline of the entire northern hemisphere.
2. Four connecting shots were taken with the focus moving down the surface of the microlith in preparation for the round of close-up horizontal shots. The camera was positioned as close as possible to the artefact to fill the frame and occasionally the edges of the microlith went out of the frame as the lens was so close. The stand was avoided at all times.
3. The microlith was then removed from the wire stand and positioned flat on the turntable, with the thickest edge facing the camera. The camera was repositioned

at a taller height with the lens pointing down to do a round of high angle shots. This round captured the surface detail of the eastern hemisphere and the entire microlith was kept within the frame at all times.

4. Four connecting shots were then taken as the camera was lowered down slightly almost to a horizontal position and moved closer for a round of close-up shots again focusing on the eastern hemisphere and the edges of the microlith.
5. The microlith was then turned upside down so the western hemisphere was showing with the same edge pointing towards the lens. The camera was kept in the same position to do a round of close-up shots of the western hemisphere.
6. Four connecting shots were taken as the camera was slowly raised to do a round of high angle shots of the western hemisphere.
7. The microlith was then repositioned onto the wire stand, this time with the southern hemisphere showing. The camera was raised and moved closer to the specimen to do a round of close-up shots. The stand was avoided and the lens was close enough that occasionally the microlith's edges were out of the frame.
8. More connecting shots were taken as the camera was raised again to do the final round of high angle shots of the southern hemisphere. The stand was avoided but the edge of the southern hemisphere was within the image frame at all times.

You will notice that no wide rounds were taken in this case study. This is because the microlith was so small that most of the images taken had edges showing so they were unnecessary. Connecting shots, however, are essential for small objects such as microliths to ensure that there is a clear progression of images from one camera position to the next. It is crucial that all the fine detail is captured seamlessly to help the software stitch it together accurately. When in any doubt about whether you should take another photograph to ensure the photos are connected, or from a different angle – take a shot.

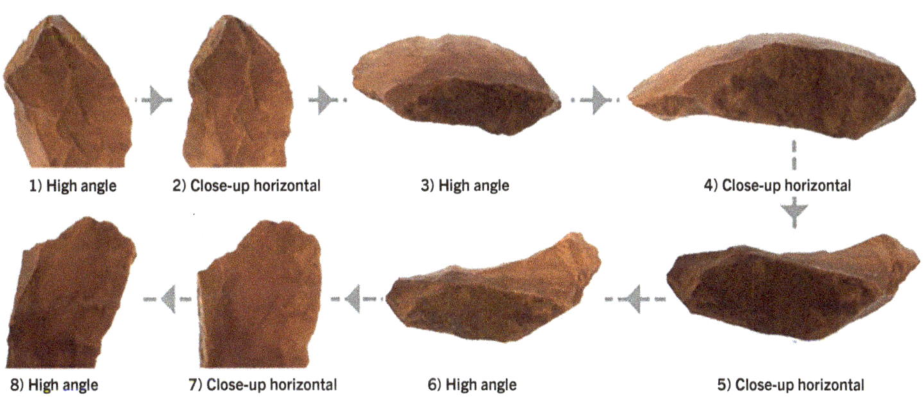

Figure 8.17 The flowchart of camera positions for a microlith.

8.3.1 Model product

The photogrammetry model of this case study (Figure 8.18) was built in Agisoft's *Metashape* Professional from 540 images taken in both RAW and Large, Fine JPEG file formats. Minor edits to the highlights were made on the RAW images, to reduce the specular reflection on the surface of the microlith. The RAW images were then converted to TIFF files for processing. Following the method outlined above, there was enough overlap from both hemispheres that all images could be run in one batch. The model was run on a high-accuracy alignment setting with "Generic Preselection" turned on. No masking was required as the stand was avoided at all times and 100% alignment was obtained due to a consistent overlap of 80% within the photos. The point cloud quality was set to high, depth filtering to mild, and depth map quality and mesh face count were also set to high. The model generated a tie point cloud of 686,683 tie points and a mesh face count of 3,782,883 faces.

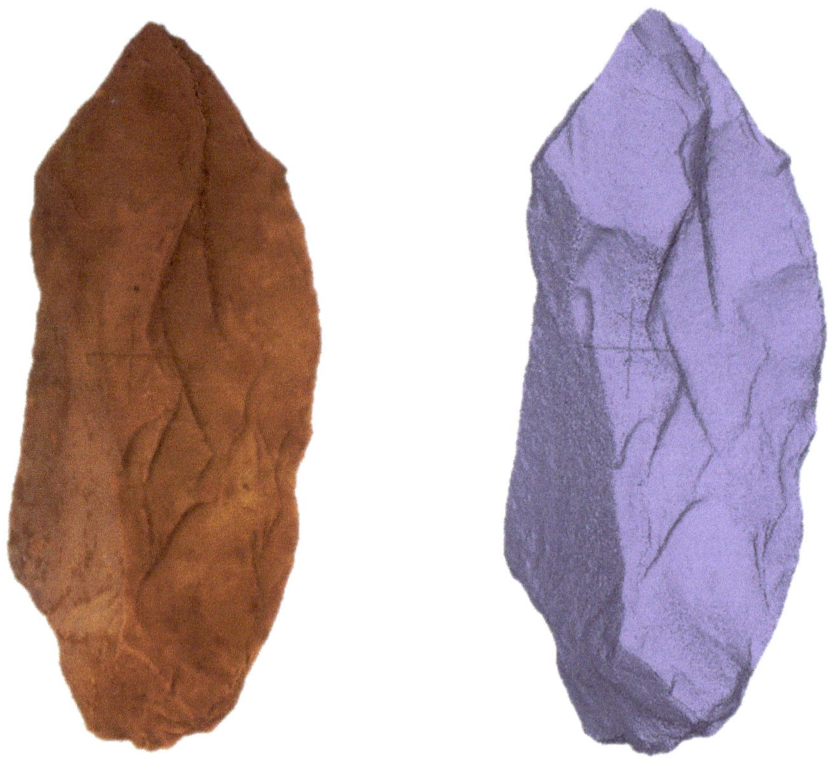

Figure 8.18 The photogrammetry model product of the microlith produced from 540 images shown in both the texture and solid mesh views. Katjarra collection, Jo McDonald, University of Western Australia.

8.4 A round object (an aryballos)

Photogrammetry works particularly well for ceramic objects as long as the surface is not too reflective. Some difficulty may arise in capturing the detail accurately if the shape of the vessel is particularly curvaceous. In the below case study, a Corinthian aryballos, there are some areas with considerable detail that are tricky to capture; therefore, the shooting method had to be expanded to include multiple rounds of high angle and close-up camera positions. The intricate yet bold detail and the matte surface of the ceramic, however, were good indications that a successful photogrammetry model could be produced.

Ten rounds were taken to capture the surface of this vessel. Both the northern and southern hemispheres were photographed as the aryballos could be safely turned upside down and supported on a mount. There is a lot of intricate detail on this case study, so several close-up rounds were taken to capture the markings correctly. Under the rim of the vessel, the neck and the inside of the handle were identified as potentially tricky sections to capture correctly so a round of low angle shots was included to specifically focus on the underside. Take note that ceramic vessels may have a lip and remember to pay them extra attention.

The order of the camera positions for this vessel was (Figure 8.19):

- Northern hemisphere:
  1. High angle
  2. Wide, high angle
  3. Close-up horizontal
  4. Low angle
  5. Close-up horizontal
  6. Close-up horizontal
  7. Horizontal wide

- Southern hemisphere:
  8. Horizontal, wide
  9. High angle
  10. High angle

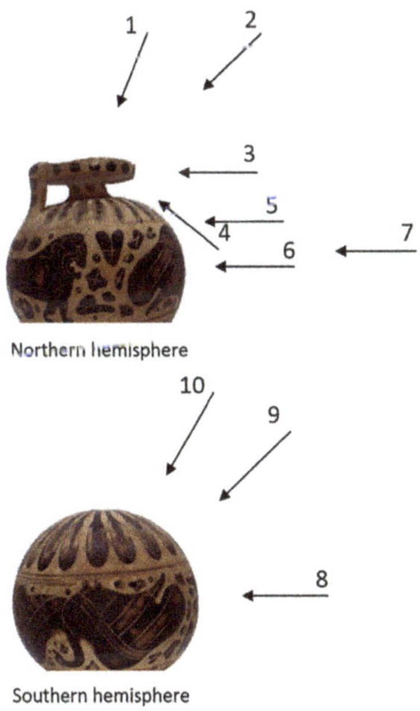

Figure 8.19 The order of camera positions required to completely capture this round vessel (a Corinthian aryballos). NM1998.27 Nicholson Collection, Chau Chak Wing Museum, the University of Sydney.

The equipment used was:

- Canon 80D DSLR APS-C camera body
- Canon 35 mm f/2.8 macro lens
- Canon ring flash with a lowered brightness intensity to -3.7 to reduce any intense reflection bouncing back from the subject's surface
- Foldio lightbox with all LED lights turned on with additional lights on either side
- White background sheet
- Foldio 360 app-controlled turntable set to 3x speed with backlight on
- Manfrotto studio tripod
- Kiwi camera rail
- Foam mount
- Scale bar

The camera settings were:

- Manual priority
- Aperture: f/13
- Shutter speed: 1/125
- ISO: 1250
- Large, Fine JPEG file format

A detailed step-by-step guide to shooting this case study is provided here (Figure 8.20):

1. For the first camera position, the tripod was extended as far as it could go with the lens pointing down to capture the flat edge of the mouth of the northern hemisphere of this vessel at a high angle.
2. The camera was then moved back slightly and the lens lowered slightly to capture a round of wide, high angle images. This round focused on the vessel's lip, shoulder and the detail of the upper body. The wide shots also capture the globular shape of the aryballos. This round of high angle shots had to be carefully taken to avoid including the turntable or the stand the vessel was resting on.
3. Due to the amount of detail on the vessel, a series of close-up horizontal rounds were taken focusing on the lip, neck and shoulder. To capture these areas, the camera was lowered and moved closer to the vessel with the lens tilted up to a horizontal position.
4. The next camera position was at a low angle to capture the detail under the lip. The camera was lowered and the lens adjusted to point up to focus under the rim. These were tricky shots to take on the tripod as there was not enough space underneath the lightbox, so the camera had to be taken off the tripod and rail and the round was taken freehand.
5. Another round of horizontal close-up photos was taken, this time focusing on the detail at the vessel's shoulder and the detail of the body. This round was important to connect to the following round of close-up shots.

6. The last round of close-up horizontal shots focused on the imagery of the body. Notice in Figure 8.20 that the neck, handle and lip were intentionally avoided in this round.
7. The final images of the northern hemisphere were a round of horizontal wide photos to capture the entire shape of the aryballos above the base. The camera had to be moved back away from the vessel and lowered slightly to fit it all in the frame.
8. The vessel was then safely turned upside down (after taking several close-up connecting shots) and repositioned on the mount so the southern hemisphere could be captured. The first round was a batch of wide horizontal photos to capture the shape of the southern hemisphere.
9. The camera was then raised and the lens adjusted downwards to take a round of high angle images. These focused on both the vessel's base and the lower half of the body. These were taken relatively close to the vessel to fill the frame with the subject.
10. For the final round, the camera was raised to its highest extent and the lens pointed down for a round of high angle shots. These images captured the top section of the southern hemisphere and all the detail on the base of the aryballos.

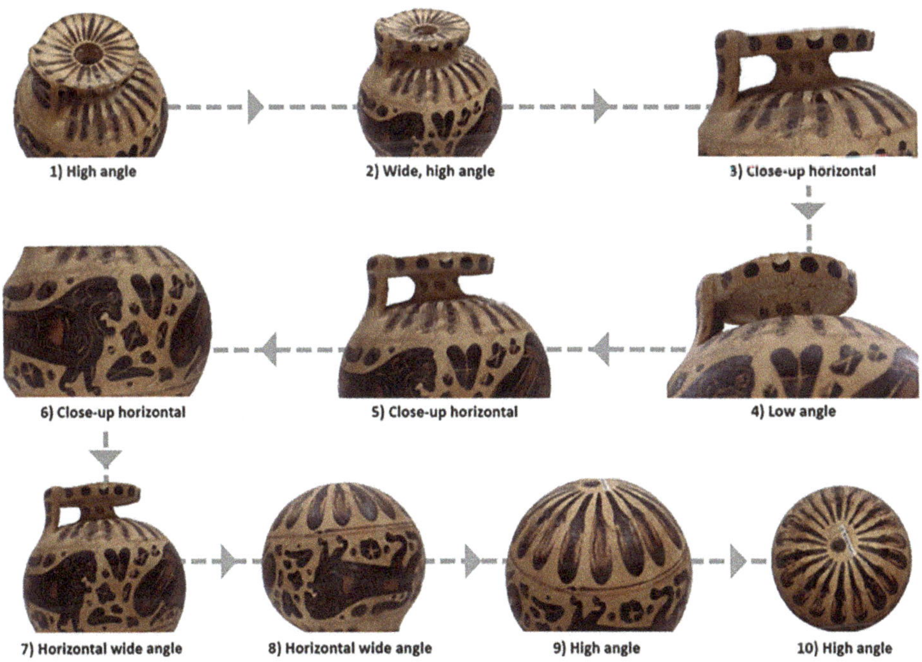

Figure 8.20 Image examples taken from each camera position required to model the Corinthian aryballos.

8.4.1 Model product

This model of a Corinthian aryballos (Figure 8.21) was processed through Agisoft's *Metashape* Professional from 319 Large, Fine JPEG images. It was processed in one batch with around 20 images containing masks of the background to run a tie point mask. The model was run on high-accuracy alignment settings with "Generic Preselection" turned on, a high point cloud quality setting, mild depth filtering, and high depth map quality and mesh face count. The model had 100% alignment, 1,623,081 tie points and 6,145,827 mesh faces.

Although ten rounds may seem excessive for such a small object, having so many camera positions ensured that the software would produce a clean and accurate reconstruction of the curved edges and the lip with detailed and high-quality mesh. It also meant there was little intervention in the processing stage, which was also improved with the addition of several masks.

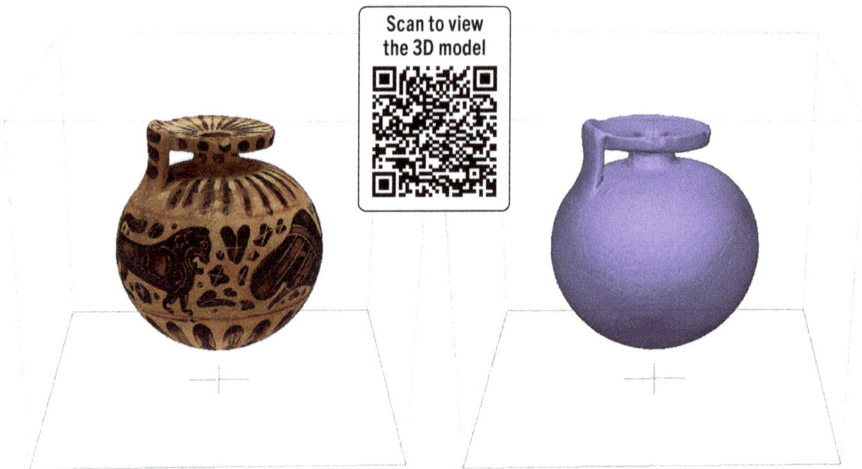

Figure 8.21 The photogrammetry model of the round aryballos produced by following the above steps. NM1998.27 Nicholson Collection, Chau Chak Wing Museum, the University of Sydney.

8.5 A long, thin artefact (bone fragment)

Long, thin objects can be particularly tricky to model as there is less surface area that can be easily captured in one image frame. As such, an additional step can be included in the shooting process to ensure that the software aligns the model correctly. This method requires the artefact to be photographed in both an upright and horizontal position; therefore a mount might be necessary for modelling long and thin objects.

For this case study, a bone fragment, the bone had to be positioned upright on a rigid PVC mount for the first five camera positions focusing on the northern hemisphere, then repositioned on its side in a second mount made of rubber (see Figure 8.22) for a series of connecting shots along the thinnest section of the bone, then turned upside down and returned to the PVC mount so the southern hemisphere could be captured.

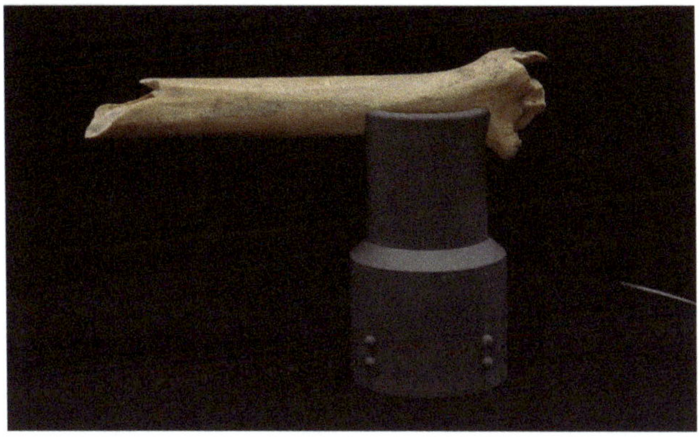

Figure 8.22 The bone fragment positioned on a rubber mount to stabilise it for the connecting shots.

The camera positions included the following:

- Northern hemisphere:
  1. High angle
  2. High angle
  3. Close-up horizontal
  4. Close-up horizontal
  5. Wide
- Eastern hemisphere (aerial view):
  6. Close-up high angle
  7. Close-up high angle
  8. Close-up high angle
- Southern hemisphere:
  9. Wide
  10. Close-up horizontal
  11. Close-up horizontal
  12. High angle
  13. High angle

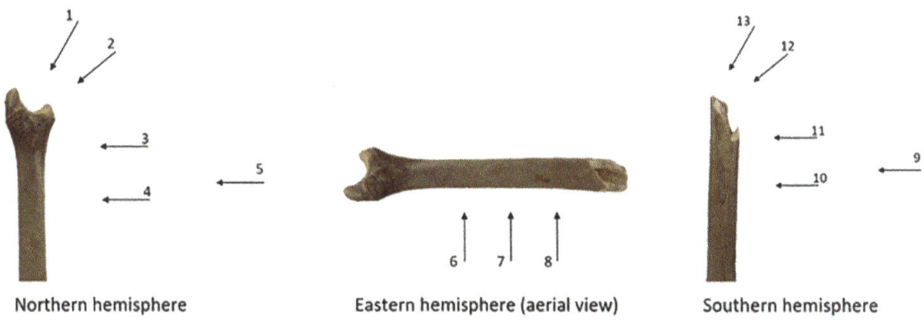

Figure 8.23 The order of camera positions required to completely capture a long, thin bone fragment. The aerial view of the bone is given for the eastern hemisphere.

Equipment used:
- Canon 80D DSLR APS-C camera body
- Canon 35 mm f/2.8 macro lens
- Canon ring flash
- Foldio lightbox with all LED lights turned on with additional lights on either side
- Black background sheet
- Foldio 360 app-controlled turntable set to 3x speed with backlight on
- Manfrotto studio tripod
- PVC mount
- Rubber mount
- Scale bar

The camera settings were:
- Manual priority
- Aperture: f/11
- Shutter speed: 1/125
- ISO: 640
- Large, Fine JPEG file format

The shooting method used to correctly model this long, thin bone was as follows (Figure 8.24):

1. The bone was positioned upright on a mount exposing around 60% of the bone so the northern hemisphere could be captured. The tripod was extended to its fullest height with the camera oriented on its side to a vertical position with the lens pointing down at the top of the bone to do a round of high angle shots. As the bone was so thin, the top edge of the bone almost touched the top of the frame to fill the image with the subject and limit the presence of the background in the shot.
2. The camera was then lowered slightly and the lens raised to do a second round of high angle shots of the northern hemisphere, still focusing on the morphology at the epiphysis of the bone.
3. For the first round of close-up horizontal photos, the camera was lowered and the lens was tilted until it was level. These images focused on the upper shaft area and where it connects to the epiphysis.
4. A second round of close-up horizontal images was required to reach just over half of the diaphysis. The camera was lowered and the lens remained in a horizontal position. The number of close-up rounds focusing on the long, thin section of the object you are modelling will depend on the length of the object. Ideally, half of this section is captured when in this orientation.
5. The final images taken of the northern hemisphere were a round of wide shots. The entire length of the bone fragment was included in the frame, but did not exceed any area that was not covered in the previous rounds.

6. The bone fragment was then placed flat on the turntable exposing the eastern hemisphere. A series of three connected images (6, 7 and 8 in Figure 8.24) were then taken along the diaphysis from a close-up high angle position. These shots connect the northern hemisphere to the southern hemisphere and should not be overlooked. If the object is short, a wide image could be taken at this point to capture the entire side of the bone in one image. This bone fragment, however, was too long to be captured well from a wide position.
7. The bone fragment was then repositioned on the mount with the southern hemisphere exposed. Again, about 60% of the bone was above the mount. The camera was readjusted to do a round of wide images. Again, these photos must overlap with the previous connecting shots.
8. The camera was then moved towards the specimen for the first round of close-up horizontal images (10 in Figure 8.24) of the southern hemisphere, focusing back on the diaphysis.
9. Raising the camera again, the second round of close-up horizontal shots (11 in Figure 8.24) was taken, continuing to capture the rest of the bone's shaft.
10. The camera was then extended further and the lens tilted downwards for the first round of high angle shots focusing on the fragmented edges of the bone.
11. The final position for this case study required the camera to be raised to the tripod column's fullest height with the lens brought down so that the top of the bone fragment could be captured at a high angle. Like in the first round of images, the top edge of the bone fragment met the top of the frame to fill the frame.

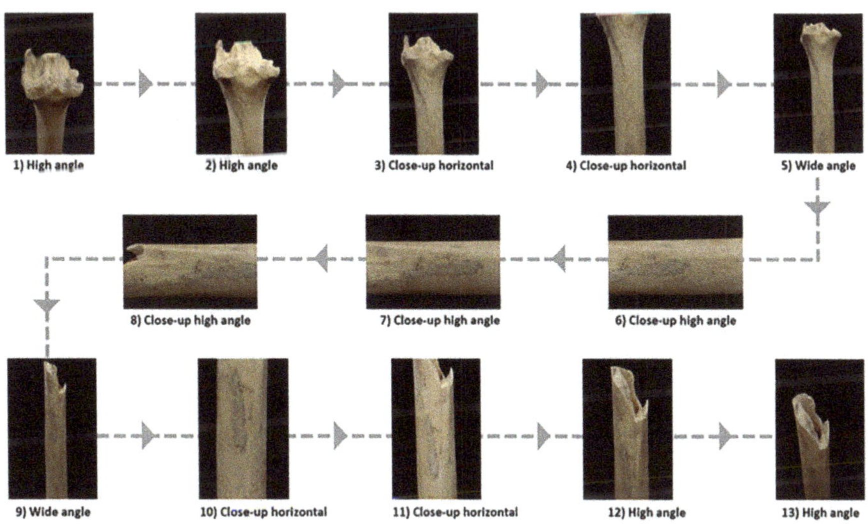

Figure 8.24 The first images from each camera position for the bone fragment.

8.5.1 Model product

This model (Figure 8.25) was processed through Agisoft's *Metashape* Professional from 522 Large, Fine JPEG images. All images were processed in one batch and around 30 photos were masked to remove the background. The model was run on medium alignment accuracy with "Generic Preselection" turned on and masked from tie points. The point cloud quality was set to medium, depth filtering was set to aggressive, depth map quality was medium and the face count was high. The model had 100% alignment and produced 248,222 tie points and a mesh count of 987,848 faces. Figure 8.25 shows the arrangement of camera positions and the final product in the textured view.

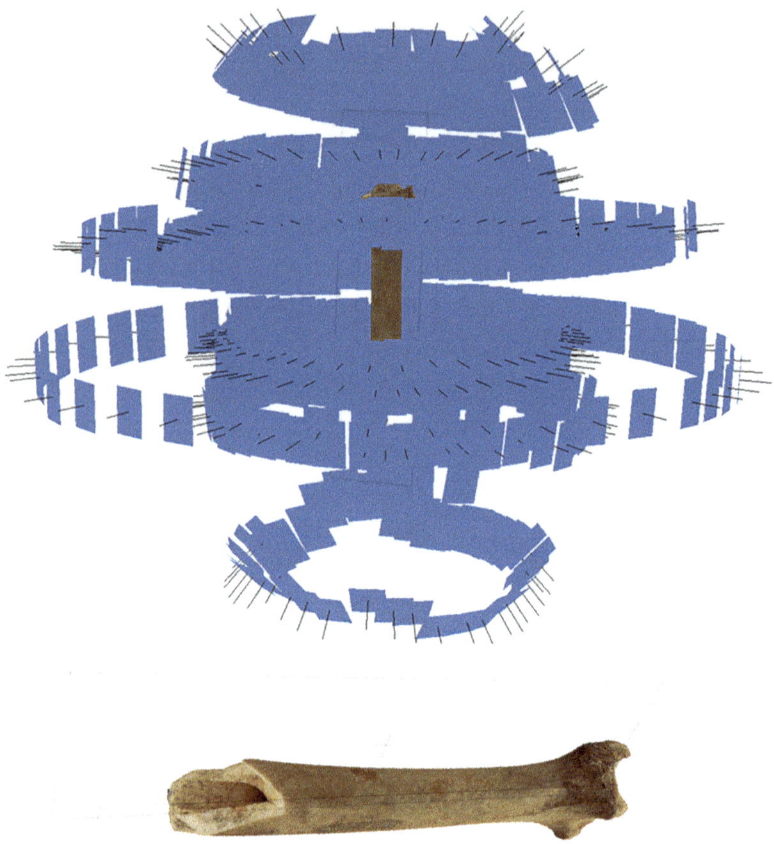

Figure 8.25 The camera locations, each represented by a blue square, around the bone fragment and the final product of the photogrammetry model produced from 522 images using the above method.

8.6 A triangular prism (lithic specimen)

Objects that are a triangular prism in shape have three sides and, as such, have a slightly different order of camera positions and object orientations. To avoid the software from potentially misaligning the object, triangular objects benefit from being photographed in both vertical and horizontal positions, as shown in Figure 8.26. In this case study, a stone tool, the northern and southern hemispheres were captured first, supported by a rubber mount. It was then positioned flat on the turntable and rotated along the x axis so the three sides could be photographed. The order of camera positions used for this case study was as follows:

- Northern hemisphere (on mount):
  1. High angle
  2. High angle
  3. Close-up horizontal
- Southern hemisphere (on mount):
  4. Close-up horizontal
  5. High angle
  6. High angle
- Face 1 (on turntable):
  7. Horizontal wide
- Face 2:
  8. Horizontal wide
- Face 3:
  9. Horizontal wide

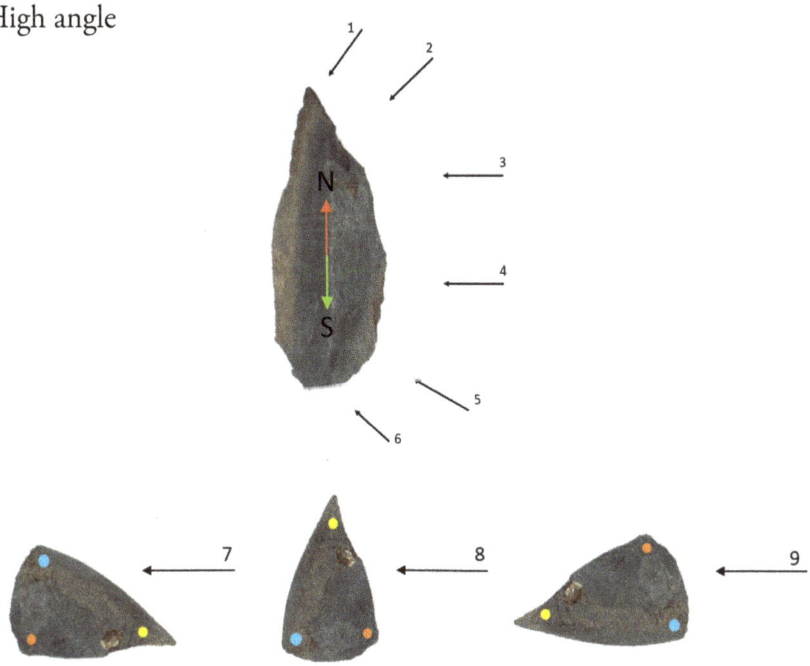

Figure 8.26 The camera positions and object orientation required to capture this triangular prismatic object. The arrows indicate the position and angle of the camera lens. Notice the rotation of the stone tool for the 7th, 8th and 9th camera positions, using the coloured dots for guidance.

Equipment used:

- Canon 80D DSLR APS-C camera body
- Canon 35 mm f/2.8 macro lens
- Ortery PhotoBench 80
- PVC mount
- Scale bar

Camera settings:

- Manual priority
- Aperture: f/16
- Shutter speed: 1/100
- ISO: 200
- Large, Fine JPEG file format

Figure 8.27 shows the first image captured from each round to provide an idea of how the object was oriented and the camera positioned.

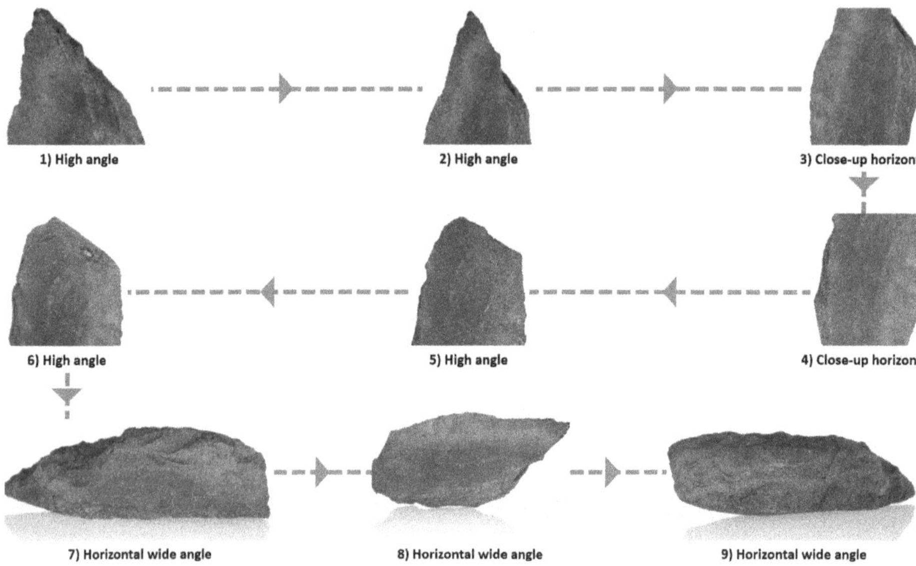

Figure 8.27 The first images taken at each camera position for the stone tool.

8.6.1 Model product

This model was processed through Agisoft's *Metashape* Professional from 324 Large, Fine JPEG images. All images were processed in one batch with one masked image from each of the horizontal wide rounds of the three faces as there was some reflection on the turntable. The model was run on high-accuracy alignment settings with "Generic Preselection" turned on, high point cloud quality, mild depth filtering, and high depth map quality and mesh face count. The model had 100% alignment, 1,303,460 tie points and a mesh face count of 2,872,888.

Figure 8.28 shows the final model product with the arrangement of camera positions used to align the triangular prismatic stone tool. The horizontal wide shots of the three faces can be seen crossing over each other at different axes.

Positioning the object horizontally and rotating it to capture the three sides may seem excessive, but the absence of any obstruction from the mount significantly aids in alignment success. Just remember, when shooting a triangular prismatic object, connecting shots must be taken between each of these orientations.

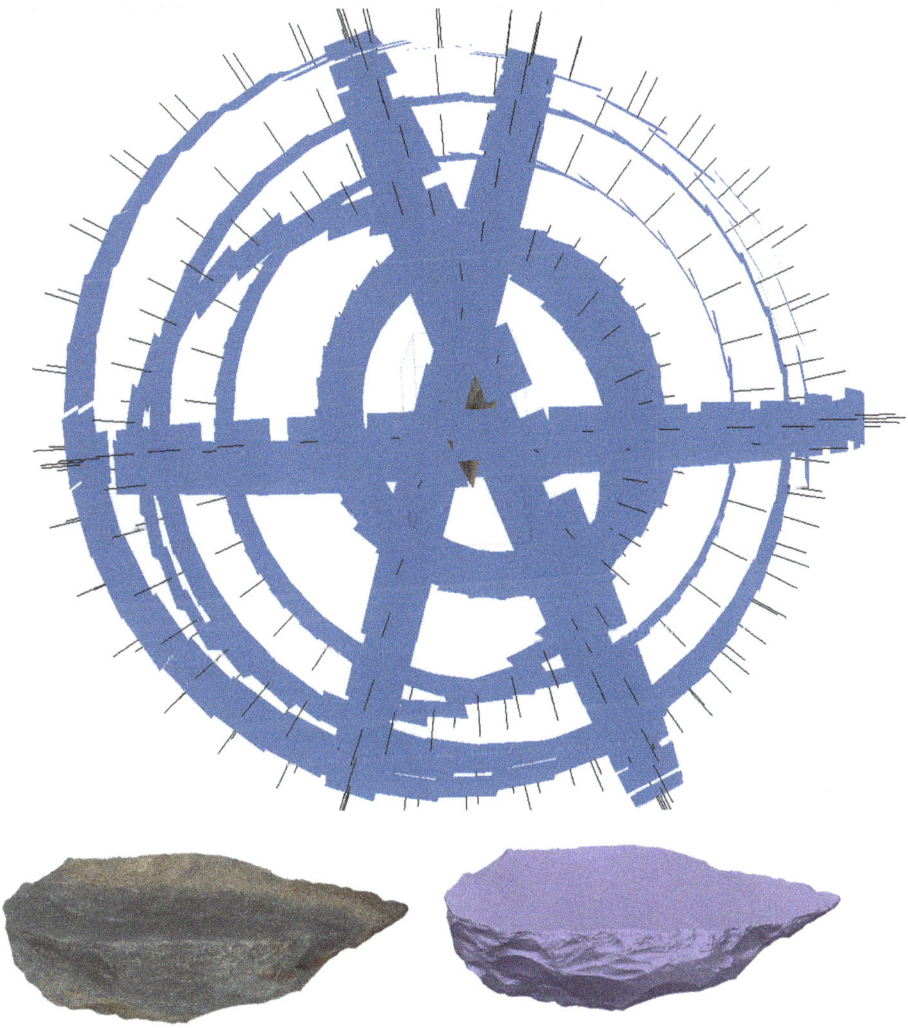

Figure 8.28 Photogrammetry model of a triangular prism artefact with the images included in three-dimensional space. Note the three rounds of photos that cross through the other axes. South Molle Island quarry "Juan knife", Lara Lamb, University of Southern Queensland.

8.7 A black, metal object shot in a semi-open environment (head of Dionysus)

Black artefacts can be incredibly hard to model, particularly if they are made from metal. This is because the lack of colour and detail in a black surface makes it hard for the software to identify key points in the object to stitch the model together. This case study, a bronze cast of the head of Dionysus, was particularly tricky as there were additional obstacles encountered in the photography process. The object could not be moved and was close to a wall, resulting in restricted access to the back of the object (see Figure 8.29). The ambient light was from cool overhead ultraviolet lights; therefore, a dampened ring flash was used to combat the lack of illumination as no studio lights were available. The bust was also on a tall plinth and a stepladder had to be used so the photographer could capture the top of the bust's head. These are the kind of obstacles that photogrammetrists may run into (particularly if the object is in a museum), so it is a good idea to be prepared for shooting in these kinds of less-than-ideal environments.

For this case study, the following camera positions were used with connecting shots taken between each camera position:

1. High angle round focusing on the crown of the head of Dionysus.
2. A second high angle round with the camera lowered to focus on the curvature of the head.
3. Close-up horizontal to capture the detail at the top section of the bust's face and hair.
4. A second round of close-up horizontal shots with the camera lowered to focus on the middle section of the bust's face and hair.
5. A third round of close-up horizontal shots with the camera lowered again to focus on the lower section of the bust's face and hair and areas around its neck.
6. Low angle round to capture detail underneath the bust's chin and hair.
7. A second low angle wide camera position with the camera moved slightly further back, close to a horizontal position (due to the height of the bust, the camera was still in a low angle position) to capture the entire shape of the bust.

In Figure 8.29, the model and camera locations can be seen from an aerial perspective. It is evident where the wall was as there is a clear gap at the back of the statue where the camera could not reach. It is also obvious from this figure that the images were not evenly spaced and appear more randomly positioned compared to an object photographed on a turntable. This is because the photographer had to step down from the ladder and reposition themselves and the ladder after each shot for the two high angle rounds and the first round of close-up horizontal

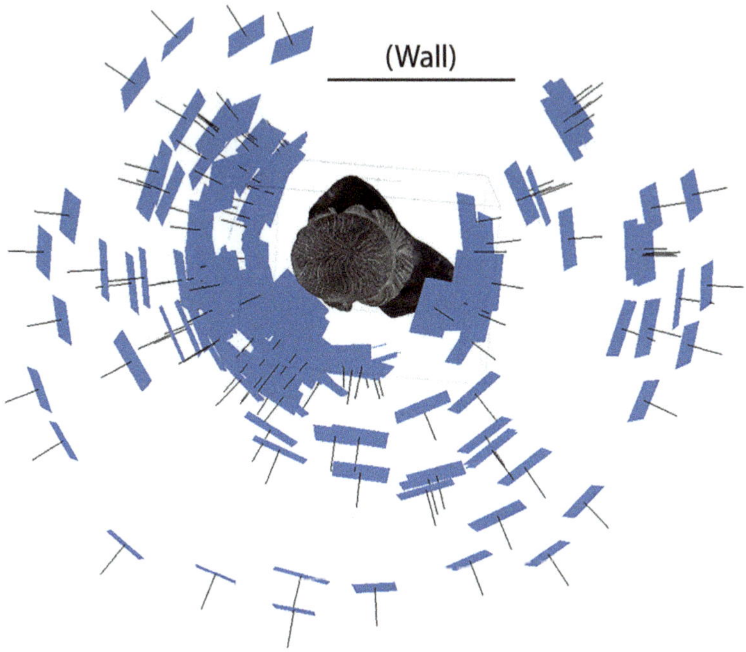

Figure 8.29 Aerial view of the head of Dionysus with the camera locations. Notice the lack of images taken at the back of the statue.

shots. To maintain overlap within each image, the photographer had to choose a point on the bust in each photo and return to the point after the ladder and camera were repositioned for the next shot. With such height variations between each camera position, connecting shots were crucial for this case study, again to ensure continuity throughout the photographs.

The equipment used was:

- Canon 80D DSLR APS-C camera body
- Canon 35 mm f/2.8 macro lens
- Canon ring flash with the lights dampened with a piece of tissue taped over the bulbs to reduce the intensity of reflection
- Scale bar

The camera settings were:

- Manual priority
- Aperture: f/7.1
- Shutter speed: 1/125
- ISO: 640
- RAW (converted to TIFF for processing) and Large, Fine JPEG file format

8.7.1 Model product

This model (Figure 8.30) was produced through Agisoft's *Metashape* Professional from 167 images shot in RAW and Large, Fine JPEG file format. Minor adjustments were made to the images in *Camera Raw* to reduce instances of specular reflection (adjusting the highlights, whites and shadows) on the metal. The RAW images were then converted to TIFF for processing. The images were run in one batch on medium alignment accuracy with key and tie point limits adjusted to 100,000 and 10,000 respectively and "Generic Preselection" turned on. The point cloud quality was set to high, the depth filtering set to moderate, and the depth map quality and mesh face count were both set to high. The model had 90% alignment with 151 images aligning correctly, generating 239,893 tie points and 17,700,201 mesh faces.

Despite the limited access, there were no holes in the mesh at the back of the model as enough surface area was captured on either side of the bust. There were issues with alignment around the bottom of the bust where the bronze became darker and flatter, resulting in images here failing to align. The tie point cloud had to be edited thoroughly with the background and plinth completely removed and outlier tie points selected and deleted by filtering them out via the "Reprojection error" and "Reconstruction uncertainty" filters under the "Gradual Selection" tool.

Black objects that are not reflective and have a rougher texture, such as basalt or wood, are more likely to produce successful models compared to reflective ones.

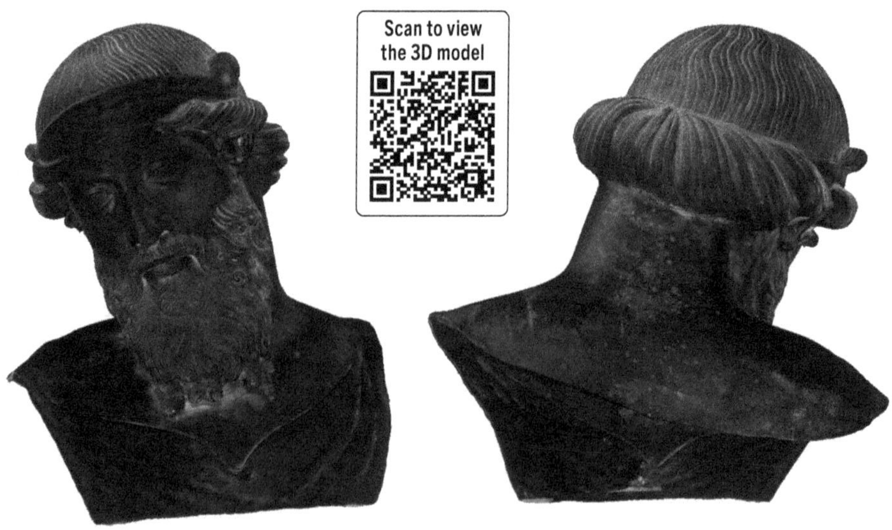

Figure 8.30 Photogrammetry model of the black bronze head of Dionysus created from 167 images. NM2008.2 Nicholson Collection, Chau Chak Wing Museum, the University of Sydney.

If the object has a very rough and matte surface, a flash may improve the alignment and quality of the model as flashes will bring out any surface detail. If you decide to use a flash, take a few shots of the object in the shooting environment with various intensities to see what setting produces the best images before you commence the shooting. If you detect any sharp reflection from the object, dampen the flash by lowering the brightness by a stop or two. If it is still not low enough, consider covering the flash with a filter or even tissue paper. Increasing the exposure on the camera will ensure surface detail is captured, and using a white background is essential to define the edges of the object. Increasing the number of photographs taken per round is helpful when modelling black artefacts, especially if they are featureless. This will help the software accurately align the model. If possible, adding targets around the object will also help in alignment success.

If the black object is reflective, featureless or slightly transparent (such as obsidian) it is incredibly difficult, if not pointless, trying to create a photogrammetry model unless a matting powder is applied to the surface.

8.8 A coin (tetradrachm)

Coins are notoriously difficult to model using photogrammetry. Shiny, small, thin and occasionally very detailed, coins can be a challenge for photogrammetrists. It is possible to make successful models of coins by following a comparatively longer shooting process and adding a specific type of mount. It is possible to create models of coins with any macro lens; however, for detail-rich and accurate mesh and texture it is recommended that a lens with a focal length of at least 50 mm is used. It is possible to model a coin with a 35 mm lens (this case study was created using a Canon 35 mm f/2.8 macro EF-S lens); however, there is considerably less detail captured. The setup should be in a lightbox with even, ambient light. Dampening the light sources for coins that are particularly reflective will help to reduce reflection.

Typically, the issues encountered when processing a model of a coin are in the alignment stage. As coins are thin, obtaining correct alignment can be difficult. Either the two faces will not align correctly due to insufficient overlap of images from one face to the other or the northern and southern hemispheres cannot merge together as there is not enough overlap on the faces of each chunk. To help with bringing the alignment together correctly, a mount with targets on it is needed. The mount can be made of any workable white material such as foam or polystyrene. Cut it into a square that is big enough so that four targets can be glued onto it. In the centre, cut out a notch that is deep enough that it can support the coin in an upright position but does not cover more than 20% of the coin's faces. It also must be able to keep the coin stable when it is being rotated on a turntable. The targets can be accessed and printed off from *Metashape* ("Tools" – "Markers" – "Print Markers") or found online if you are using different software. If using *Metashape*, you can input the radius of the inner circle of the target; the ones shown in Figure 8.31 have a radius of 2 mm.

In the case study here, a c. 400 BCE tetradrachm from Athens, the following equipment was used:

- Canon 80D DSLR APS-C camera body
- Canon 35 mm f/2.8 macro
- Canon ring flash dampened with tissue paper over the bulbs
- Foldio lightbox
- White background
- Foldio 360 turntable
- Manfrotto tripod
- Kiwi camera rail
- Square polystyrene mount with 2 mm radius targets glued to the corner
- Scale bar

The camera settings were:

- Manual priority
- Aperture: f/13
- Shutter speed: 1/125
- ISO: 125
- RAW and Large, Fine JPEG file format

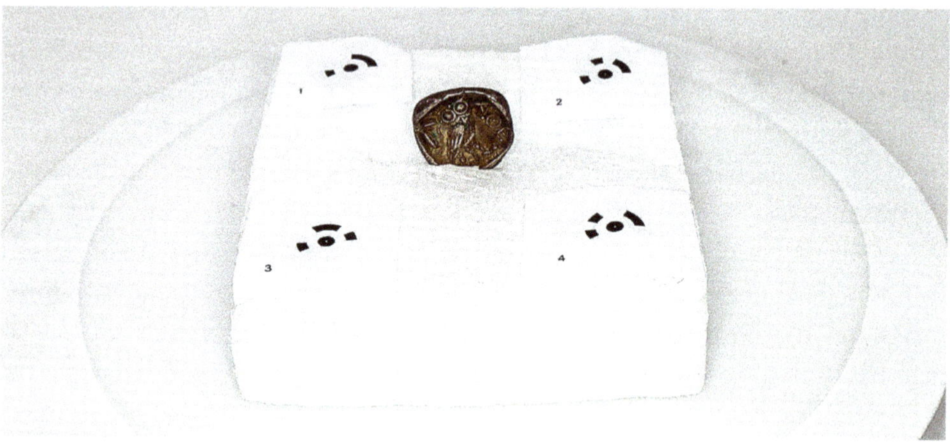

Figure 8.31 A polystyrene mount with targets glued to the corners. A tetradrachm coin is positioned in the groove cut out in the centre. NM2004.655 Nicholson Collection, Chau Chak Wing Museum, the University of Sydney.

To model a coin, both the northern and southern hemispheres need to be captured following this method:

1. A wide, high angle round that captures the top edge and rims of the coin and the entire mount and the targets.
2. A second wide, high angle round with the camera slightly lowered, capturing the rim and the upper areas of the coin's faces and the mount and targets.
3. A third wide, high angle round with the camera lowered again to focus on the centre of the coin's faces, again including the mount and targets.
4. A close-up high angle round to capture more of the intricate detail of the coin's edge and rims.
5. A second close-up high angle round focusing on the rim and upper sections of the coin's faces.
6. A close-up horizontal round to capture the detail of the coin's faces.
7. Close-up connecting shots.
8. Take the coin off the mount and place it flat on the turntable; take a round of close-up shots of the entire face filling the frame with the camera lens directly above the coin.
9. Turn the coin upside down and repeat this sequence for the southern hemisphere.

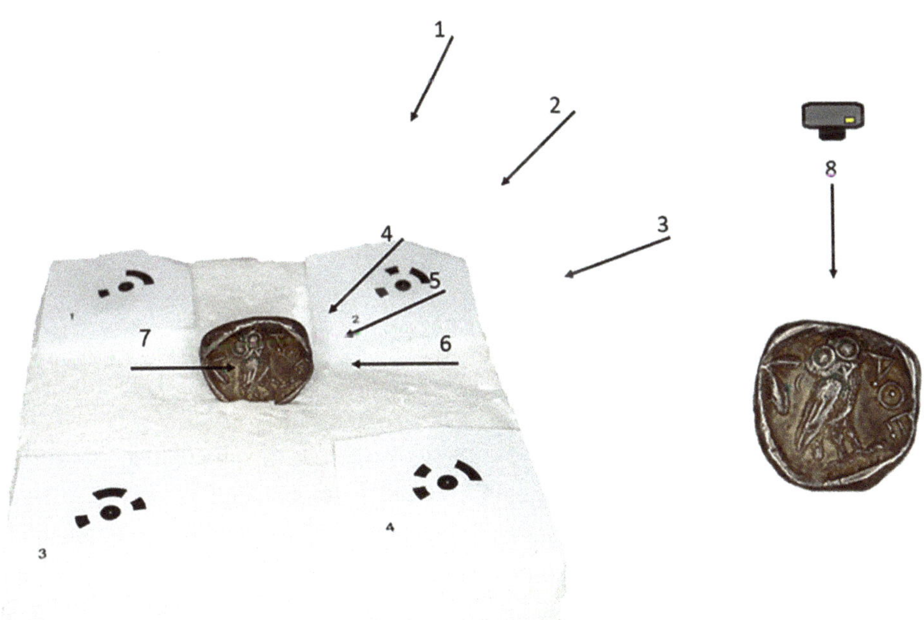

Figure 8.32 The camera positions for capturing one hemisphere of a coin. Notice for camera position 8 it is taken off the mount and placed flat on the turntable and captured from above.

With this method, the aim is to capture the mount and targets as the targets help with the alignment of the tie point cloud. The reason there are several rounds of high angle and close-up camera positions is to ensure that the coin's surface is completely captured and enough overlap of the central areas of the faces has been obtained in the hemispheres to allow for a successful alignment of them. If the coin is particularly small or detailed, it might be fitting to include more rounds to ensure that there is clear overlap from one side to the other.

When it comes to processing the images, run the two hemispheres as separate chunks at a low or medium alignment accuracy and process to the mesh stage. The models of each hemisphere, with camera location turned on, should look like Figure 8.33.

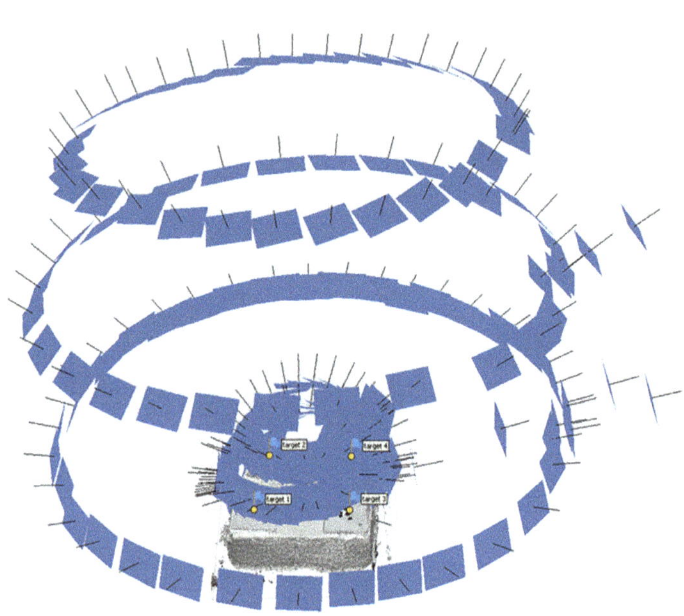

Figure 8.33 The camera positions required to photograph one hemisphere of a coin.

As shown in this figure, the six camera positions can be identified (three high angle and three close-up) and the mount with the targets is also included. From here, duplicate the two models (so the originals are untouched and saved) and in the copies of these two chunks, select and delete the entire mount from the model in the mesh view, leaving only the coin. You will need to cut out the section of the coin that is covered by the mount so both hemispheres look like Figure 8.34.

Once this is done, run a mask from the model (right-click on an image – "Masks" – "Import masks" – "Method: From Model") for both chunks. Move the images from both of these chunks into a new chunk by selecting all the images,

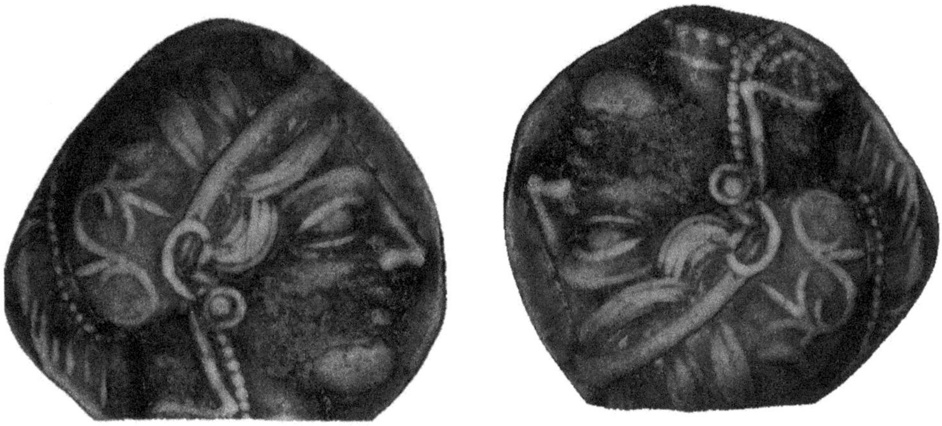

Figure 8.34 The two modelled hemispheres of the coin with the mount, targets and bottom sections of the coin selected and deleted from the model. These two models will be masked to build the final model.

right-clicking one and selecting "Move cameras" – "New chunk" and rerun the entire batch process from alignment to texture with masks applied to the key points. Through this method, only the coin should be rendered and the mount and targets are completely ignored.

Small objects are significantly harder to model than larger objects. As discussed in 8.3, you are working with less surface area on a much smaller scale, which can be tricky to capture. The correct gear is also essential to create an accurate model. For projects like these case studies, it is important to remember that when in any doubt about whether you should do another round or capture from a different angle – take a shot. It is always preferable to overshoot than undershoot, especially for small, finely detailed objects like coins.

8.8.1 Model product

Following the above process produced the model (Figure 8.35) comprising 449 Large, Fine JPEG images. The alignment setting was high, "Generic Preselection" turned on, depth filtering set to moderate and depth map quality and mesh face count set to high. There was 100% alignment success producing a final model of 313,860 points and 699,994 mesh faces. There are slightly blurred sections of the model; however, this would be minimised if a lens with a longer focal length was used.

As shown in Figure 8.36, turning on the camera locations for the final product shows the arrangement of camera positions around the coin. The high angle and the close-up rounds can be seen on either side of the coin.

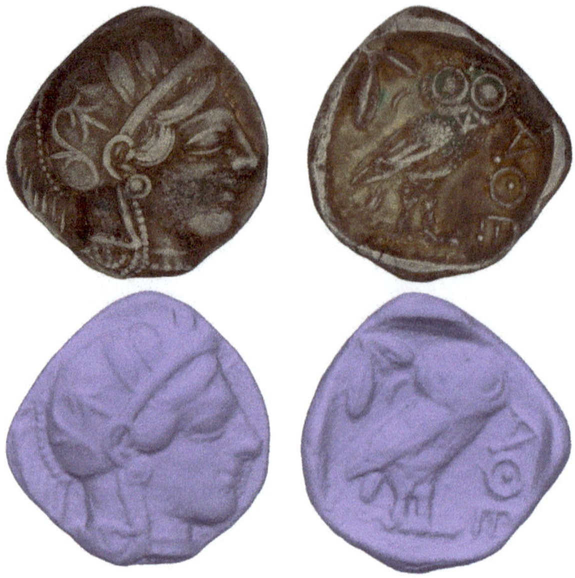

Scan to view the 3D model

Figure 8.35 The final model product of the tetradrachm. NM2004.655 Nicholson Collection, Chau Chak Wing Museum, the University of Sydney.

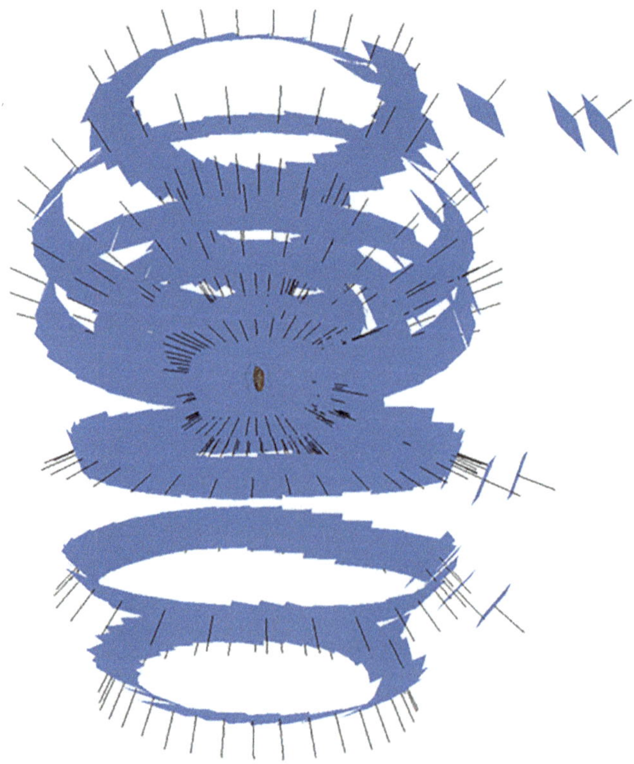

Figure 8.36 The arrangement of camera positions used on either side of the coin.

8.9 An excavation pit

While not the focus of this manual, knowing how to photograph an excavation pit or any terrestrial feature is useful for any archaeologist exploring photogrammetry. Photographing an excavation will follow some combination of high angle, horizontal and wide camera positions to achieve an accurate 3D model. Capturing excavations and terrestrial features in an exposed open environment can be harder and more time-consuming compared to shooting an artefact in a controlled environment, so it is important to plan accordingly. You must consider the time of day (preferably at the solar zenith or early morning or late afternoon to avoid intense shadows), the weather (preferably overcast), and how best to capture the necessary high angle shots – by hand, with a tall monopod with a remote shutter, or even a drone. A standard or wide angle lens is essential for modelling excavations; just remember to not adjust the zoom throughout the shooting process.

As stated previously, a tripod is less useful in the field if you are constantly moving around a pit, so freehand shooting or using a monopod is preferable. A monopod will ensure the images are at a consistent height and is also useful in taking high angle aerial-view shots if using a drone is not possible. Just remember to have someone spot the photographer or help in holding the monopod, particularly if the monopod is at its longest extension. Holding a monopod with a heavy DSLR and lens in the air can be painful if carried for a while!

Camera settings will be slightly different and will depend on light availability. The aperture setting can be lowered, to around f/5 is acceptable; however, the most suitable aperture will depend on the lens attached, the type of camera (full-frame or cropped), the light availability and how close the subject is to the lens. It is good practice to play with the settings before shooting an open excavation. Take several test shots with different apertures while keeping the shutter speed above 1/100 of a second and the ISO as low as possible to maintain clear, detailed photographs. If the light source is the sun and you notice there is changing cloud cover (and therefore changing light intensities), consider changing the ISO to Auto so the camera can balance exposure for you. If this is done, remember to check the images frequently to ensure they are consistently balanced and, if not, change the ISO back to a well-exposed setting.

The order and number of camera positions required in the shooting stage will depend on variables such as the size, shape and depth of the pit, so the method provided here is simply a breakdown of the primary camera positions and movements needed to capture the walls and the base of the pit accurately, and may likely need to be modified to suit the pit being modelled. The five primary stages are to capture the perimeter of the pit, the edges between the ground and the walls, the detail in the walls, the connection between the walls and the bottom, and finally the base of the pit. These camera positions are illustrated in Figure 8.37.

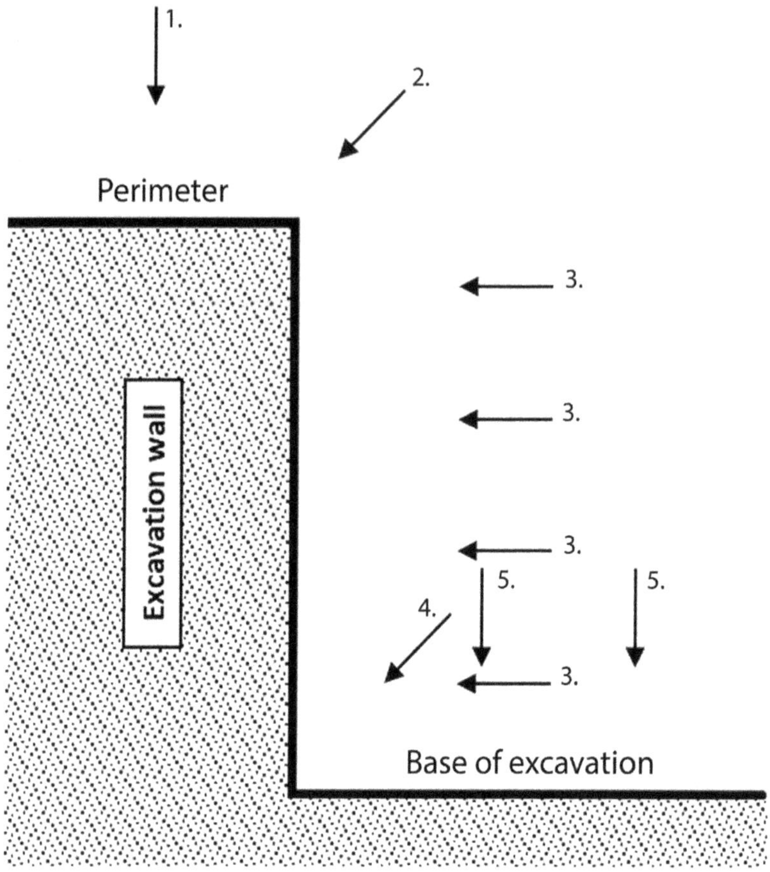

Figure 8.37 Camera positions for shooting an excavation pit, aerial view.

1. Perimeter

The first step is to define the border of the area you want to be modelled, typically this will be the ground area around the excavation. Aim to include 15–20% of the edge of the excavation in each image. Start at one corner (make a note of which corner you started at), point the lens to the ground (high angle position) and walk around the edge completing a circuit around the pit, taking consistent photos with around 70% overlap. Depending on whether you are shooting freehand or higher up with a monopod, with a wide lens or with a standard kit lens, the distance between each image will be different to achieve the 70% overlap. Continue to take photos until you end where you started.

2. Ground to walls

Once the perimeter has been photographed, the edges of the pit need to be photographed. Depending on the pit's depth, this can either be done standing inside the pit with a monopod or freehand, or standing on the edge with the lens pointed down. The focus of this step is to capture the intersection of the wall and the surrounding ground. This round of edge shots and the previous round of the perimeter should be a seamless sequence of images that are at least 70–80% overlapping, connecting the ground to the wall. Again, images should start at one corner, move around the entire pit, and finish where you started. If the pit is shallow and there is not much depth to the wall, these edge shots will also capture the base of the pit, possibly meaning the next step can be missed. If the walls are deep, however, the next step is to photograph the stratigraphy.

3. Walls

Depending on the depth of the excavation walls, this could be just one round of images or several. If it is possible, stand inside the pit, position the camera so it is facing the wall and the lens is parallel to the ground and photograph it with around 70–80% overlap around the pit. Remember, the closer the lens is to the wall, the more detail will be captured. If you cannot easily fit inside the pit, shoot from the top of the pit with the lens pointing down to the wall from above. When shooting the walls, it is up to you, the photographer, whether you want to shoot one wall at a time moving from the top of the wall and working your way down to the bottom or travel around the pit in one direction capturing one layer at a time and slowly creating a spiral of images to the bottom of the pit. Whichever method is chosen, ensure there is consistent overlap.

4. Walls to base

Once you have arrived at the base of the wall, a round of shots needs to be taken that includes 50% of the base and 50% of the wall. Depending on the size of the pit, this might be very difficult so try your best to capture this intersection between the floor and the wall. Again, start from where you have just finished your shots from the previous step, and continue to work around the edges of the base of the pit, finishing where you started.

5. Base of the pit

The last step to shooting an excavation pit is photographing the base. Like the walls, the route to capture the floor is up to you as several different paths can be chosen. Depending on the size of the pit, the photographer can choose to move up and down the length of the pit, as shown in Figure 8.38a. Alternatively, if the

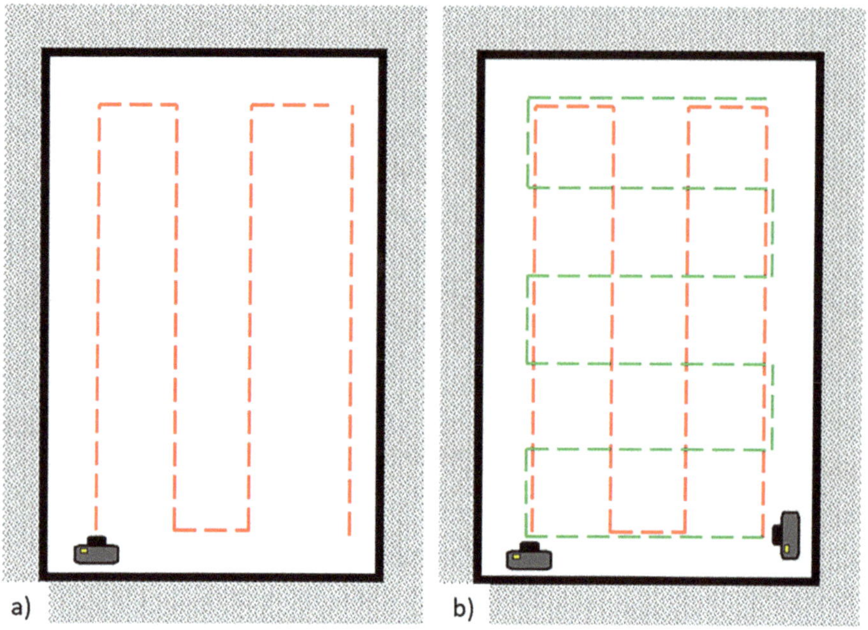

Figure 8.38 Photographing the bottom of an excavation pit can either be done a) lengthways or b) in a grid pattern.

pit is larger and there is more area to cover, following a grid pattern (as shown in Figure 8.38b) might be a better option. Whatever path is chosen, just ensure that it is consistent and with at least 70% overlap in each shot.

When the entire excavation pit has been photographed, it is good practice to take a step back and take some photos of the entire site from a variety of angles. These do not need to be included in the modelling software to be processed (although they of course can be added), but they are useful reminders of what the original site looked like, and what you should expect the model to look like too.

Depending on the soil type of the excavation, walking around creating footprints is not ideal when it comes to creating photogrammetry models. In these cases, the best method may be to simply capture as much as possible from the top of the pit and to move around the perimeter shooting from a high angle position. It's also useful to have a brush on hand to brush away any obvious footprints before you shoot, as these will be present in the model if captured. If you are digging in very sandy soil, not only are hand and footprints left very easily but it can be dangerous to shoot from the edges of the pit as it is very easy to fall in and wreck the walls. Always take precautions when photographing a deep excavation and have someone with the photographer if there is a danger to them, the equipment or the excavation.

8.9.1 Model product

For this case study, the following equipment was used to photograph a 2.5 m by 2 m pit:

- Canon 80D DSLR APS-C camera body
- Canon 18-135 mm kit lens with the focal length set to 25 mm
- Two Arlec portable lights
- Scale bar and targets with a centre diameter of 20 mm

Camera settings:

- Manual priority
- Aperture: f/4
- Shutter speed: 1/125
- ISO: 1000
- Large, Fine JPEG file format

The photogrammetry model (shown in Figure 8.39) of this excavation was built from 1,705 images in Large, Fine JPEG format processing in one batch. The model was run on medium alignment accuracy with "Generic Preselection" turned on. The point cloud quality was set at high, the depth filtering set to moderate, and the depth map quality and mesh face count both set to high. The model had 99% alignment (1,691 of 1,701 aligned) generating 8,393,549 points and 49,133,872 mesh faces.

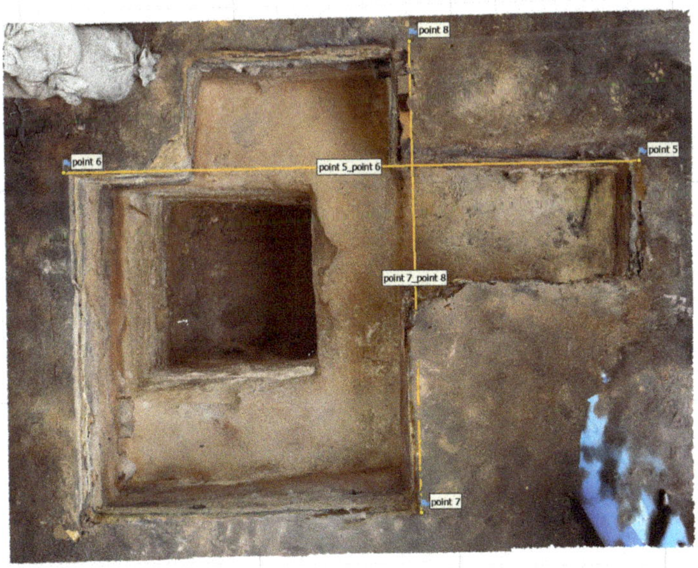

Figure 8.39 Model product of an excavation produced by following the above method. The process had to be repeated to capture the second step.

8.10 A terrestrial feature

Shooting a topographical feature or multiple topographical features in one model can follow a similar pattern to what is proposed for an excavation pit. The camera settings should be adjusted to suit the environment by decreasing the aperture (again around f/5 is suitable) and increasing the shutter speed. Having a higher shutter speed is essential if you are shooting freehand. Again, if you are in an environment where the light is noticeably changing, consider setting the ISO to Auto so the camera can balance the exposure for you.

If the features are quite tall, a monopod might be essential to capture the highest areas of the features; however, the shooting method will be the same. A standard or wide angle lens is the most typical option for capturing topographical features; however, your choice of lens may depend on the feature(s). If the subject is relatively small and has a lot of fine detail that you want to capture in the model, opting for a wide angle macro lens might be necessary. This choice is up to you, however, and the availability of lenses in your kit. If a macro lens is selected, however, it may be wise to skip the first two steps below – otherwise you may be shooting the ground for a considerable amount of time!

1. Perimeter

The first step in capturing topographical features is to photograph the perimeter of the area in which the feature is situated. This step, and step two, is to give the model some context but can also be removed later if preferred. It helps if this area is a square or rectangle so you can follow a grid pattern when capturing the area within the perimeter. In Figure 8.40, this first step is labelled 1 and is red.

2. Ground area

The next step is to shoot the ground area within this perimeter to capture all the surface detail within this region (labelled 2 in blue in Figure 8.40). These shots will include the feature(s) in them. Depending on the size of the site, the ground can be captured from either moving up and down the area moving left to right, or in a grid-like pattern where you move up and down the area moving left to right, then cross back going from the bottom to the top of the area, as shown in Figure 8.40. Smaller areas may only need one run from left to right; however, if you want to increase the accuracy and the resolution of the model, follow the grid pattern to capture your images.

3. Capturing the feature

The final step is capturing the detail of the feature or features. Before moving straight to the first feature, you, the photographer, have to photograph the path taken to reach the feature to ensure all images are connected – think of these as connecting shots.

The size and shape of the feature will dictate how many steps are involved in covering its entire surface. If the feature is small and close to the ground, a series of horizontal images taken of the object's circumference and another round of high angle photographs of the top regions may suffice. If the feature is larger, a series of low angle, horizontal and high angle photographs might be needed to completely cover the subject. Start by photographing the lower sections of the feature, connecting to what was previously photographed on the ground, then proceed up the sides of the object, finishing with a few rounds of high angle shots.

If there are multiple features you want to model, remember to connect them by taking photographs of the ground that separates them; that is, after the first feature is completely captured, take photos moving down its side to the ground, then move while taking photos of the ground to the next feature, where you can proceed to capture it. Do not jump across to the second feature without connecting them. This path can be seen by the green dotted lines labelled 3 in Figure 8.40.

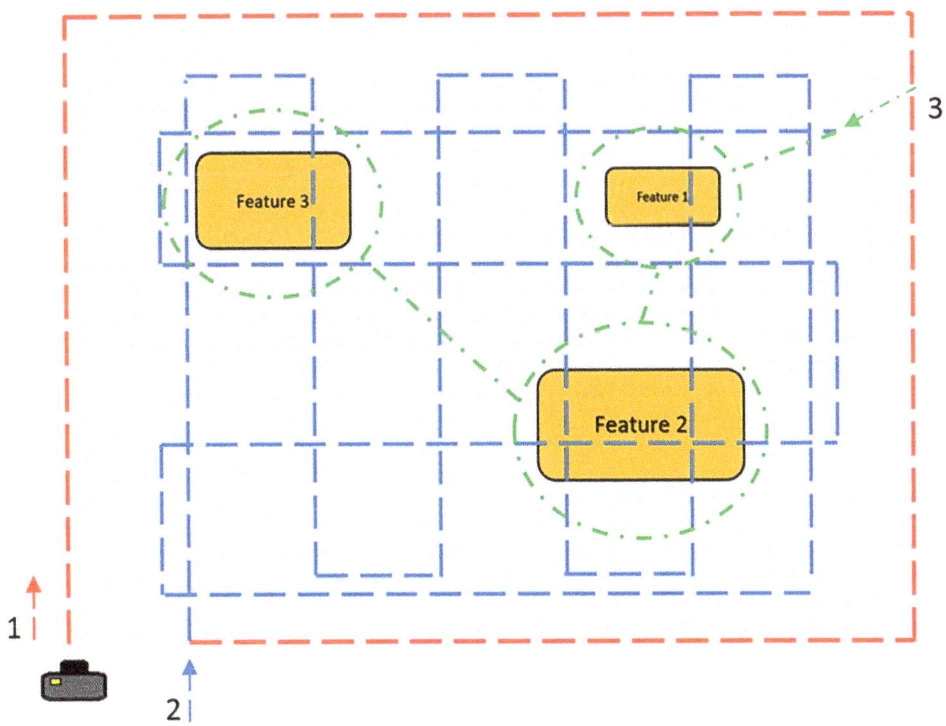

Figure 8.40 Shooting path to capture terrestrial features.

8.10.1 Model product

For this case study, a stone structure on an area of grass with an adjacent tree, the following equipment was used:

- Canon 5D Mark IV full-frame camera body
- Canon EF 24-70 mm L Series lens set to 24 mm
- Scale bar

Camera settings:

- Manual priority
- Aperture: f/5.6
- Shutter speed: 1/160
- ISO: 500
- Large, Fine JPEG file format

This topographical model (Figure 8.41) was created from processing 336 Large, Fine JPEG images in *Metashape* Professional. The settings included an alignment accuracy of medium, the default key and tie point settings (40,000 and 4,000, respectively), high point cloud quality, mild depth filtering, and depth map quality and mesh face count were both set to high. The final product had 100% alignment and generated 272,817 points and 55,575,789 mesh faces.

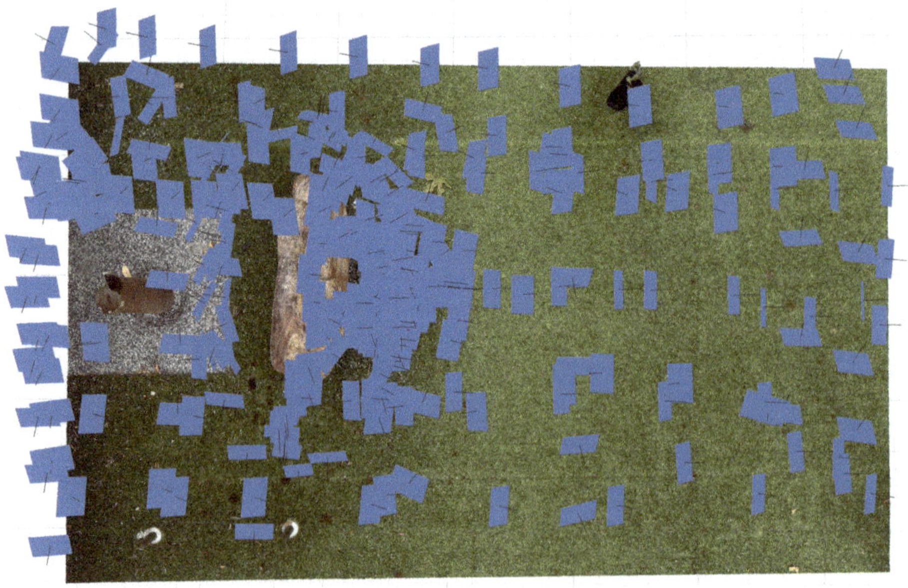

Figure 8.41 Aerial view of a topographical model showing camera locations taken in the grid format. Notice the cluster of images taken around the stone feature.

8.11 A walled structure with corners

Capturing interior and exterior walls is a straightforward process for photogrammetry modelling. Depending on the height of the wall it can be conducted freehand, with a monopod, or on a tripod. Again, a standard or wide angle lens is ideal. Like with an excavation pit or topographical feature, the aperture settings can be lowered to an f-stop of around f/5, the shutter speed increased if shooting freehand, and the ISO can either be set to Auto to adjust for any light changes, or set to an ISO value that balances the aperture and shutter speed settings.

1. Capturing walls

All that is required to capture flat walls is two camera positions. The first is a series of overlapping horizontal photographs moving across the wall at the same distance away, and the second is with the camera set further back away from the wall to capture more of the wall, the ceiling or sky, and the ground in the image.

In Figure 8.42, a simple aerial diagram has been drawn to give you an overview of these camera positions indicated by the coloured arrows. You can see that for the blue, green and red walls, there are two sets of camera positions. In this example, the shorter red and green walls only need two photos in the first position and one wider image per wall. The blue wall needs five horizontal shots with two wide images as it is longer.

If the wall is particularly tall, two rounds of the first camera position can be taken, with the first round pointed to the lower half of the wall and the second pointing to the upper half. This method can also be chosen if you want to capture more detail on the walls by being closer to it. If detail is what you are after, however, see step 3 – capturing detailed walls.

2. Capturing corners

The corners of rooms and the corners of walls require more attention than the walls. Anywhere where one wall transitions to another in a different direction requires angled shots to be taken so the photogrammetry software can accurately capture the changing morphology. In Figure 8.42, these angled shots are coloured orange. For inside corners (labelled a), the camera needs to be pointed directly at the corner before moving on to the next wall. For outside corners (labelled b), three shots moving from one side over to the other are needed to correctly capture the angle of the corner.

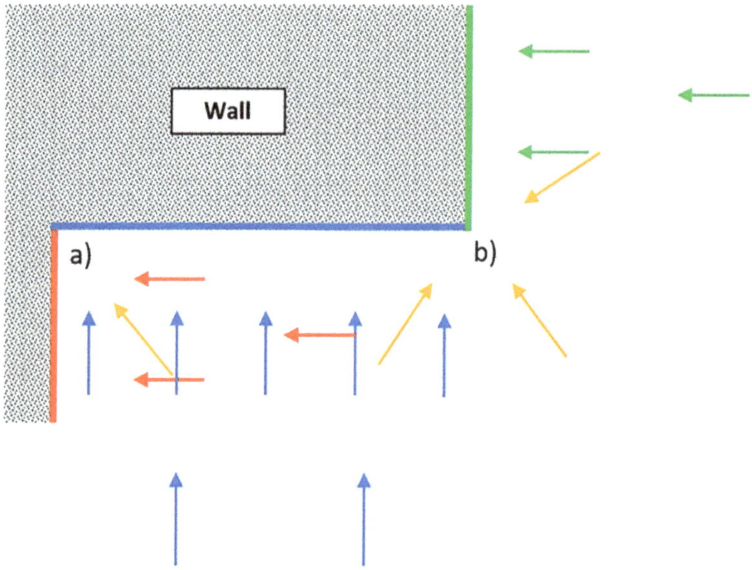

Figure 8.42 Aerial view of the camera positions required to capture three walls. Red arrows capture the red wall, the blue arrows are for the blue wall, and the green arrows are the camera positions for the green wall. Note the orange arrows are the positions required to capture the corners a) and b).

3. Capturing detailed walls

Walls with more detail such as carvings, paintings or any kind of important decoration or masonry on them need to be captured with greater care, and it may be necessary that you use a macro lens if this detail is crucial in your models. Firstly, you will need to move much closer to the wall so more detail is in the frame. Focus on one wall at a time and take photos in a zigzag-like pattern moving down the wall, as shown in Figure 8.43. Take note that you might need to crouch down to capture the bottom sections of the walls. Once you have completed this, take several wide images by moving the camera back and capturing either the entire wall in one shot, or several photos focusing on larger sections of the wall in each image.

This method was used to model Figure 8.43. Two walls were captured with one wall containing an archway. The first wall was captured following the zigzag-like pattern, then the corner of the room was photographed with the camera moving up the wall to ensure the detail was photographed carefully. This pattern was repeated to capture the wall with the archway, with the photographer moving around underneath to capture the interior of the archway.

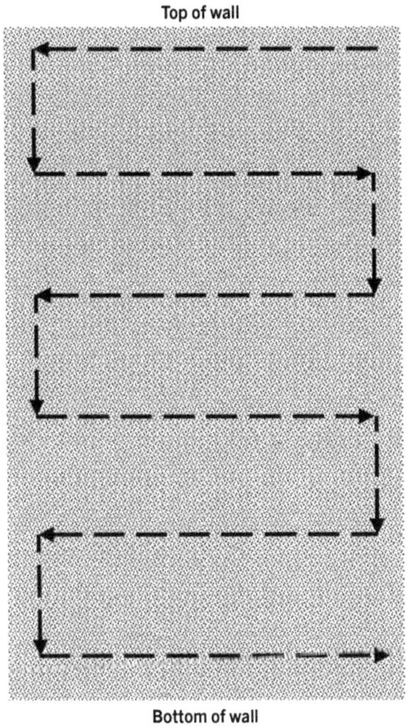

Figure 8.43 The progression of images required to capture a tall wall. Ensure there is consistent overlap of at least 70% in each image.

The main concern with interior walls is ensuring there is enough light. Using studio lamps will help with even illumination of the walls or even a dampened flash if there is no alternative. Lighting is particularly important if you are photographing rock art. It is crucial that a colour checker is used if modelling rock art – obtaining the correct colour is fundamental to recording any rock art sites.

8.11.1 Model product

This case study, of two connecting walls with an archway in one, required the following equipment:

- Canon 80D DSLR APS-C camera body
- Canon EF 18-135 mm standard lens with focal length set to 20 mm
- Scale bar

Camera settings:

- Manual priority
- Aperture: f/5.6
- Shutter speed: 1/200
- ISO: 1000
- Large, Fine JPEG file format

The model product of two adjacent walls with an archway (Figure 8.44) was built from 238 Large, Fine JPEG images using a Canon 80D with a standard 18-135 mm kit lens set to a focal length of 20 mm. Photos were taken freehand and on a cloudy day. As there was a relatively low number of photos, the alignment setting was set to "Highest", the key and tie point limits set to 0, and the depth filtering was moderate, and depth map quality and mesh face count were set to high. The final model contains 1,142,780 tie points and 23,331,416 mesh faces which were then decimated down to 3,335,510.

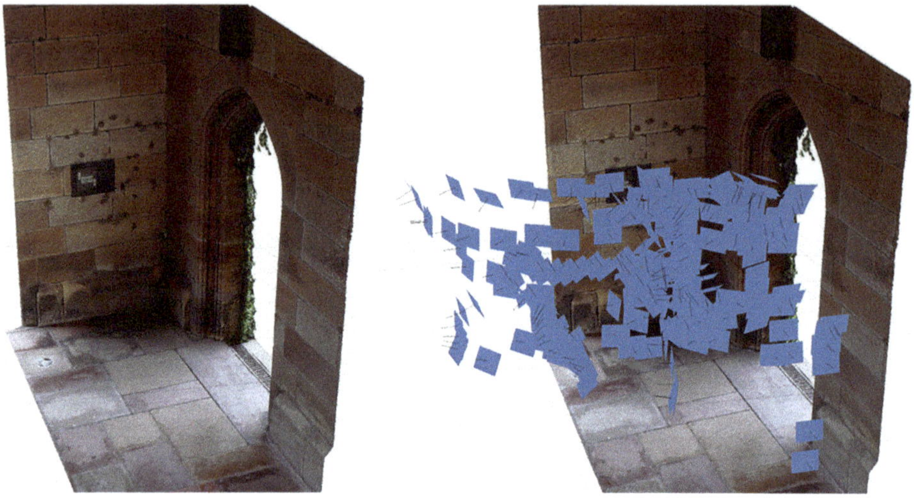

Figure 8.44 Photogrammetry model of a wall.

8.12 Next steps

Your photogrammetry career may likely span beyond the variety of archaeological examples shown here; however, hopefully these case studies provide you with a framework that can help with your own projects. Remember that the photogrammetry process is flexible; the photography setup, equipment, and the order and number of camera positions can all be adapted to the project to better capture the object at hand. You, the photographer, have complete control over the process, so follow your gut – if you think you should conduct another round of shots to better cover a particular section, then do. If you think you need to reshoot the whole object with a different lens, then change the lens. It is all a learning experience and the more you explore and experiment, the better a photogrammetrist you will become. Just remember the mantra – when in doubt, take a shot!

It is likely, however, that at some point you will run into an issue or two with the model products after you process your images. In the following chapter, the typical problems encountered by beginner photogrammetrists are listed and discussed, with suggested causes of the problems, how to fix them, and how to avoid them in the future.

Chapter 9

COMMON MODEL ISSUES

Errors in the alignment, mesh or texture of a generated photogrammetry model are common, and it is very likely that a beginner photogrammetrist will encounter a number of issues when they start out. Photogrammetry model problems are likely due to mistakes made in the shooting stage, but luckily most errors can be rectified by editing the model in photogrammetry software. The process of resurrecting a failed or incorrect model may not be very obvious to a novice, so the most common issues have been outlined in this chapter with visual examples of what they look like, how to fix them and how to prevent them in the future. In this chapter, Agisoft *Metashape* is again used.

The range of issues covered are:

9.1. Only one side of the model has aligned
9.2. The turntable has merged with the subject
9.3. The background (or elements of the background) is showing in the model
9.4. The mount has merged with the subject
9.5. The model is not the correct colour
9.6. The edges have incorrectly aligned

9.1 Only one side of the model has aligned

A common issue that frequently arises is that the photogrammetry software aligns and stitches together half of the model. There are two varieties of this issue; the first is where only roughly 50% of the images have aligned (see Figure 9.1), and the second is where *all* the images have been incorrectly aligned to only one side of the artefact, resulting in again only half a model. In this case, the software has determined that all detail captured solely originates from one side of the artefact. Beginners often encounter this particular problem, especially when modelling small, thin materials.

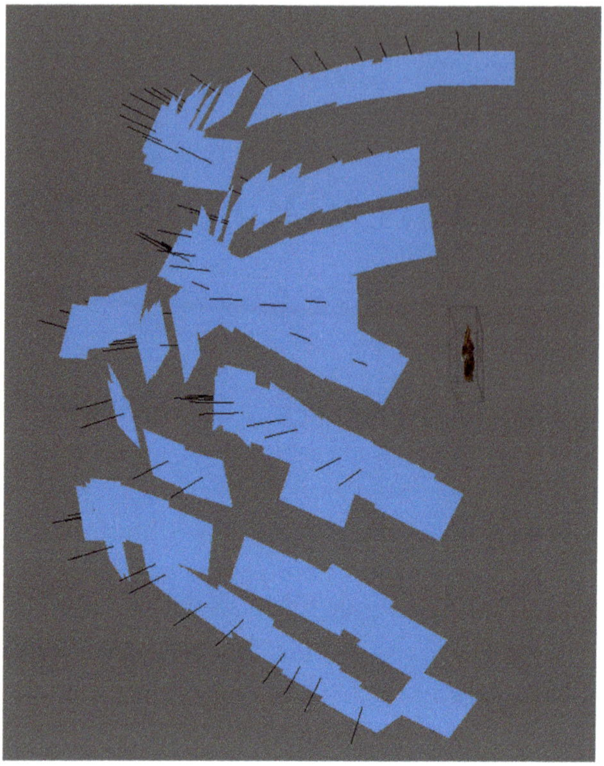

Figure 9.1 A photogrammetry model of a lithic specimen where only half of the images have aligned.

9.1.1 Causes

The most likely reason why only half of the model has aligned is a lack of detailed close-up and wide angle shots that focus on the edges or areas that connect one face to another. This lack of photographic overlap in these areas is likely to be the cause, which is why edge and connecting shots are crucial in photogrammetry shooting.

This issue could also be from a lack of even lighting illuminating the entire object. If an artefact casts a shadow on the edges or areas that connect one face to another, the likelihood of the software identifying key points in these sections is low. If the camera cannot clearly see the surface due to shadow, the software is not going to either. If the brightness of the surface drastically changes when the artefact is repositioned, again the software is going to struggle to detect consistent features to connect the two sides. The likely outcome will be a darker, half-formed model with blurred edges.

This issue may also occur when the wrong lens is used. Using a kit or standard lens for close-range photogrammetry on artefacts that need a macro lens will not provide the detailed close-up images that may be needed for successful alignment. Using the incorrect lens will result in the model seen in Figure 9.2.

The replica Neanderthal skull shown in Figure 9.3 was photographed with a Canon 18-135 mm lens but should have been photographed with a macro lens for photogrammetry modelling. By using an 18-135 mm lens (set with a focal length of 18 mm), only half of the model was created, as shown in Figure 9.2 where only 154 of the 356 images have aligned. The photographs produced were simply too far away from the object for the software to detect the key and tie points required to connect the northern and southern hemispheres.

This issue is also relevant and quite common for photogrammerists modelling rooms or buildings. When shooting confined spaces that move from one interior or exterior space to another, the points of transition – that is, doors and windows – must be thoroughly covered in photographs from different perspectives and angles to indicate to the software how the different spaces relate and connect. Otherwise, it is likely the software will stitch all the images into one space.

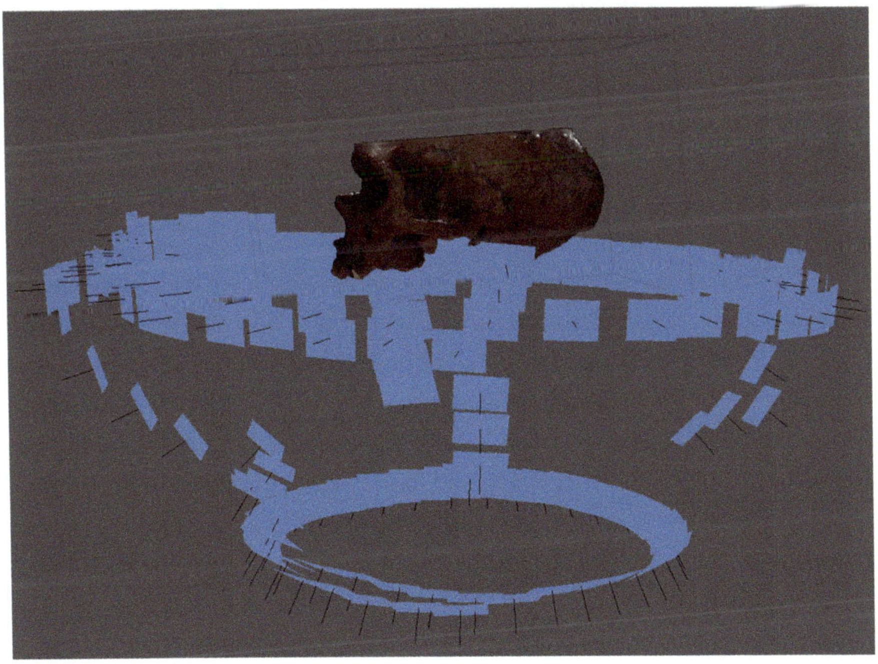

Figure 9.2 By using the wrong lens type, only half of the model was built.

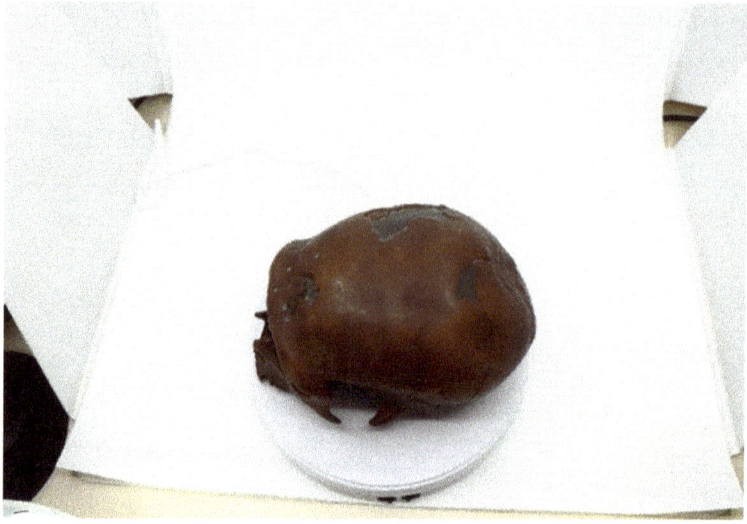

Figure 9.3 A 18-135 mm lens was used to photograph this replica Neanderthal skull. A macro lens is a better choice. Discipline of Archaeology reference collection, the University of Sydney.

9.1.2 How to fix

The simplest way to fix this issue is to do another trial run focusing on edges and areas that connect one face or hemisphere to the other. Ensure the shooting environment is well-lit and the camera settings are suitable for the environment. In this example, taking more close-up shots using a macro lens of the skull's sides and face moving from the top of the skull to the underside would fix this problem. If a macro lens is not available, taking more photographs at the minimum focusing distance around the transitionary areas in a well-lit environment will enable a complete model to be built.

If it is not possible to reshoot, then the model will have to be salvaged from the photogrammetry software. Unfortunately, this is one of the harder issues to fix solely with software as the problem is due to a lack of decent, well-positioned photographs. There are a few tactics that may readjust the alignment that are worth exploring. The first is to rerun the model with a different accuracy setting in the "Align Photos" job. If high accuracy was initially set, rerun on medium or vice versa. If this is also unsuccessful, rerun the model with the "Generic Preselection" tool turned off. This method of trying to fix the model will take longer; however, it may save the model.

Another method is to run two separate chunks, one of the northern hemisphere and one of the southern hemisphere. Mask the background out from both chunks, then move these images to a new chunk and rerun again. This method is outlined in 8.8 for modelling a coin.

There is another method of rebuilding the alignment of a model – the marker-based alignment method – that is similar to what is outlined in 7.15.2; however, instead of adding in new images, markers are manually added to the existing photographs to realign the photographs in the model. Although it may be somewhat time-consuming (depending on how many photographs are accurately aligned) it might also be a faster, more accurate method than rerunning the model on a multitude of different settings hoping for perfect alignment.

9.1.3 How to avoid

This is a simple issue to avoid in future trial runs. Firstly, increase the number of photographs taken in areas that connect one side of the artefact to the other, or from one hemisphere to the other – this is done by decreasing the distance and/or angle between each shot. Additionally, do not forget to take the connecting shots every time you move the camera's position or the artefact. Ensuring that the environment is well-lit, shadows are avoided at all costs, and the right lens is used will also improve model alignment quality and the overall aesthetic of the rendering.

9.2 The turntable has merged with the subject

If no mount is required and the archaeological object is placed straight onto the turntable, occasionally the artefact can be modelled with the turntable attached and part of the final product. Typically, this is a result of the use of incorrect camera positions, or the images were processed without any masking conducted on them. This problem can either be very obvious (as shown in Figure 9.4) or only slightly apparent in the mesh; therefore careful observation should be made in the mesh wireframe and solid views. If you are shooting an object in one orientation (i.e. only the northern hemisphere is photographed), this problem is more likely to occur if no masking has been conducted on the images. The turntable will have to be masked before you process, as it is essential to take photos of where the object comes in contact with the turntable for the model to be complete. If you are capturing both the northern and southern hemispheres, the merging of the turntable is less likely to occur as you are capturing the underside of the object; however, it is still possible for sections of the turntable to merge into the main model.

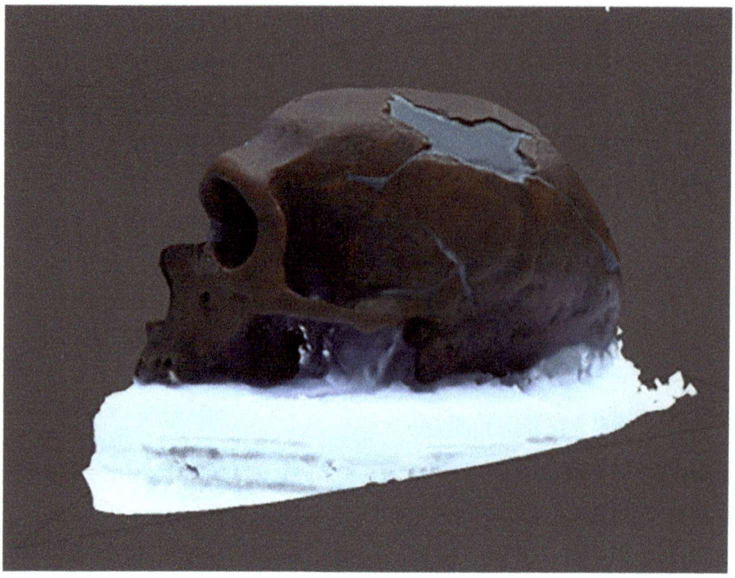

Figure 9.4 The turntable has merged into the model of the replica Neanderthal skull.

9.2.1 Causes

The main cause of this issue is when too many photographs were processed that feature the turntable and artefact together and, more specifically, photographs that include shadows cast by the artefact onto the turntable. The software cannot identify any clear edges of the object and any shadows will obscure the division between the two; consequently the software will merge the artefact to the turntable unless the turntable is masked. This issue is most likely to occur in the wide shots where more of the artefact is being included in the frame.

9.2.2 How to fix

Regardless of whether you are shooting in one or two orientations, the editing process will be the same. The first method is to run a tie point mask in the alignment stage. Before rerunning the alignment job, mask the turntable in a subsample of the total batch, ensuring at least one image from each camera position is masked. Aim to mask around 5–10% of the total number of images and then rerun the process (be sure to select "Apply masks to tie points" in the "Align Photos" job). The various ways to mask in *Metashape* are outlined in Chapter 7. Remember to enable "Strict volumetric mask" when you move on to the "Build Model" job as this will ensure cleaner edges.

If this is unsuccessful, run a mask on the entire photo batch following the instructions outlined in Chapter 7 such as the "Mask from model" method (7.14.5). Run the alignment and point cloud processing settings on low, and clean up as much of the model as possible through either the colour selection tool or the standard free-form selection tool. Once the turntable is completely deleted from the model, run the mesh job – "Build Model". Here, create a mask by right-clicking and selecting "Import Masks" – "From Model". This will mask every single image in the batch. From here, duplicate this chunk so the masks are kept in the copy and rerun the new model from the beginning ("Align Photos") on higher settings and set "Apply masks to key points". The new model will be produced without the turntable and therefore can be run to the texture job.

If only a little of the turntable is attached to the model, the colour selection tool may be enough to delete it. Go into the point cloud view and navigate to "Tools" – "Point Cloud" – "Select Points by Color" and select the dominant colours of the turntable to delete them, then rerun the mesh and texture.

9.2.3 How to avoid

There are two primary ways to reduce the chances of the turntable merging with the model in the photography stage. Firstly, try placing the object on a mount to separate it from the turntable, giving it some height and reducing the likelihood of it appearing in any wide images.

The second avoidance measure is regarding the camera positions. Repositioning the camera closer to completely avoid the turntable will mean you won't have to mask any images – remember, if it is not captured, it will not be modelled. It will not be difficult to avoid the turntable in the close-up and low angle rounds, but it can be in the wide and high angle camera positions. Figure 9.5 is an example of an incorrectly positioned camera for a wide horizontal round. The turntable is seen in every single image, along with a lot of background, and without masking it will definitely be included in the photogrammetry model. By moving the camera closer and lifting the lens so the bottom of the frame is in line with the bottom of the artefact, the turntable can be avoided. Figure 9.6 shows what should be in the image frame, denoted by the red outline. There is a lot of wasted space in that image of background and turntable when only the replica skull needs to be captured.

If you are shooting the object in two orientations, you can completely avoid the bottom of the artefact to cut out the turntable completely. Do not worry that the bottom section of the artefact is being ignored in the images – when it is turned upside down, it will be captured. As long as clear connecting shots are taken, the

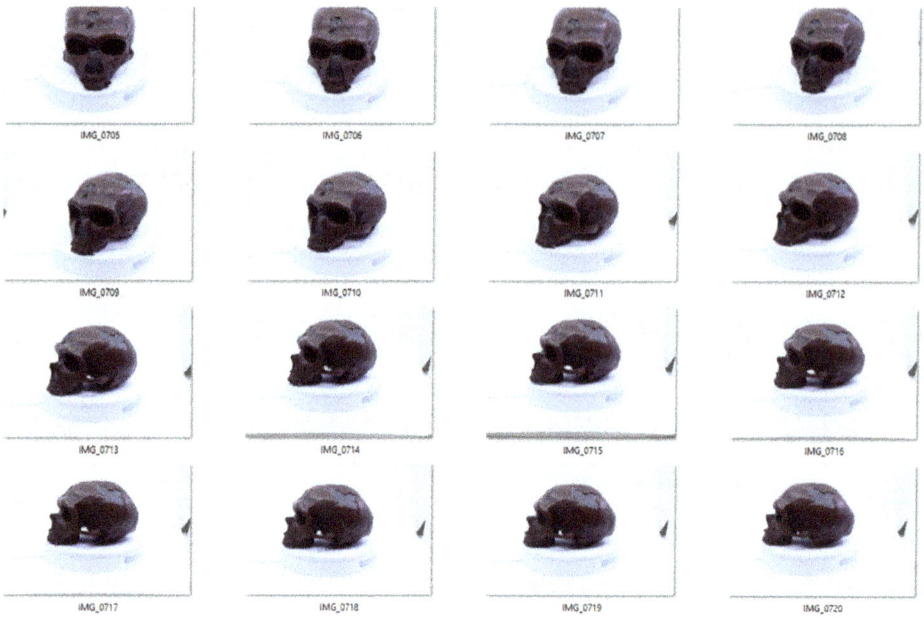

Figure 9.5 Examples of images that will lead to the turntable merging into the main model.

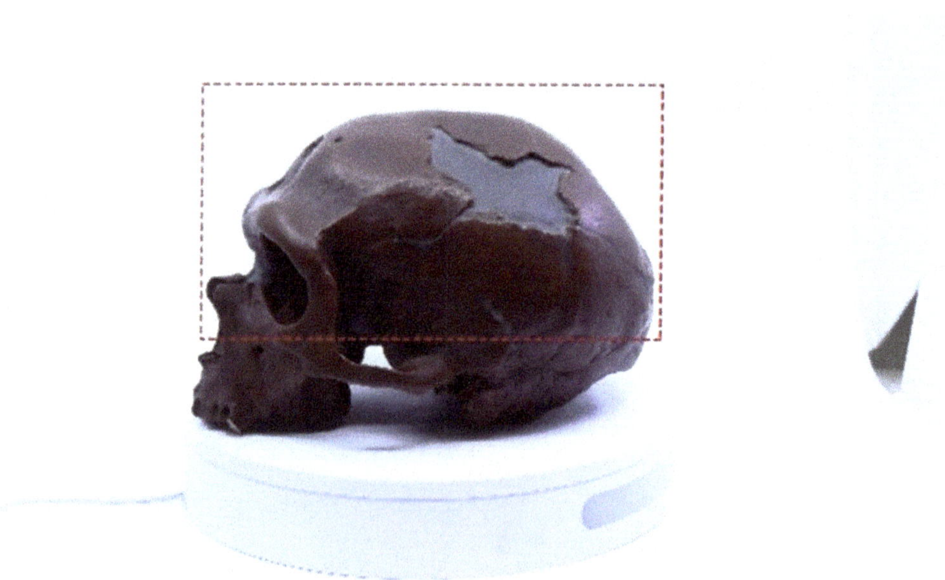

Figure 9.6 The red square in this image shows what should be in the frame.

two hemispheres will align correctly. If you are photographing the object in one orientation, however, some masking or model editing might be needed, especially if the object is complex or detailed where it comes into contact with the turntable.

With the high angle camera position, again move closer to the object's surface and readjust the angle of the lens to avoid capturing the turntable. It is unlikely you will avoid it completely, and this is why it is imperative that the turntable be a contrasting colour to the artefact. The software needs to be able to identify it as a separate feature, and, if it is still included in the rendered model, it can be easily edited out from the model.

If you are not using a macro lens, you will find it difficult to fill the frame with the subject and will spend more time editing. Between the options of capturing more background or turntable, opt to capture the background over anything the object is sitting on. The simple reason is that seamless backgrounds are less likely to be included in the model and, if they are, they are easier to mask or edit out than turntables or mounts.

9.3 The background (or elements of the background) is showing in the model

Occasionally models are generated with traces of the background included, either attached to the model or as small fragments of mesh floating in digital space (Figure 9.7). This can happen when shooting an object in one orientation or two; however, depending on the severity there are multiple solutions to this problem.

9.3.1 Causes

There are many reasons why this issue could occur; however, it is typically due to the background featuring heavily in the photographs. If most of the images taken show a significantly high percentage of background relative to object, the software is more likely going to detect a key point in the background, therefore increasing the chances of the background being included. If the background is not seamless or there are noticeable features in the background, the likelihood of the background being rendered will also increase. Other reasons might be if there is little contrast between the object's colour and the background colour or if the edges of the artefact are a similar shade or slightly transparent.

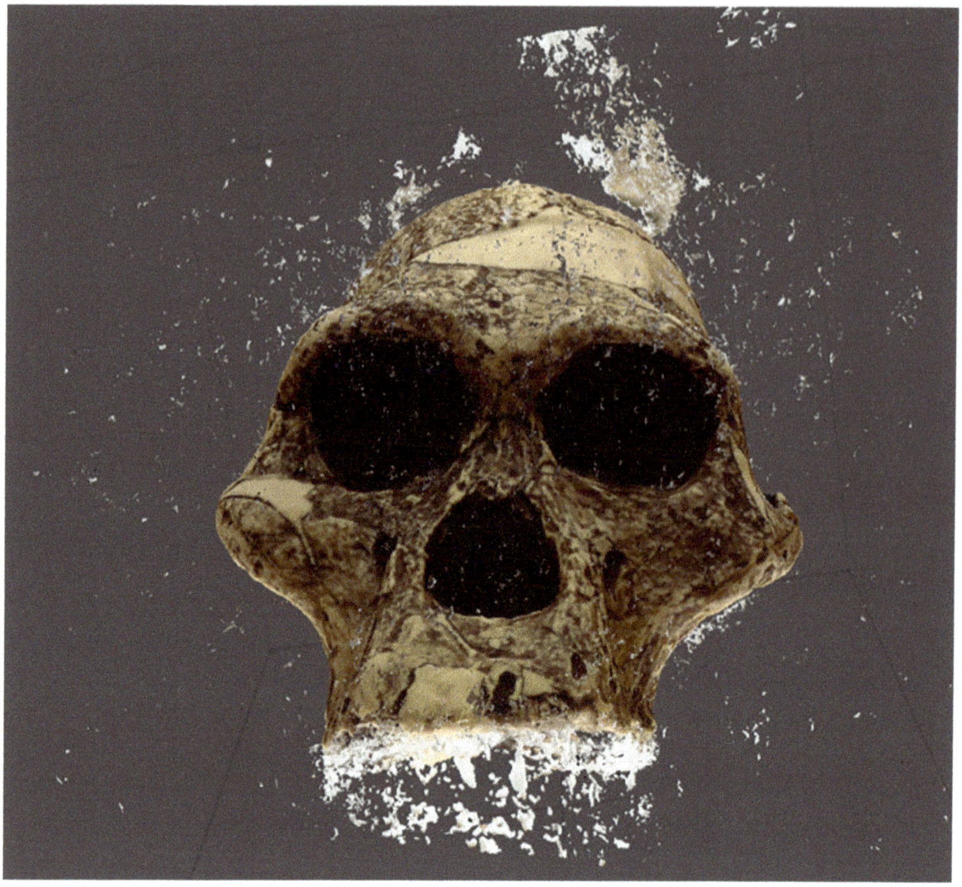

Figure 9.7 Floating mesh from the background has been included in this model of a replica *Australopithecus africanus* skull. Discipline of Archaeology reference collection, the University of Sydney.

9.3.2 How to fix

Like the issue in 9.2, this problem can be easily fixed by using several of the editing options in *Metashape* software. If the background cannot be easily selected and deleted from the model, then the best method to remove it all is via a masking method. Run a tie point mask in the alignment stage by masking the background out of a subsample (5–10%) of the total batch, ensuring at least one image is masked from each camera position (remember to tick "Apply masks to tie points" if this is the method chosen). Alternatively, mask the *entire* batch of images before processing the model by following one of the methods outlined in Chapter 7, such as the "Mask from model" method (7.14.5). If all images are masked, remember to select "Apply masks to key points" in the alignment stage. Removing any background from the images is a foolproof way to ensure it will not be rendered in the final model.

If you find it particularly difficult to remove all traces of the background, another option is to run the colour selection tool in the point cloud (outlined in 7.8.2). You can select all points that are the colour of the background and delete them; from there, the mesh and texture can be rerun.

If there are floating mesh clumps of background unattached to the main model, a simple trick to quickly remove them all is to select "Model", "Gradual Selection", and under the "Criterion" option select "Connected component size". Here you can increase the threshold filter to select isolated fragments that are not part of the main model. Once they are all selected, you can delete them.

9.3.3 How to avoid

There are several simple ways to avoid this issue. Firstly, position the camera closer to the object to fill more of the frame with the subject and reduce the amount of background in the shot. Try to have at least 75% object to 25% background in the frame at all times. Ensure that the background is a seamless sheet that contrasts with the subject. If the artefact you are shooting has sharp edges that are a similar shade to the background or are transparent, take a series of well-exposed and sharp edge shots that clearly show a distinction between the object and the background.

9.4 The mount has merged with the subject

This problem has similar causes and solutions to the problem of the turntable being included in the model. The severity of the issue could be minor, as shown in Figure 9.8, where only traces of the mount have merged, or it could be more prominent, where the entire mount has been modelled.

9.4.1 Causes

Like the causes outlined in 9.2, the most likely reason for this issue is that too many images were taken showing the mount supporting the archaeological object. Figure 9.8 is the result of including wide shots that feature the mount too prominently (a result of the setup shown in Figure 9.9). The outline of the PVC mount can be seen in the point cloud, and due to the shadows it cast onto the skull, it cannot be easily edited out.

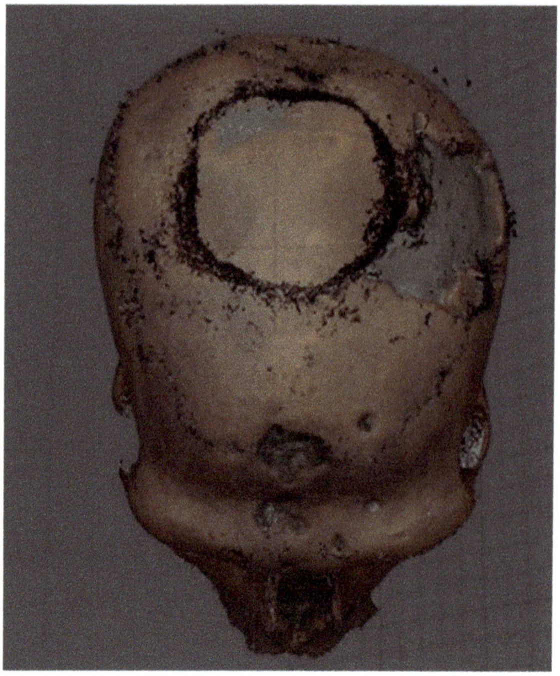

Figure 9.8 The outline of a mount on the model of a replica Neanderthal skull.

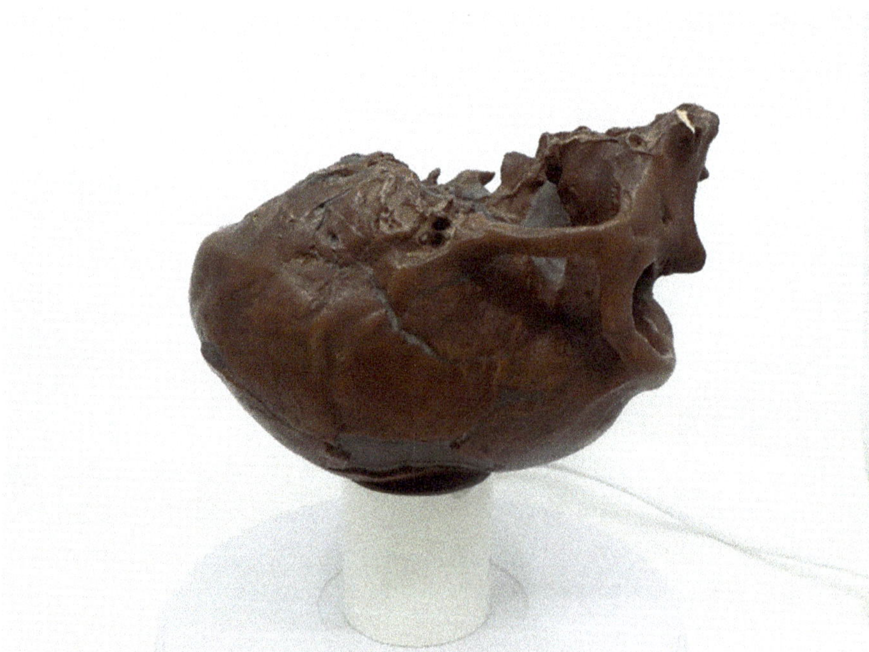

Figure 9.9 An incorrectly captured wide shot. The mount should not be included and will result in the mount merging into the main model.

9.4.2 How to fix

Try the methods listed in 9.2.2 and 9.3.2: mask a couple of images and run a tie point mask or create a mask from the entire object and rerun the entire process with a key point mask applied (methods outlined in 7.14). The colour selection tool is the other option if the mount is a clearly contrasting colour and can be completely selected and deleted; however, the presence of any shadows may make this difficult (as they will not be selected) and the outline of the shadows will remain. If these solutions do not solve this problem and there is still a faint but distinguishable outline of the mount in the model product, the images will need to be reshot with an adjusted camera position, as detailed below.

9.4.3 How to avoid

The primary method to avoid this issue is to ensure that no images contain the mount in them. This means readjusting your camera positions if the mount can be seen in the frame. For close-up and wide camera positions, move the lens considerably closer to the object and angle the lens up to cut the mount out from the field of view. This will mean that you will have to take more images of the object's surface, as the camera is closer, and possibly use another camera position or two. It will also result in the section closest to the mount not being photographed. This area, plus the area that the mount is covering, will therefore need to be photographed without the mount entirely. The object will need to be repositioned upside down (if possible) to expose this area so that it can be captured with a couple more rounds. Just remember to take close-up connecting shots if you do reorient the subject.

Ideally, your object mounts are smaller than the object itself, meaning that they cannot be seen in any high angle shots. If the mount can be seen in the high angle shots, consider fashioning a smaller mount or you will likely have to mask these images so the mount is not included in the model.

It is highly recommended that a macro lens is used when photographing objects for photogrammetry modelling to avoid issues such as this one. It will be considerably more difficult to model an object with a standard lens, as without the macro function you cannot be as close to the subject with the camera focused. With a standard lens, you will need to position the camera further back so the lens can focus on the subject, resulting in more of the shooting environment (such as the background, turntable and mount) being captured in the frame. If a standard lens is all that is available, still prioritise avoiding the mount in all photographs. This will likely result in more of the background featuring in the images – do not worry as backgrounds are considerably easier to edit out than mounts and turntables!

9.5 The model is not the correct colour

Images that have a warm or cool colour cast will create a model that is tinted reddish-orange or blue respectively. Without being corrected, the model is not a true representation of the original archaeological artefact.

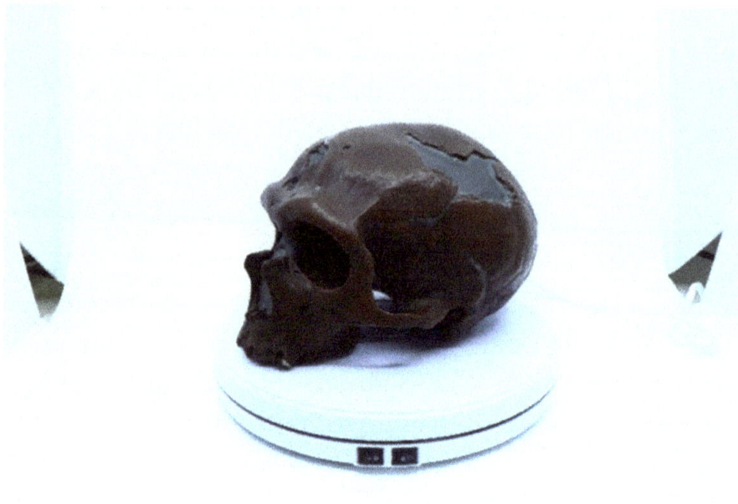

Figure 9.10 The Kelvin setting on the white balance is too low, producing an image with a cool colour cast.

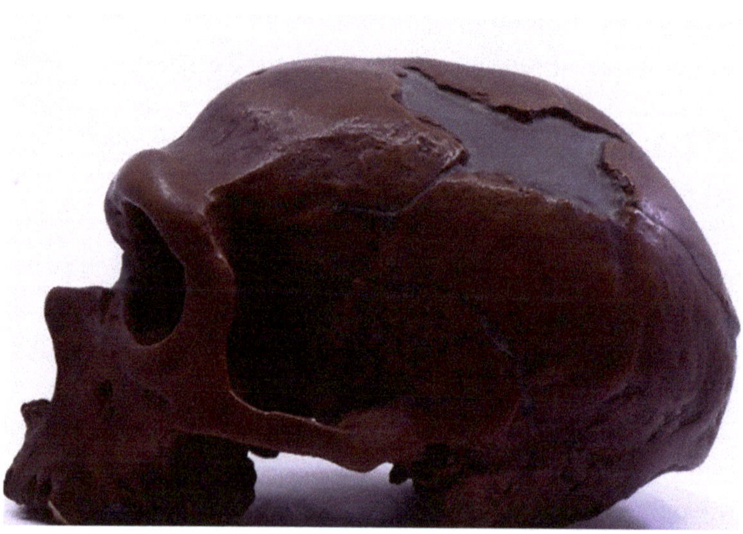

Figure 9.11 The Kelvin setting on the white balance is too high, producing an image with a warm colour cast.

9.5.1 Cause

This problem is a direct result of not setting the white balance correctly on the camera. If the white balance is incorrect, images and the resulting model will have reddish or bluish tints as shown in Figures 9.10 and 9.11. This is problematic as it is not an accurate representation of the original subject's surface.

9.5.2 How to fix

Luckily this problem can be fixed with image editing software. The photos need to be selected as a batch and have the colour temperature adjusted in software such as *Camera Raw* accessed through *Bridge*, or via *Lightroom* or *Photoshop* – programs in Adobe's *Creative Cloud* suite. In *Camera Raw*, select all the images, then adjust the colour temperature balance manually. This will simultaneously change all images. Alternatively, in *Lightroom*, one image can be adjusted and the changes copied and pasted to the rest of the images, or in *Photoshop* a batch process of adjusting the white balance can be recorded and saved, then applied to the entire image folder. For more information and directions on how to adjust the colour temperatures of a batch of images, see Chapter 6. If you do not have access to image editing software, you will have to reset the white balance on your camera to suit the shooting environment (method outlined in 5.2.2) and reshoot the object for processing.

If a colour checker chart was included at the beginning of the shooting process (see 6.2), a colour profile can be created, saved and imported into image editing software such as *Lightroom* to adjust the colour cast of the rest of the images. This is the best method to ensure you have accurately captured the correct colours of your artefact and all serious photogrammetrists should endeavour to include a colour checker in their photography kit.

9.5.3 How to avoid

Before every shooting session, ensure the white balance has been set correctly by positioning a piece of paper in the shooting environment, taking a photo of it, and setting the white balance to that image through the "Custom White Balance" option. This is a more reliable method than choosing one of the white balance options on the camera. The custom option configures the settings to the actual conditions you are shooting in and will produce more accurate images. If possible, also include a colour checker chart in the shooting environment and follow the steps in 6.2 to readjust the colours in the images. This will ensure that not only your white balance is correct but all other colours in your images are also correct.

9.6 The edges have incorrectly aligned

9.6.1 Causes

This is a common problem for novice photogrammetrists modelling artefacts with sharp or thin edges. Typically, this issue is caused by an inadequate number of close-up and well-exposed photographs that focus on the edges of an artefact and that capture the surface information from one face moving to the other. As you can see in Figure 9.12, the edges of the two faces of this artefact do not align perfectly, creating two distinct peaks. This indicates that the images have failed to align correctly and need to be rectified.

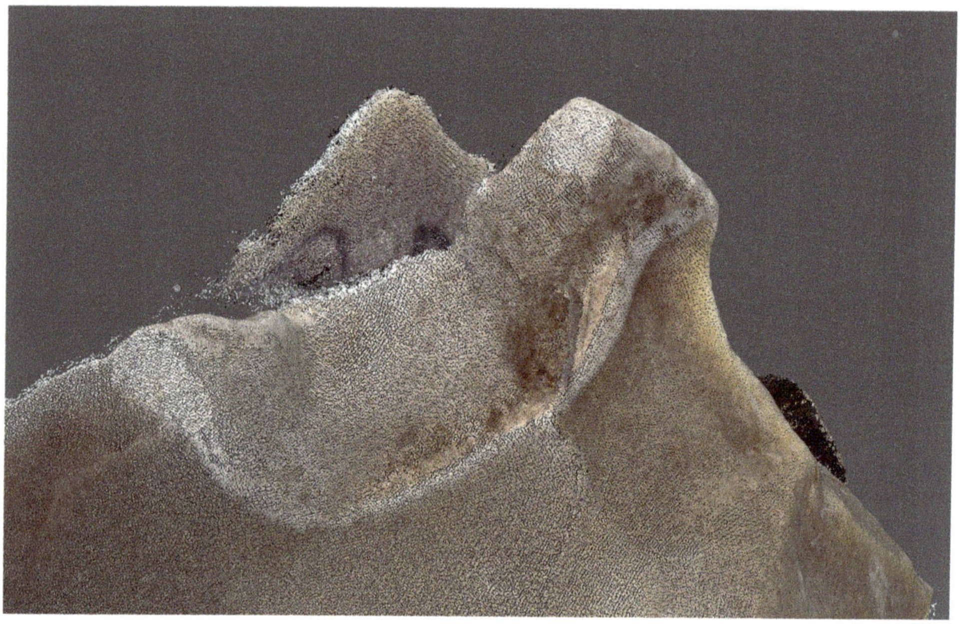

Figure 9.12 An incorrectly aligned model of a lithic artefact shown in the point cloud view. Tabun collection, Art Jelinek, Steve Kuhn, University of Arizona, Tucson.

9.6.2 How to fix

It is faster and easier to fix this problem by reshooting the artefact rather than trying to manually realign the images in *Metashape*. Realigning the images can take considerable time and effort and if not done correctly the edges may still be incorrect. If it is not possible to return to the shooting stage, apply the method listed in 9.1 – rerun the model in photogrammetry software with a different accuracy setting in the "Align Photos" job; that is, if high accuracy was initially set, rerun on medium or vice versa. If this is also unsuccessful, rerun the model with the "Generic Preselection" tool turned off. This is a slow method and it may not be successful, and for this reason, it is safer and recommended to return to the shooting stage and take some more images of the edges to fix the problem.

If you are able to reshoot the object, it is not necessary to capture the entire object again; simply focus on the areas that were incorrect in the model. Ensure the shooting area is well-lit and the camera is set to a balanced exposure in keeping with the settings that were used in the previous shooting session. Position the camera as close as possible to the artefact's edge, and following the method outlined in 5.6.7, capture the object's edge moving from one side of the artefact to the other moving along the edge. Ensure that enough of the sides of the artefact are covered so the images can be aligned easily with the rest of the model. If you are unsure whether you need to photograph from a different perspective, or more of the edges need to be captured, just remember the mantra – when in doubt, take a shot. It is always better to overshoot than undershoot.

It is likely that you will have to rerun the entire modelling process from the alignment stage with the new images to be correctly stitched together. If the area that has been incorrectly meshed is not that severe, however, it may be possible to simply select and delete the areas that failed to align properly in the model and import the new images by following the steps outlined in 7.15.

9.6.3 How to avoid

For any object that has thin, sharp or transparent edges, take a series of well-exposed and close-up edge shots to ensure that the edges of the object are completely captured. For particularly problematic objects, take edge shots from multiple positions and angles and avoid including too much of the background in the frame. Edge shots can be taken at any time during the shooting stage; just make sure that the images sequentially connect to the rest of the photos of the object. Ensure you also have a suitable macro lens for objects with thin edges – standard lenses may not capture the detail of edges, which may also contribute to the issue of failed alignment.

9.7 Concluding notes

Most errors or issues that occur in photogrammetry models are due to mistakes made in the shooting stage. Common mistakes include the camera being in the wrong position or angle during a shooting round, an insufficient number of images were taken, the camera was set up incorrectly, or an incorrect lens was used. Fortunately, most modelling issues can be easily rectified in photogrammetry software. It is recommended that you become familiar with the editing tools in your photogrammetry software so you can understand how to resolve future issues with your models, even if it is for simple touch-ups. Knowing how to identify a potential problem at the time, however, such as an incorrect camera position or camera setting, comes with experience. Your confidence in shooting and processing will simply evolve and grow with practice.

If you have images of an object that cannot be improved by image editing software and therefore are unusable for model-building, you may have to reshoot the object. Problems such as significant camera blur in all or most images, or when the object has not been captured correctly, resulting in unconnected photos or gaps in object coverage, are examples of issues that are irreparable using editing software and the object must be photographed again. It is therefore crucial that before you commence shooting, double-check the settings on the camera and create a workflow of the shooting process (i.e. order of camera angles and number of rounds) just to avoid any potential issues occurring in the processing stage. The freedom to conduct countless trial shooting runs may not always be available. Depending on where you are capturing archaeological material, for example away in the field or in a museum, you typically only have a limited time with the material. As such, make it a priority to take the time to capture the objects correctly and to do a quality check of the images as you are shooting to mitigate the chances of major problems occurring down the processing line. And just remember the mantra – when in doubt, take a shot!

Chapter 10

PHOTOGRAMMETRY SOFTWARE

A variety of structure-from-motion (SfM) photogrammetry software is currently available for desktop and laptop computers. Some software are licensed-based while others are open-source. Each operates in different ways, with distinct workflows and command structures, and all have different hardware requirements. As a result, they all create models with subtly different characteristics. This chapter provides a review of a collection of the main software choices currently available. As photogrammetry software will likely develop rapidly in the coming years, this comparison is to provide you with some understanding of the programs available in 2024.

The software that is evaluated in this chapter is Agisoft *Metashape*, Capturing Reality *RealityCapture*, *Pix4DMapper*, AliceVision *Meshroom* and *Regard3D*. For each of these photogrammetry software programs, the system requirements have been listed (10.1). A comparison of each is then presented with assessments based on published reviews, specifically looking at the geometric accuracy of models, processing time, and cost of each software (10.2). More comprehensive reviews of two of the most commonly used software options – *Metashape* (10.3) and *Meshroom* (10.4) – are then presented. Towards the end of this chapter (10.5), a simple workflow for creating a model in *Meshroom* is summarised for those interested in exploring this software. The model produced from following this workflow is compared to the model generated in Case study 8.8 in *Metashape*, using the same images to compare the processing time, image alignment accuracy, and the produced tie point and mesh face numbers.

10.1 Photogrammetry software and their system requirements

All the currently available photogrammetry software options have different requirements to run efficiently. Your choice of both hardware and software will be influenced by the size of the photogrammetry models you are planning on processing and the extent of work planned. Confirm what hardware requirements are necessary to efficiently run a particular program before investing in a computer. The main computing requirements for photogrammetry modelling are RAM (the computer's short-term memory), the operating system and the GPU (the graphics card). Aim for a minimum of 32 GB of RAM and a relatively high-end GPU (such as NVIDIA GeForce RTX series or the AMD Radeon RX models) for processing photogrammetry models.

Licensed-based software including *Metashape*, *RealityCapture* and *Pix4DMapper* can all be purchased online; however, take note that most of these options are not compatible with macOS or Linux systems, only Windows. This should be taken into consideration if you are deciding which operating system to run your licensed-based photogrammetry software. The various free options of software, such as *Meshroom* and *Regard3D*, tend to be more compatible with the three most common operating systems – Windows, macOS and Linux.

Information on the current recommended specs and compatible operating systems to efficiently run the software *Metashape*, *RealityCapture*, *Pix4DMapper*, *Meshroom* and *Regard3D* is summarised below.

Agisoft *Metashape*

www.agisoft.com
Available for Windows, macOS and Linux OS
Recommended specs for basic configuration (laptop or desktop) ("System Requirements", Agisoft, 2023):
GPU: NVIDIA or AMD with 1024+ unified shaders
RAM: 16–32 GB
CPU: 4–12 core Intel, AMD or Apple M1/M2 processor, 2.0+ GHz

Recommended specs for advanced configuration (desktop or workstation):
GPU: 1–2 NVIDIA or AMD with 1920+ unified shaders
RAM: 32–128 GB
CPU: 6–32 core Intel or AMD processor, 3.0+ GHz

Recommended specs for extreme configuration (server):
GPU: Quadro, Tesla, Radeon Pro or Instinct GPUs

RAM: 128 GB minimum
CPU: A dual-socket Intel Xeon or AMD EPYC based servers, 3.0+ GHz

RealityCapture

capturingreality.com
Available for Windows 7/8/8.1/10/11 64-bit or Windows Server version 2008+
Recommended specs for basic configuration ("OS and Hardware Requirements", CapturingReality, 2023):
GPU: NVIDIA with CUDA 3.0+ capabilities and 1GB VRAM
RAM: 8 GB minimum
CPU: 4 core processor minimum

Pix4DMapper

pix4d.com
Available for Windows 10 (recommended) and 11; however, a Beta macOS version of *Pix4DMapper* is available
Recommended specs for basic configuration ("Computer Requirements", Pix4D, 2021):
GPU: NVIDIA GeForce GTX compatible with OpenGL 3.2
RAM: 8 GB (small projects under 100 images)
16 GM (medium projects between 100 and 500 images)
32 GB (large projects between 500 and 1,000 images)
64 GB (very large projects between 1,000 and 2,000 images)
CPU: 4–6 core Intel i7/Intel i9/Threadripper/Xeon processor

Meshroom

alicevision.org
Available for Windows and Linux OS (macOS with specific hardware and drivers)
Recommended specs for basic configuration ("Requirements", Meshroom, 2020):
GPU: NVIDIA with CUDA 2.0+ capabilities
RAM: 32 GB
CPU: Intel i7 or AMD Ryzen 7 processor

Regard3D

www.regard3d.org
Available for Windows and macOS, compatible with 64-bit versions only
Recommended specs for basic configuration ("Download", Regard3D, no date):
GPU: openGL capable graphics card or chip
RAM: 8 GB recommended

Some software options, like *Metashape* and *Pix4DMapper*, allow for cloud-based processing, which means model-building can be done with a computer that does not meet the recommended specifications listed here. For cloud-based processing, however, you will want an internet connection with sufficient speed and data allowance, as you will need to upload the images to the cloud and download the completed model. This method is advantageous for financial reasons as the best computers for local 3D rendering (largely gaming computers) have powerful GPUs and processing systems with significant amounts of RAM and naturally come with a higher price tag. If you intend to conduct some photogrammetry shooting in a remote location without or with limited internet connection, consider purchasing or building a computer that can take on the workload locally so you can monitor the quality of photographs taken. Even running low-quality models to confirm they are aligning correctly is a good idea. Returning from the field to process images and finding them unusable is not an ideal situation to be in!

10.2 Comparing photogrammetry software

Due to the rising popularity of SfM technology in a variety of industries, and the increasing dependence on three-dimensional modelling and digitisation in cultural heritage, there are a number of published studies comparing photogrammetry software. Typically, assessments are based on model accuracy via geometric accuracy and sparse cloud comparisons, processing time and cost. The terms "sparse cloud" and "dense cloud" will be used in this chapter instead of *Metashape*'s revised terms "tie point" and "point cloud", as these are the common terms that are used by most software.

The primary commercial SfM software used in cultural heritage that will be discussed here are Agisoft *Metashape* (previously named *Photoscan*), *RealityCapture*, *Pix4DMapper*, and the open-source programs AliceVision *Meshroom* and *Regard3D*. *Metashape* is the most commonly critically-assessed software, particularly when the appraisal concerns archaeological material and sites, and is frequently used as the basis of comparison with other photogrammetry programs (Barbasiewicz, Widerski and Daliga 2018; Cutugno, Robestelli and Pugliano 2022; Davis et al. 2017; Đurić et al. 2021; Hendrickx et al. 2019; Kingsland 2020).

There has been mounting interest in measuring model accuracy for both object-based and aerial photogrammetry models. Generally, assessments focus on one type of photogrammetry modelling, such as object-based, large-scale or uncrewed aerial vehicle (UAV)/aerial photogrammetry. Each type can look at specific criteria; for example, recent developments in assessing the quality of object-based modelling (particularly concerning cultural heritage and archaeological material) focus on the quality of mesh and texture mapping as well as reconstructed colour accuracy of three-dimensional models (Dostal and Yamafune 2018; Felicísimo and Polo 2022; Polo, Felicísimo and Durán-Domínguez 2022). The basis of determining geometric accuracy of UAV and aerial imagery of topography or architecture largely relies on measuring GCPs, CPs or GPS data (Barbasiewicz, Widerski and Daliga 2018; Becker, Galayda and MacLaughlin 2018; Cutugno, Robestelli and Pugliano 2022; Jaud et al. 2016; Verykokou et al. 2021). There are other criteria, however, that appear in all assessments, such as image alignment accuracy, sparse cloud generation and overall visual evaluations. The discussion here is not restricted to scholarship concerning just one application of photogrammetry modelling (i.e. object-based, large-scale or aerial photogrammetry) but is open to assessments that address the overall performance of all types of photogrammetry software.

Metashape is photogrammetry software for beginners and professional users. It is strong in sparse point and dense cloud generation, image alignment and mesh reconstruction accuracy (Barbasiewicz, Widerski and Daliga 2018; Georgopolous et al. 2016; Kingsland 2020). Specifically for small-scale modelling, it has been shown to produce the most successful image alignment accuracy, which is particularly useful for those wanting to create photogrammetry models of archaeological artefacts (Kingsland 2019). There are mixed reviews of the quality of texture resolution compared to competitors; however, its versatility in accepting various forms of data (close-range, UAV, fish-eye, 360, thermal, etc.) identifies it as a leader in the field of 3D image reconstruction and is another reason why it is so popular among professional users (Becker, Galayda and MacLaughlin 2018; Kingsland 2020; Reljić, Dunđer and Seljan 2019). *Metashape* offers the greatest amount of control throughout the process in terms of settings and editing and allows for the workflow process to be saved and reapplied to other projects (Kingsland 2019, 2020). *Metashape* does tend to perform slower than *RealityCapture* and *Pix4DMapper*; however, studies have shown that *Metashape* requires significantly less manual post-processing editing compared to competitors and as such reduces the overall time to produce a complete model (Georgopoulos et al. 2016; Kingsland 2019, 2020).

RealityCapture is software known for its processing speed. It is consistently faster than competing products, and therefore is an asset for photogrammetrists who need to produce a large number of models very quickly (Kingsland 2020). This feature is also beneficial for archaeologists working on-site who have limited time in the field to generate models. Mesh and texture resolution accuracy are comparable with other commercial software; however, as with all software, this is dependent on the quality of the images (Kingsland 2020; Reljić, Dunđer and Seljan 2019; Remondino et al. 2017; Verykokou et al. 2021). *RealityCapture* has internal editing functions in the software, which means no additional software is required to edit the models (Kingsland 2020).

Pix4DMapper is a good option for users looking to model UAV data. *Pix4DMapper*'s texture reconstruction has been reviewed to be visually superior to other software, and its alignment accuracy and sparse cloud generation are comparable to *Metashape* (Alidoost and Arefi 2017; Becker, Galayda and MacLaughlin 2018; Georgopolous et al. 2016). This software allows for georeferencing and scaling of models and, according to publications, *Pix4DMapper* produces low error rates and decent geometric accuracy (Alidoost and Arefi 2017; Georgopolous et al. 2016; Lau, Ariff and Razali 2022). Its processing speed has been evaluated to be faster than *Metashape*; however, the generation of dense clouds is not as well performing nor are the results as consistent (Georgopolous et al. 2016; Kingsland 2020).

Prices of pay-to-use photogrammetry software depend on what internal licensing option you choose and the version type. All the programs discussed so far come at a hefty cost, typically a one-off purchase of a few thousand Australian or US dollars. Luckily more and more software are offering free or cheaper educational licences, for example, *RealityCapture* has introduced free downloads for students and education institutions, and businesses with revenue below US$1 million. Additionally, some programs will offer versions of the software at a cheaper price with limited or reduced options or processing capacities, such as Agisoft *Metashape*, whose Standard Edition is considerably cheaper compared to the Professional Edition. Tiered versions of software provide greater accessibility to a wider range of users, but often the trade-off in price means a limited range of functionality. For infrequent users and those who require less functionality, free alternatives should be considered. These may not have the advanced functionality, data extraction, editing capabilities and model accuracy of commercial software, but are readily accessible and easier on the wallet.

Meshroom by AliceVision is a popular, free, open-source program that supports the easy creation of textured photogrammetry models. When model-building is successful, the accuracy of the model's mesh and texture has been reviewed as being high quality, but success is not always certain as it is dependent on object geometry, complexity, number of images and quality of the images (Đurić et al. 2021; Kesack 2022; Reljić, Dunđer and Seljan 2019). *Meshroom* cannot use or measure ground control points (GCPs), meaning accuracy assessments must be conducted using alternative methods (Đurić et al. 2021; Verykokou et al. 2021). There is also a lack of scaling capabilities or the capacity to generate orthomosaics.

Another free open-source software is *Regard3D*, which evaluations conclude is well suited for beginners (Elkhrachy 2022; Vacca 2019) as the interface is incredibly user-friendly and intuitive. The stages of model generation are comparable to *Metashape*; however, the terminology is slightly different. The main stages are "Compute Matches" – where key points are identified, "Triangulate" – where the tie point cloud is created, "Densification" – the creation of a dense cloud, and "Surface Generation" which processes the mesh and texture. There is also the convenient option to export straight to the software *MeshLab* after the dense point cloud has been generated for further post-processing. The online tutorial found on their website ("Tutorial", *Regard3D*) additionally provides files that are downloadable so you can process the images they have captured, allowing you to follow along and produce the model they use in their tutorial.

The accuracy of successful models generated in *Regard3D* has been reviewed to be superior to other open-source software alternatives; however, these assessments have shown that the error ratings are still not of the standard of commercial software (Elkhrachy 2022; Setiyadi, Mukhtar and Cahyadi 2021; Vacca 2019). Similar to *Meshroom*, models cannot be scaled, nor can GCPs be input (Elkhrachy 2022). Like *Meshroom*, no editing or filtering options are offered; however, optimisation of the model is possible (Đurić et al. 2021; Vacca 2019). The processing speed of *Regard3D* has been assessed to be slow to average for open-source software (Rahaman and Champion 2019; Setiyada, Mukhtar and Cahyadi 2021; Vacca 2019) and, unsurprisingly, considerably slower than commercial software (Elkhrachy 2022). Unlike *Meshroom*, however, every step has to be manually run as no batch processing is offered, inevitably increasing the overall time of model completion.

The range of photogrammetry software currently available all have their benefits and drawbacks, but the three major concerns – accuracy, processing time and cost – ultimately divide them. For curious beginners, an open-source option like *Meshroom*, *Regard3D* or the free demo of *Metashape* is recommended to provide a basis to become familiar with the terminology and stages in the model-generation process. For advanced users, functionality and performance are more likely to be influencing factors in software choice; therefore the lack of editing capabilities common in open-source software reflects why professional users are recommended to opt for commercial licences. Overall, the performance of commercial options is impressive and will only continue to improve with each update. The main discriminating variable between each choice for photogrammetrists will likely, and simply, come down to cost.

The functionality and system requirements of these five software types have been compiled into Table 10.1 to help you compare each program and decide

Software	Operating systems	Licensing options	Model types	Internal editing capabilities	Measuring capabilities	Georeferencing	Orthomosaic or orthophoto generation
Metashape	Windows, macOS, Linux	Professional and Standard Licences. Educational licences available	Close-range and aerial	Yes	Yes, only in the Professional Edition	Yes, only in the Professional Edition	Yes
RealityCapture	Windows, macOS is possible via additional software	Annual subscription option with free downloads for students, educators, hobbysists and companies from institutions under a certain annual revenue	Close-range and aerial	Yes	Yes	Yes	Yes
Pix4DMapper	Windows, Beta macOS version of *Pix4DMapper* 3.0 is available	Monthly and annual subscription licences or a one-off perpetual licence. Educational licences available	Aerial	Limited	Yes	Yes	Yes
Meshroom	Windows, Linux, macOS is possible using additional hardware and drivers	Open-source	Close-range and aerial	No	No	No	No
Regard3D	Windows, macOS	Open-source	Close-range and aerial	No	No	No	No

Table 10.1 A comparison of the functionality and operating systems of the five software programs.

which one might be the best choice for you. The factors that have been considered here are model type (close-range or aerial), operating system, licensing options, capability to edit and scale internally, if georeferencing is possible, and whether orthomosaics or orthophotos can be produced. Again, these specs are from software versions available at the time of publication.

10.3 Agisoft *Metashape* pros and cons

Agisoft *Metashape* is one of the most commonly used software for photographic 3D reconstruction for both novice and professional photogrammetrists in cultural heritage (Kingsland 2020). Its popularity is largely due to *Metashape*'s consistent and reliable performance of the primary aspects of consideration in SfM software – ease of use, accuracy of model generation, editing capabilities and processing time. Exploring these criteria further reveals the benefits and capabilities of *Metashape*; however, through this investigation, some drawbacks are uncovered that first-time users should be aware of.

A commonly viewed advantage of *Metashape* is the ease with which models can be generated and edited, and how the interface is uncomplicated and intuitive (Verykokou et al. 2021). The background colour and interface theme can be changed, and the panes can be rearranged or removed to suit your preferences. Creating a batch process is a simple task and the added ability to save a previous batch process that can be reused for other models is a helpful and time-saving function. The frequent updates and changes to settings and jobs in *Metashape* can be disruptive to regular users of the software, however. With the update to version 2.0.0 in December 2022, one of the numerous changes included a surprising change of standard terminology – "sparse point cloud" and "dense point cloud" became "tie point cloud" and "point cloud", respectively. This was an adjustment that took users by surprise. Another considerable update occurred in December 2023, to version 2.1.0, again changing some names of functions, like "Build Mesh" to "Build Model" and the addition of several new setting options in the model workflow. Little direction to the changes has been offered to users when updates occur, meaning *Metashape* users must conduct their own research to become familiar with the updates and how to use and implement the updated functions and settings.

A photogrammetry model's geometric accuracy is essential for all 3D model analyses and, consequently, there has been a growth in the methods of testing the reconstruction accuracy of models. *Metashape* has earned a reputation for consistently producing geometric accuracy through published comparisons to other commercial software, typically through measuring the accuracy of GCPs in large-scale models or visual and geometric assessments of the spatial accuracy of points in point clouds (Alidoost and Arefi 2017; Kingsland 2020; Verykokou et al. 2021). *Metashape*'s feature-detection algorithm generates reliable point clouds (which is particularly useful for generating and editing small-scale objects) with consistently high image alignment accuracy (Alidoost and Arefi 2017; Barbasiewicz, Widerski and Daliga 2018; Kesack 2022; Kingsland 2020). The reproducibility of results is also strong, with research showing minimal variation between repeated model reconstructions based on assessing GCP x, y and z coordinates and their respective error ratings (Hendrickx et al. 2019; Kingsland 2020).

Where *Metashape* excels is the fast and easy editing tools that can significantly improve the overall appearance of a model very quickly. The various editing options can be applied to different stages of the process to allow the user greater control over the quality of the final product. From closing holes and smoothing mesh, to deleting floating mesh, changing the brightness and contrast, and removing lighting, there is a reasonable supply of post-processing functions. Surprisingly, there is no ability to manually reconfigure or design the mesh layer, and similarly, there is little ability to manipulate the appearance of a model's texture in *Metashape*. *Metashape* aims to build accurate digital reconstructions of real-life objects, and if you want to redesign or distort them you will require additional software. If 3D graphic design capabilities such as mesh and texture alteration are desired by users, software such as *Geomagic*, *SketchUp*, *Blender*, *ZBrush* and *Autodesk Maya* can be included in the workflow once *Metashape* has processed and exported the model.

Of particular note is *Metashape*'s vast variety of mask-making options. Masks can be generated manually from images and then applied to key or tie points, produced and applied to the images from the meshed models themselves, or can be created externally in other image editing software and imported. Masks can also be exported and reimported to be reapplied on repeated model trial runs. This diversity of choice is really helpful and the ability to use masks in *Metashape* to improve image alignment and mesh accuracy is a really useful tool (see 7.14).

Metashape's processing speed has been assessed as being about average for commercial software; however, it is still faster than open-source alternatives (Georgopoulos et al. 2016; Kesack 2022; Kingsland 2020; Verykokou et al. 2021). Using some editing tools on particularly large models or while another model is being processed, however, can significantly slow down the speed of editing functions. Processing time overall, however, is dependent on the processing power of the computer being used and the number and quality of images (Georgopoulos et al. 2016).

Overall, *Metashape* is a reliable and user-friendly option for processing photogrammetry models that, despite some minor drawbacks, is a recommended software for processing cultural heritage photogrammetry models for analysis and research purposes.

10.4 AliceVision *Meshroom* pros and cons

Meshroom by AliceVision is a simple and straightforward open-source software for photogrammetry model processing. *Meshroom* is compatible with Windows and Linux operating systems and will only run on a macOS machine with additional hardware set up (*Meshroom*, macOS 2020). The interface is well organised and displays workflow windows in an uncomplicated arrangement that allows for easy navigation. When *Meshroom* starts up, a default workflow is provided in the interface that can be run after images are loaded. The customisable node-based system is easy to understand and follow, and particularly useful for beginners and occasional users, as there is no need to remember the multiple steps, settings or parameters. Where the software becomes more complicated is when a user needs to reconfigure the node-based pipeline for models of greater complexity or that require different or specific settings. Redesigning the pipeline will require the user to understand the functionality of the parameters and settings and how they connect and fit into the workflow. This will add significant learning time for the user and will increase processing time (Kesack 2022).

A useful feature of *Meshroom* is the ability to interact with the interface while a model is being processed. This is very advantageous as it allows you to analyse the progress of the model so far and confirm the settings are correct without having to stop the progress of the model. This is unlike other software, where you are locked out of the processing as soon as it commences. Progress can be followed by the coloured bar at the top of the interface, which is useful; however, there is no estimation of time left to process, so it is hard to schedule your processing sessions or other activities in your day (Kesack 2022; Verykokou et al. 2021).

Meshroom's main shortcoming is the inability to edit models. All post-processing adjustments must be coordinated through additional software. Other limitations include the inability to mask the model or the images, models cannot be scaled or georeferenced, and GCPs cannot be added or measured (Verykokou et al. 2021). This means that confirmation of model accuracy has to be conducted slightly differently for *Meshroom*, and again via external software. We know that *Meshroom* models typically have high geometric model accuracy; however, accuracy is dependent on the object's shape (i.e. how simple is its geometry), the method of image capture, and the amount of image data uploaded into the software (Đurić et al. 2021). As free software, *Meshroom* offers you a lot, but if you are processing large models with complex morphology, you may find licence-based software a better option (Kesack 2022).

10.5 Basic *Meshroom* workflow

Since we have looked at the pros and cons of *Meshroom*, a basic workflow for version 2023.3.0 has been supplied here. As *Meshroom* processes models locally and does not currently offer cloud processing, your computer needs to have adequate processing power (see 10.1).

10.5.1 *Meshroom* interface

Meshroom interface displays six customisable panels. On the left-hand side (labelled 1 in Figure 10.1), the panel labelled "Image Gallery" is where you drag and drop photographs. The second panel, labelled "Image Viewer", shows a selected image in a larger view. A third panel, labelled "3D Viewer", will display the model when it is generated. A fourth panel, within the "3D Viewer" panel, displays the metadata of the model, that is, the number of dot points, aligned photographs, and the mesh faces under the heading "Scene". It also contains buttons to control the display of the grid, trackball, and x, y and z axis origins displayed in the "3D Viewer" panel under the heading "Display". A fifth panel, which has two tab headings labelled "Graph Editor" and "Task Manager", exhibits the default nodes that comprise the photogrammetry modelling process, which is referred to as a "pipeline". The order of the default nodes is "CameraInit" (a contraction of Camera Initiation), "FeatureExtraction", "ImageMatching", "FeatureMatching", "StructureFromMotion", "PrepareDenseScene", "DepthMap", "DepthMapFilter", "Meshing", "MeshFiltering", and finally "Texturing". The order, number and arrangement of nodes in the pipeline are customisable and each has a variety of settings that can be changed to suit the parameters of the model and the processing speed.

When a node is selected, a sixth panel with the heading "Node" will show the settings, parameters and metadata for that node. This information is under six tabs: "Attributes", "Log", "Statistics", "Status", "Documentation" and "Notes". Before a node is processed, the parameters of that node can be adjusted to more desirable settings under "Attributes". The following tab "Log" displays all the processing information once the node has finished running. The "Statistics" tab displays a series of graphs showing the time and percentage of intensity usage of the CPU,

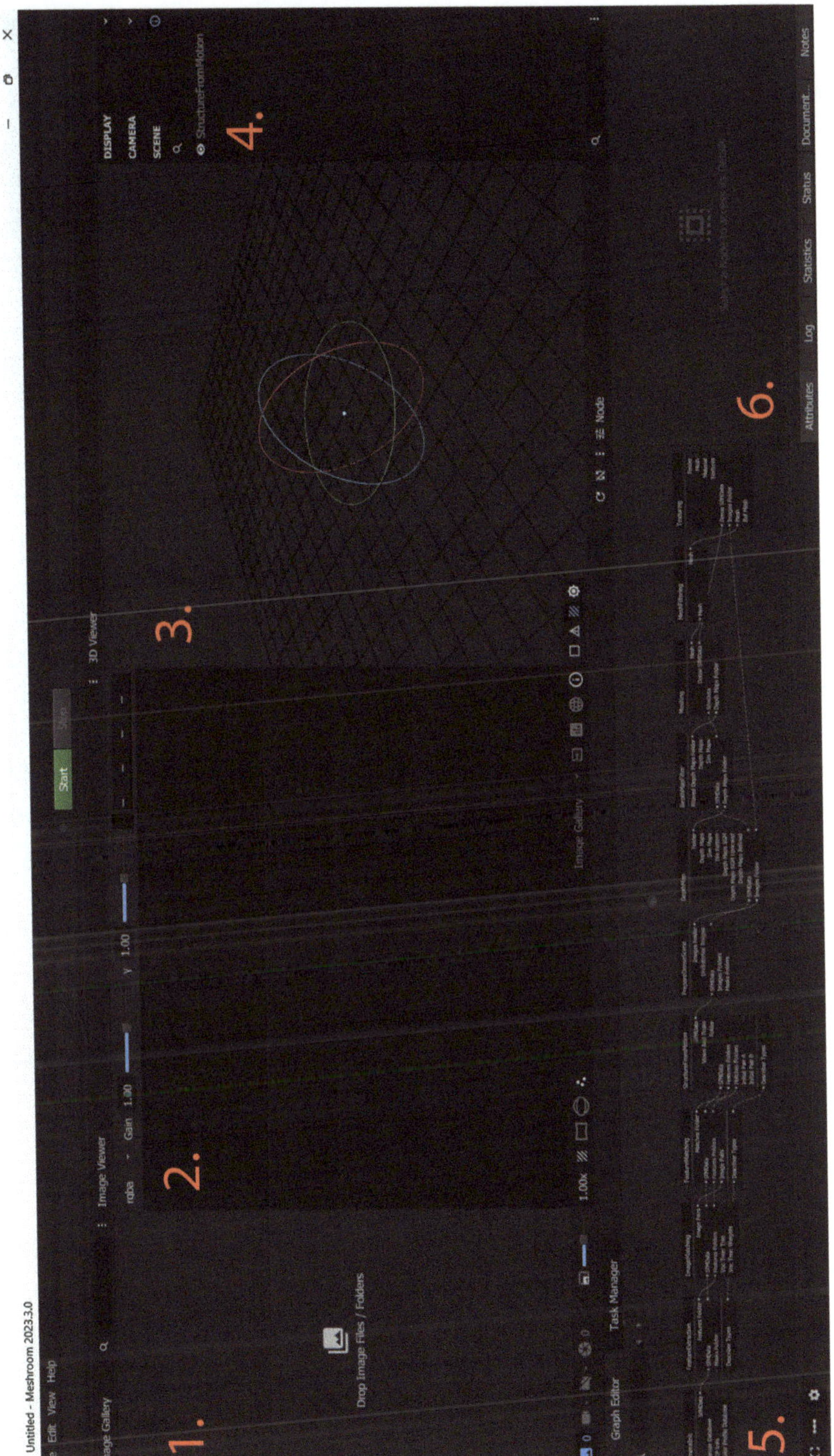

Figure 10.1 *Meshroom*'s workspace interface.

RAM and GPU during the processing of the node. The "Status" tab displays a table of metadata, such as whether the node was successful in its processing, the node's name, the start and end time, and the total processing time. "Documentation" lists the steps involved in the node and provides detailed information about each step. The last tab, "Notes", is where the user can leave comments regarding changes or settings of the node for future reference, the colour of the node and its label.

Do not be put off by all the variety of changeable parameters and settings of the nodes. Depending on the desired quality and size of the model, the model might benefit from having adjusted settings; however, it is not essential to change them.

10.5.2 Import photos

The first step in processing a model in *Meshroom* is to import the photos. This can be done by either dragging and dropping the images from the folder in which they are saved into the "Images" pane in *Meshroom* or by heading to "File" – "Import Images" and selecting and importing the photos from there. The images will appear on the left-hand side with the first image enlarged in the second window and the total number of images identified under the smaller photo thumbnails. Once the photos have been uploaded, save the model in a folder where the photos are located.

For the example here, the photographs used in Case study 8.1 of the *Australopithecus africanus* replica skull processed in *Metashape* Professional were imported and processed in *Meshroom* 2023.3.0 (see Figure 10.2).

10.5.3 Node system and settings

To produce a basic model, the default settings do not necessarily need to be adjusted, and at this point, you can start processing the model by clicking the green "Start" button at the top of the interface. If you want to improve the basic workflow, some useful adjustments are suggested here to increase the alignment success and the model quality. In the pipeline, the nodes can be selected and the settings updated. By selecting the "FeatureMatching" node, the "Attributes" pane to the right of the pipeline will show a setting labelled "Guided Matching". This is a useful function to enable as it will increase the number of image matches, therefore producing a model with better alignment; however, it can significantly increase the processing time. Another useful function to enable is the "Keep Only the Largest Mesh" under the "MeshFiltering" node as this will clear all floating mesh that is not part of the main model. This is comparable to *Metashape*'s "Connected Component

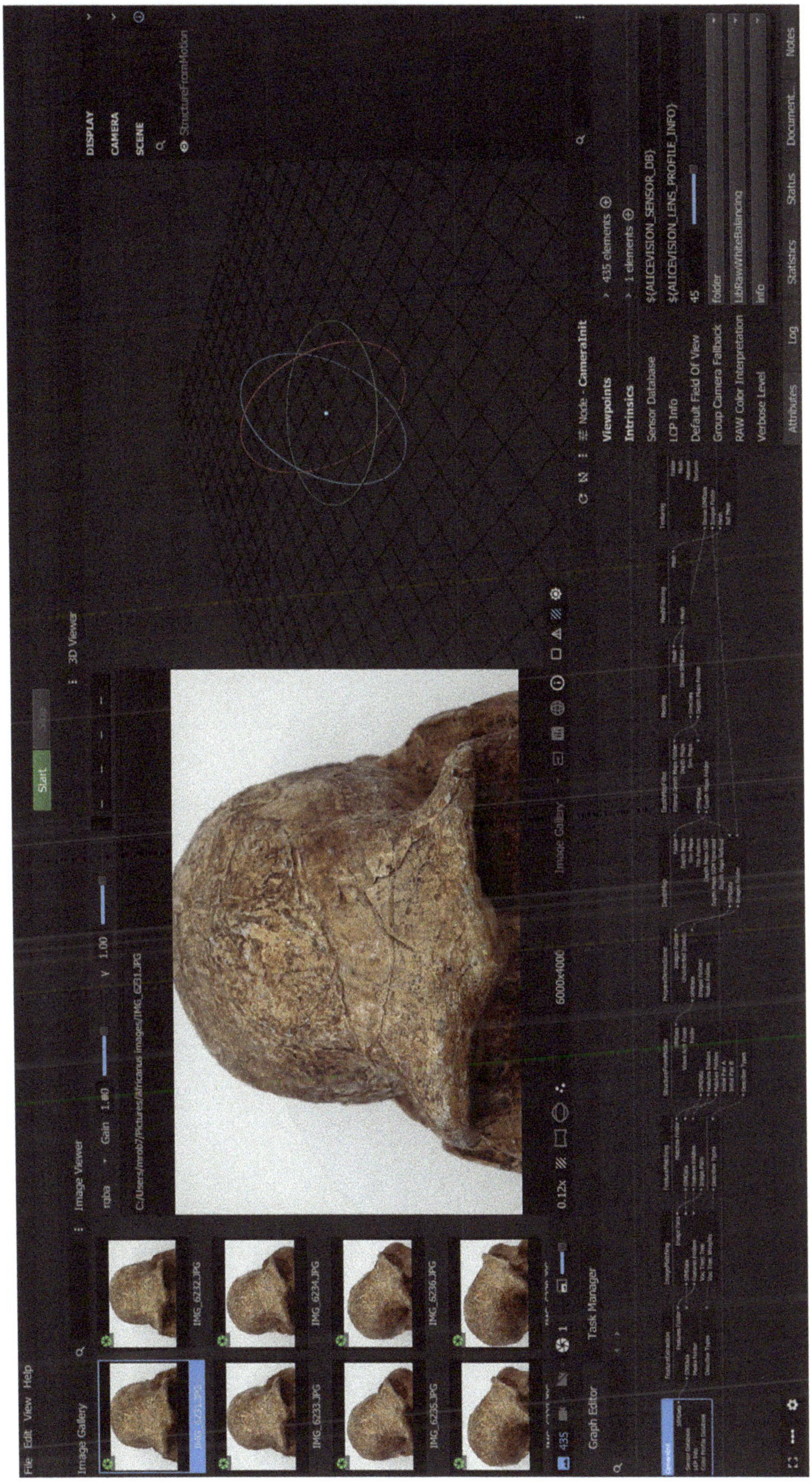

Figure 10.2 *Meshroom*'s interface after importing images of the replica *Australopithecus africanus* skull.

Size" in the "Gradual Selection" tool. There is also the option to remove triangles of a certain size (again similar to *Metashape*'s "Polygon Size" tool under "Gradual Selection") under the same node. In the final node, "Texturing", there is a useful option to reduce the resolution of the texture quality if you need to lower the file size of the model, for example from 8192 (the default) to 4096 texture resolution, and the ability to close mesh holes with the "Fill Holes" option.

As the pipeline is customisable, new nodes can be added. Simply right-click on the grey space in the "Graph Editor" window, which will provide options for additional nodes. Once a new node has been selected, you can reposition it to fit in the pipeline by clicking and dragging the nodes to make space. New nodes need to be connected to the pipeline system. This is done by using the connecting line to link up the nodes – click on one of the outputs of the previous node and join it to the inputs of the new node. Repeat this step from the new node to the next node in the queue to ensure the processing continues through the pipeline.

An example of a useful node to include in the pipeline is the "Publish" node which allows the model to be saved to other 3D model editing software. Right-click in the bottom pane, type in the search bar "Publish" and select the option that appears. Align it to the end of the pipeline and connect to the "Texturing" node by clicking on "Mesh" and connecting the line to "Input Files", and then the same for "Material" and "Textures" (see Figure 10.3). Select the node and in the "Attributes" pane, you can input the folder to which you want to export the files. Unfortunately, you cannot browse the folder directly, but you can paste

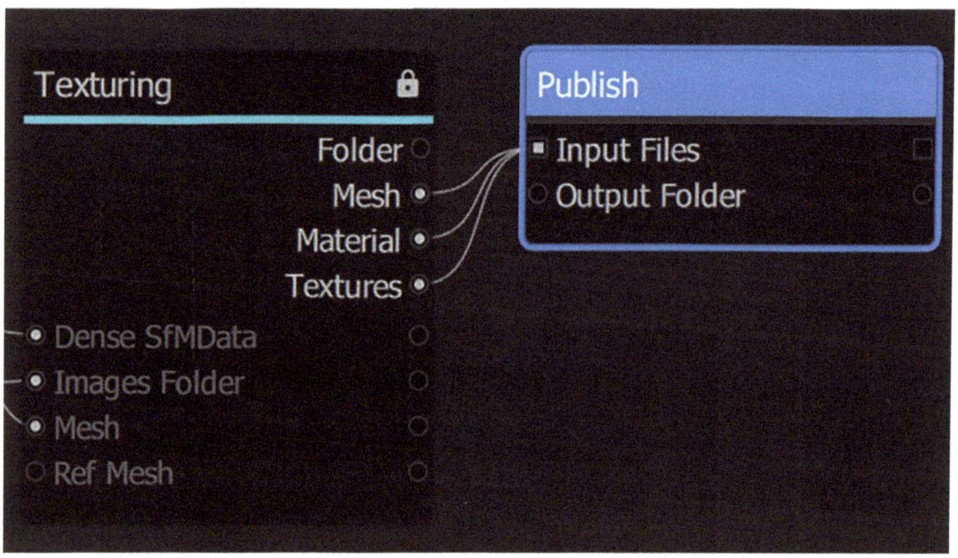

Figure 10.3 The additional "Publish" node added to the end of the pipeline.

the address of the folder into the text box. To do this, open the file explorer on your computer and navigate to the folder to which you want to export the files. In the address bar at the top where the folder paths are shown, right-click and select "Copy address". Return to *Meshroom* and paste the address in (Control + V) next to the "Output Folder". From here, you can continue to process the model.

Once all the settings have been adjusted, click the green "Start" button at the top of the page, which will start the processing of the model from the first node through to the last. You will notice a blue processing bar underneath. As the processing progresses, the green bar will grow to show that certain jobs have been completed and the orange bar will move towards the right, indicating what node is currently being processed. The corresponding node in the bottom pipeline will also show an orange bar, with the previous node showing green and the following node blue. If you only want to process a subset of the nodes, right-click on the last node that you want to run to and select "Compute". *Meshroom* will start the process from the beginning to that point.

As each node is completed, the progressive stages of the model will appear in the "3D Viewer" pane. As soon as the SfM node has finished processing, the sparse point cloud (the same as *Metashape*'s tie point cloud) will appear and can be viewed. To adjust the size of the sparse points, use the top slider on the right-hand side to increase, decrease or remove the dot points. The second slider adjusts the size of the camera icons surrounding the model – these can be seen configured around the model in Figure 10.4. Once the mesh and texture have finished processing, these layers can then also be viewed in the pane. Once the model has finished processing, the model can be explored and exported.

10.5.4 Model product

Once all the nodes are processed and indicated with a solid green bar, the textured model will appear in the "3D Viewer" pane. There is the option to analyse the model in solid, wireframe and texture formats by selecting the corresponding icons in the bottom left corner. To navigate around the model, click and move the mouse to change the view. To pan across the model, press the central button on the mouse (or the scroll wheel) and move the mouse. Alternatively, press the Shift key and move the mouse to pan. Incidentally, this is also how you can reposition the node pipeline. Scrolling the mouse wheel will zoom in and out of the model (or the pipeline) or you can press the Alt key, right-click, and move the mouse to zoom in and out. Finally, double-clicking on a point on the model will adjust the centre view to that point.

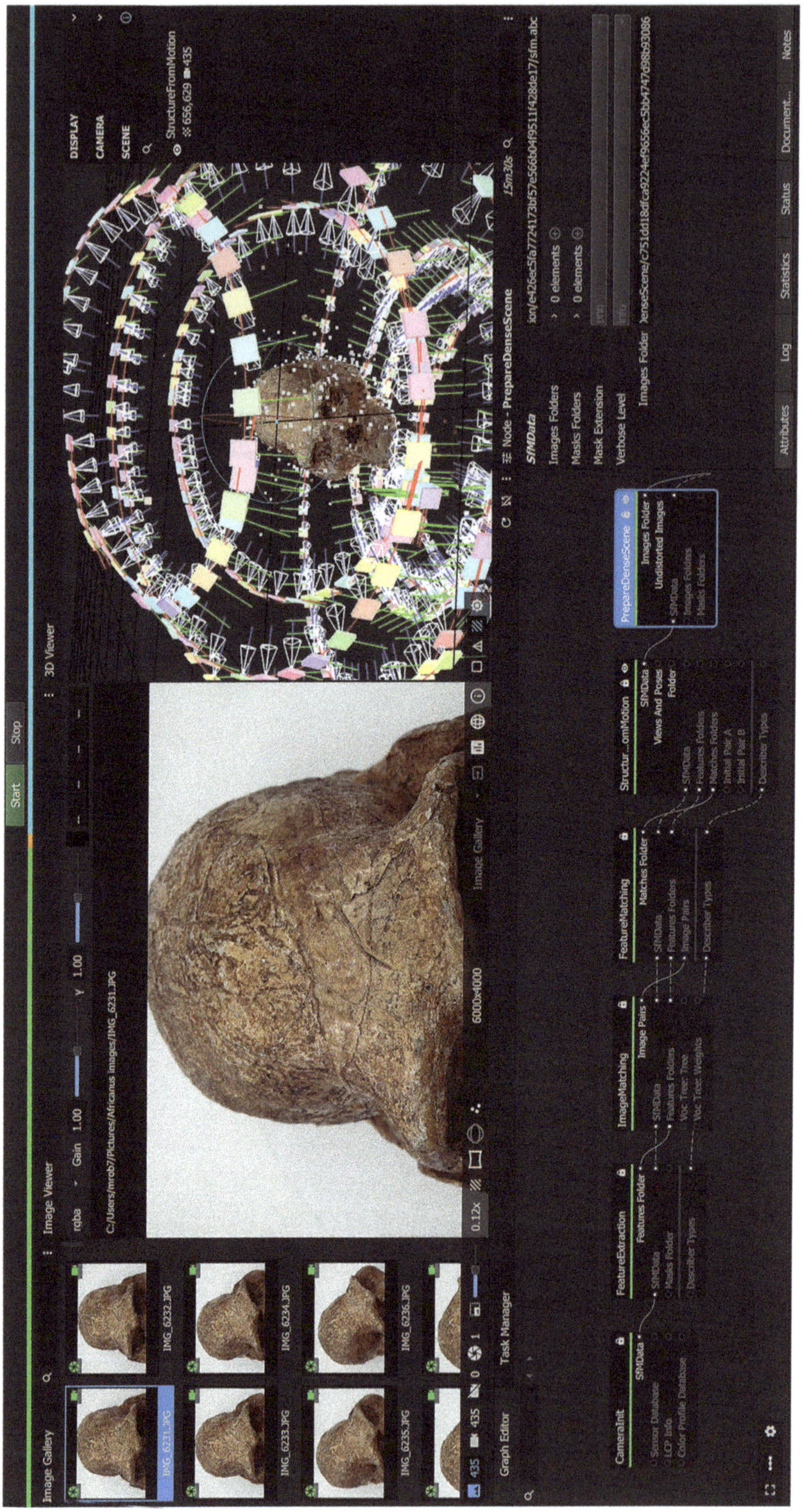

Figure 10.4 *Meshroom*'s interface during a model being processed.

This model of a replica *Australopithecus africanus* skull was created from 435 images with 100% alignment success. The final model had a total of 656,692 points, 4,910,159 mesh faces, and a total processing time of around 9 hours and 30 minutes. The same images run on *Metashape* Professional (using the same computer and with comparable settings) produced a total of 1,909,552 tie points and 11,358,878 mesh faces in a total of 3 hours 41 minutes. This is a considerable difference; however, for open-source software, this is still an impressive model to generate.

Through a thorough inspection of the model, there are no holes in the mesh, the texture has been applied correctly, and the resolution is sharp and clear. There was no floating mesh as the function to eliminate any unattached mesh was enabled and the final model also did not require further masking to remove the background or turntable.

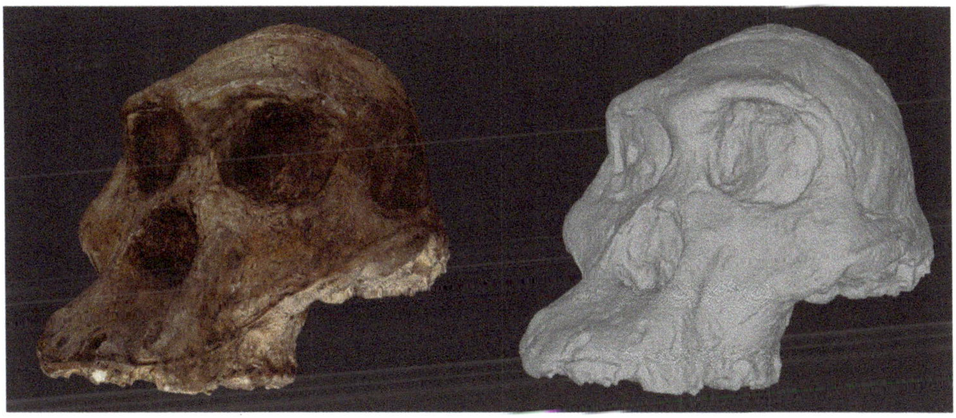

Figure 10.5 The final model product of the resin skull produced using *Meshroom* in both texture and solid formats.

10.6 Concluding advice

There is a growing number of photogrammetry software on the market, providing users with a remarkable range of choices to suit various budgets, computing specs and operating systems. It is recommended for all users, from beginners to advanced, who are considering purchasing a commercial licence, to first explore the free or demo versions before making a financial commitment. This will help ensure that the software produces models at the standards and speed required, as well as offering the types of functionality that are necessary for your modelling projects. This chapter's look into open-source options shows that they can be trusted alternatives if your main concern is cost; however, be aware that most free options, like the two discussed here, are likely to lack a variety of useful functions required for more advanced photogrammetry modelling. For beginners wanting to explore photogrammetry modelling in an environment that is easy to operate and navigate, however, the simplicity of *Meshroom* means that it is a great place to develop a foundation. Just ensure that your computer can efficiently run whatever software you choose if you are processing models locally on your computer.

Chapter 11

CONCLUDING THOUGHTS

Photogrammetry is a game-changing tool for archaeologists. The technology's numerous benefits and opportunities can be applied to all areas of archaeology and their practice. From excavation sites to museums, cultural heritage conservation, archaeological research, education and outreach, photogrammetry can strengthen our understanding and exploration of the human past.

Photogrammetry has the power to digitally preserve cultural material and archaeological sites so that they are impervious to degradation and can withstand the test of time. Assessments can be conducted on photogrammetry models without the worry of subjecting the object to any danger or impacting it in any way. The shooting stage of the photogrammetry method is also unobtrusive. The positions and locations of the photography gear (and the photographer!) are flexible and portable and can be easily adjusted to limit the interaction with an object or site to maintain its protection. The captured data is also powerful and incredibly useful – accurate measurements and dimensions can be obtained, fine surface rugosity revealed, and imperceptible detail easily missed by the naked eye can be identified for the first time by stripping back the texture to view the raw mesh surface underneath. Additionally, photogrammetry is particularly well suited for archaeological material. The technology excels in generating high-quality models of materials with rough and unreflective surfaces, capturing fine details effectively. Objects or features with intricate or complex surfaces are more likely to produce models that successfully align, resulting in accurate mesh and texture representation. In particular, objects made of bone, stone, wood and unglazed clay fall into these categories and are coincidentally materials commonly handled by archaeologists.

In light of the difficulties and pressures brought on by the COVID-19 pandemic, now more than ever we are realising the importance of accessibility to cultural heritage sites and objects. 3D modelling and the platforms that allow for the easy and costless dissemination of 3D models were instantly recognised for their valuable use and application in cultural heritage education as they enabled tertiary classes and courses to continue throughout the impacted years. They provided students and others with the experience of working with archaeological material despite being unable to physically see or handle the material themselves. The interactive nature of photogrammetry models gave them the added benefit of allowing the examination of entire objects, inspecting the high-resolution surfaces to a degree that perhaps would not have been permitted at a museum, and is equally impossible from 2D images. Online photogrammetry catalogues are growing in popularity and more institutions are choosing to showcase their models on 3D modelling platforms such as *Sketchfab* and *Pedestal*, in a way advertising the material the institutions contain. The public can now access, view and interact with objects that are physically behind glass or are possibly not even on display. The accessibility that photogrammetry and other forms of 3D modelling provide to everyone is why, at the core, this is such a powerful tool.

A model may not replace the real object; however, it does provide viewers with a connection to cultural material – all that is needed is a screen. It is for this reason that the developing field of smartphone photogrammetry is promising. In recent years, smartphone photogrammetry has been growing in popularity, and while smartphone camera technology and processing capabilities are still improving, it does mean that photogrammetry modelling is becoming available to more people and industries. Additionally, it will ensure more objects and sites of significance are digitally recorded to some degree. The standard photogrammetry kit can be expensive; therefore the introduction of smartphone-based photogrammetry reduces the cost pressures and enables photogrammetry to become more than just a niche technology that only a few can utilise.

As time progresses, the models produced through photogrammetry are being utilised in more and more ways. 3D printing of photogrammetry models is becoming more commonly used in research and education, and the incorporation of photogrammetry into augmented reality (AR) and virtual reality (VR) has been done successfully across the globe for years. We are now seeing models used in interactive displays in museums and similar institutions, AR models projected into public spaces, VR experiences, and even virtual walk-throughs of museums and cultural heritage sites. Photogrammetry models are now able to be merged with other forms of 3D modelling, such as laser scans from LiDAR (Light Detection and Ranging), and computerised tomography (CT) scans (see Figure 11.1) to analyse the surface and interior of sites and objects in further depth. Public access to 3D visualisations of archaeological sites and objects means that cultural heritage is quite literally at the fingertips of anyone with an internet connection.

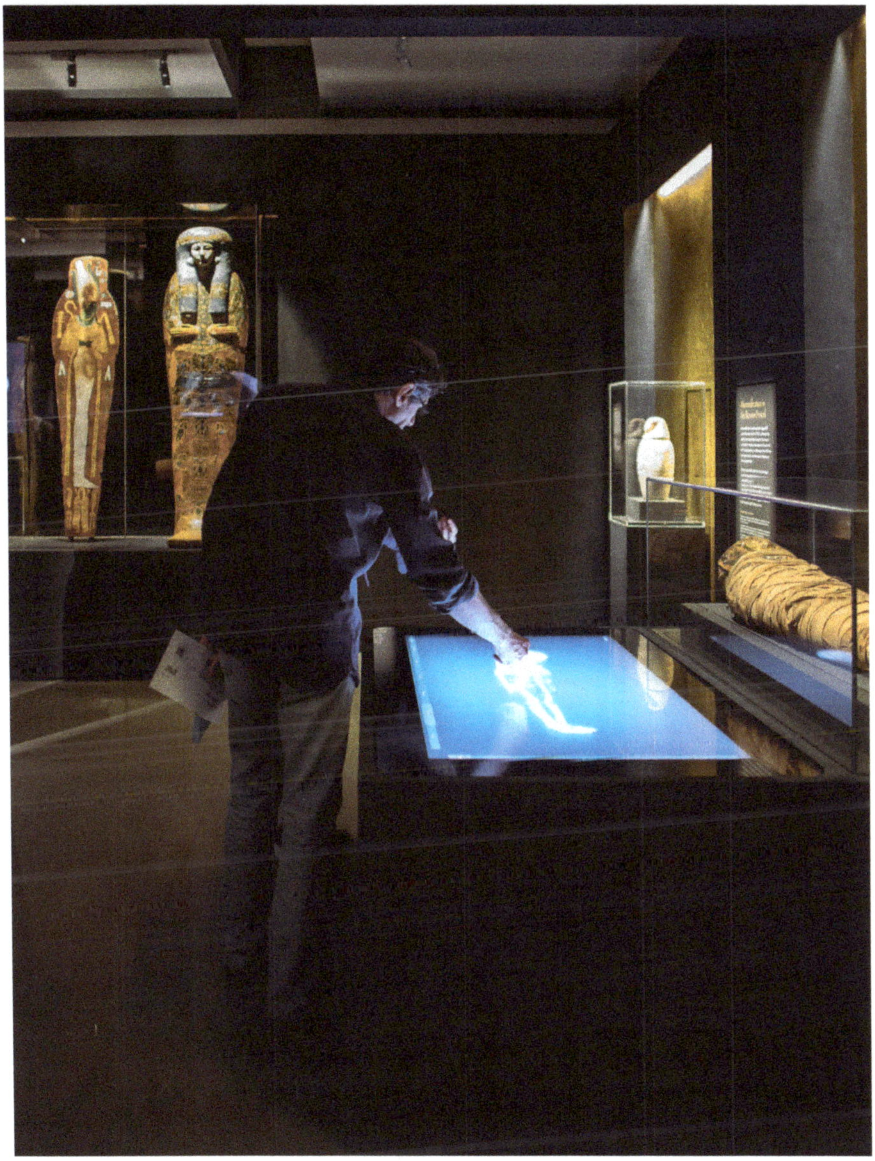

Figure 11.1 An interactive touch table of a photogrammetry model that can be manipulated to show the interior CT scan of an Egyptian mummy. Image: Photographer David James, Courtesy of the Chau Chak Wing Museum, the University of Sydney.

There are so many opportunities in the fields of photogrammetry and 3D modelling that can be very effectively and readily applied in archaeology and cultural heritage conservation, leaving us with no doubt as to why archaeologists have embraced the technology so quickly. As uptake expands and technology improves, however, so will the applications for photogrammetry within archaeology. It is for this reason that it is quickly becoming essential for archaeologists, particularly those exploring digital and geospatial archaeology, to develop a foundation in photogrammetry. This is why this manual has been developed – to provide this foundation. With no expectation of prior knowledge or understanding of photography or photogrammetry on the reader's part, this manual has taken you through an introduction to the science of photography and the key terms and settings when it comes to taking a good photo. It has explored the kinds of equipment you could include in your kit to capture archaeological objects, how to set up a shooting environment using a lightbox and without one, and how to navigate shooting in an uncontrolled environment. The steps for accurately capturing an object for photogrammetry modelling have been described, with the aid of the essential "golden rules" of photogrammetry, which are necessary to follow for successful model generation. Tips for editing your images prior to processing have also been included. A comprehensive guide on processing your models in Agisoft *Metashape* has been provided as well as an introduction to processing in the free, open-source alternative software AliceVision *Meshroom*. To help plan your own photogrammetry exercises, a series of case study examples have been included in this manual, covering a wide range of archaeological material. Additionally, to help troubleshoot any model issues you might run into, a compilation of the most common errors and how to fix them has been included. We have also explored other alternative photogrammetry software options currently available, delving into their specific specifications and analysing their advantages and disadvantages.

There is a common assumption that photogrammetry is simply taking photos of an object with the software stitching a model together for you, but as we have seen, there is so much more to photogrammetry than this. The essential prerequisites of knowledge, such as understanding how to set up a digital camera correctly, what the exposure triangle is and how it affects the images you take, and where to position the object, the lights, as well as your camera to capture the correct shots, comprise only half the journey of creating accurate photogrammetry models. We have seen that model success and accuracy come down to various factors and considerations that can occur at any stage of the photogrammetry process – considerations that you are now privy to and can prepare for. This book has also shown that a range of budgets can support photogrammetry modelling. It is essential to recognise that not many people, especially students of archaeology, are going to have access to professional photography equipment. That is why steps to create DIY lightboxes and artefact mounts have been included, as well as some direction as to what household items can double up as useful photography gear, such as car windscreen sunshades as light reflectors, and shower cap camera flash diffusers. There are numerous ways to build your photogrammetry kit inexpensively and creatively and still produce successful models.

Having covered the primary steps to create photogrammetry models – from capturing to processing – you now possess the foundations to progress beyond what is covered in this book. This guide can be taken with you to refer to, wherever you may be capturing or processing models – in a museum, in a lab or in the field – whenever you need some direction. From close-range to aerial photogrammetry, and from modelling sites above ground to shooting underwater, armed with the information in this book, you will be equipped to confidently explore the growing field of photogrammetry and its applications, wherever your archaeological research takes you.

And just remember – when in doubt, take a shot!

REFERENCES

Agisoft (2024). *User Manual: Professional Edition, Version 2.1.0.* https://www.agisoft.com/pdf/metashape-pro_2_1_en.pdf.

Alidoost, F. and H. Arefi (2017). Comparison of UAS-Based Photogrammetry Software for 3D Point Cloud Generation: A Survey over a Historical Site. *4th International Geoadvances Workshop – Geoadvances 2017: Isprs Workshop on Multi-Dimensional & Multi-Scale Spatial Data Modeling* IV-4/W4: 55–61. https://doi.org/10.5194/isprs-annals-IV-4-W4-55-2017.

Barbasiewicz, Adrianna, Tadeusz Widerski and Karol Daliga (2018). The Analysis of the Accuracy of Spatial Models Using Photogrammetric Software: Agisoft Photoscan and Pix4D. *Seminary on Geomatics, Civil and Environmental Engineering* (2017 ESG) 26. https://doi.org/10.1051/e3sconf/20182600012.

Becker, R.E., L.J. Galayda and M.M. MacLaughlin (2018). Digital Photogrammetry Software Comparison for Rock Mass Characterization. Paper presented at the 52nd US Rock Mechanics/Geomechanics Symposium, Seattle, Washington, June.

"Computer Requirements, Pix4Dmapper," Pix4D Documentation, Pix4D (updated 2021). https://support.pix4d.com/hc/en-us/articles/115002439383-Computer-requirements-PIX4Dmapper.

Cutugno, Matteo, Umberto Robustelli and Giovanni Pugliano (2022). Structure-from-Motion 3D Reconstruction of the Historical Overpass Ponte Della Cerra: A Comparison between Micmac (R) Open Source

Software and Metashape (R). Drones 6(9). https://doi.org/10.3390/drones6090242.

Davis, Annabelle, David Belton, Petra Helmholz, Paul Bourke and Jo McDonald (2017). Pilbara Rock Art: Laser Scanning, Photogrammetry and 3D Photographic Reconstruction as Heritage Management Tools. *Heritage Science* 5(1). https://doi.org/10.1186/s40494-017-0140-7.

Dostal, Christopher and Kotaro Yamafune (2018). Photogrammetric Texture Mapping: A Method for Increasing the Fidelity of 3D Models of Cultural Heritage Materials. *Journal of Archaeological Science-Reports* 18: 430–36. https://doi.org/10.1016/j.jasrep.2018.01.024.

"Download," Regard3D (n.d.). https://www.regard3d.org/index.php/download.

Đurić, Isidora, Ivana Vasiljević, Miloš Obradović, Vesna Stojaković, Jelena Kićanović and Ratko Obradović (2021). Comparative Analysis of Open-Source and Commercial Photogrammetry Software for Cultural Heritage. Paper presented at the eCAADe 2021 International Scientific Conference, University of Novi Sad, Novi Sad, Serbia, 8-10 September 2021, proceedings of the 39th eCAADe Conference 2: 243–52. https://doi.org/10.52842/conf.ecaade.2021.2.243.

Elkhrachy, Ismail (2022). 3D Structure from 2D Dimensional Images Using Structure from Motion Algorithms. *Sustainability* 14(9): 5399. https://doi.org/10.3390/su14095399.

"Features," Agisoft (updated 2024). https://www.agisoft.com/features/compare/.

Felicísimo, Ángel M. and María Eugenia Polo (2022). Measurement and Control of Colour Fidelity in Scanned 3D Models for Heritage Conservation. *Journal of Cultural Heritage* 56: 159–66. https://doi.org/10.1016/j. culher.2022.06.010.

Georgopoulos, A., C. Oikonomou, E. Adamopoulos and E.K. Stathopoulou (2016). Evaluating Unmanned Aerial Platforms for Cultural Heritage Large Scale Mapping. *International Archives of the Photogrammetry, Remote Sensing and Spatial Information Sciences – ISPRS Archives* 41(B5): 355–62. https://doi.org/10.5194/isprsarchives-XLI-B5-355-2016.

Hendrickx, Hanne, Sebastián Vivero, Laure De Cock, Bart De Wit, Philippe De Maeyer, Christophe Lambiel, Reynald Delaloye, Jan Nyssen and Amaury Frankl (2019). The Reproducibility of SfM Algorithms to Produce Detailed Digital Surface Models: The Example of Photoscan Applied to a

High-Alpine Rock Glacier. *Remote Sensing Letters* 10(1): 11–20. https://doi.org/10.1080/2150704X.2018.1519641.

Jaud, Marion, Sophie Passot, Réjanne Le Bivic, Christophe Delacourt, Philippe Grandjean and Nicolas Le Dantec (2016). Assessing the Accuracy of High Resolution Digital Surface Models Computed by Photoscan® and Micmac® in Sub-Optimal Survey Conditions. *Remote Sensing* 8(6): 465. https://doi.org/10.3390/ rs8060465.

Kesack, Rob (2022). Processing in Progress: A Benchmark Analysis of Photogrammetry Applications for Digital Architectural Documentation. *Technology | Architecture + Design* 6(1): 118–22. https://doi.org/10.1080/24751448.2022.2040313.

Kingsland, Kaitlyn (2020). Comparative Analysis of Digital Photogrammetry Software for Cultural Heritage. *Digital Applications in Archaeology and Cultural Heritage* 18. https://doi.org/10.1016/j.daach.2020.e00157.

Kingsland, Kaitlyn (2019). A Comparative Analysis of Two Commercial Digital Photogrammetry Software for Cultural Heritage Applications. *New Trends in Image Analysis and Processing – ICIAP 2019* 11808: 70–80. https://doi. org/10.1007/978-3-030-30754-7_8.

Lau, Bik Sing, Mohd Farid Mohd Ariff and Ahmad Firdaus Razali (2022). Comparison between AliceVision Meshroom and Pix4Dmapper Software in Generating Three-Dimensional (3D) Photogrammetry. *Journal of Advanced Geospatial Science & Technology* 2(2): 117–38.

Meshroom, "AliceVision," macOS, updated 2020. https://meshroom-manual.readthedocs.io/en/bibtex1/ install/osx/osx.html.

"OS and hardware requirements," CapturingReality, updated 2024. https://support.capturingreality.com/hc/en-us/articles/115001524071-OS-and-hardware-requirements.

Polo, María-Eugenia, Ángel M. Felicísimo and Guadalupe Durán-Domínguez (2022). Accurate 3D Models in Both Geometry and Texture: An Archaeological Application. *Digital Applications in Archaeology and Cultural Heritage* 27.

Rahaman, Hafizur and Erik Champion (2019). To 3D or not 3D: choosing a photogrammetry workflow for cultural heritage groups. *Heritage* 2(3): 1835–51. https://doi.org/10.3390/heritage2030112.

Reljić, Ivan, Ivan Dunđer and Sanja Seljan (2019). Photogrammetric 3D Scanning of Physical Objects: Tools and Workflow. *Tem Journal-Technology*

Education Management Informatics 8(2): 383–88. https://doi.org/10.18421/Tem82-09.

Remondino, Fabio, Erica Nocerino, Isabella Toschi and Fabio Menna (2017). A Critical Review of Automated Photogrammetric Processing of Large Datasets. *Icomos/Isprs International Scientific Committee on Heritage Documentation (Cipa) 26th International Cipa Symposium – Digital Workflows for Heritage Conservation* 42(2W5): 591–99. https://doi.org/10.5194/ isprs-archives-XLII-2-W5-591-2017.

"Requirements," AliceVision (updated 2020). https://meshroom-manual.readthedocs.io/en/ bibtex1/install/requirements/requirements.html.

Setiyadi, Suto, Husneni Mukhtar and Willy Anugrah Cahyadi. "A Comparative Study of Affordable Photogrammetry Software for Reconstructing 3D Model of a Human Foot." Paper presented at the IEEE 7th International Conference on Smart Instrumentation, Measurement and Applications (ICSIMA), Bandung, Indonesia, September 2021. https://doi.org/10.1109/icsima50015.2021.9526314.

"System Requirements," Agisoft, updated 2023. https://www.agisoft.com/downloads/ system-requirements/.

"System Requirements," Bentley, updated 2021. http://tiny.cc/xai4vz.

"Tutorials," AliceVision, updated 2020. https://meshroom-manual.readthedocs.io/en/latest/ tutorials/tutorials.html.

Vacca, G. (2019). Overview of Open Source Software for Close Range Photogrammetry. Foss4g 2019 – Academic Track 42-4(W14): 239–45. https://doi. org/10.5194/isprs-archives-XLII-4-W14-239-2019.

Verykokou, Styliani, Sofia Soile, Fotis Bourexis, Panagiotis Tokmakidis, Konstantinos Tokmakidis and Charalabos Ioannidis. "A Comparative Analysis of Different Software Packages for 3D Modelling of Complex Geometries." Paper presented at the Digital Heritage. Progress in Cultural Heritage: Documentation, Preservation, and Protection: 8th International Conference, EuroMed 2020, Virtual Event, November 2020, revised Selected Papers 2021.

INDEX

Index

Index

PHOTOGRAMMETRY KIT

1. Quick reference guide to setting up and shooting for close-range photogrammetry
2. Quick reference guide for processing in Agisoft *Metashape*
3. 8 cm scale bar with greyscale and colour reference chart
4. 15 cm scale bar with greyscale and colour reference chart
5. 5 mm targets
6. 10 mm targets
7. Chessboard for lens calibration
8. White page for white balance calibration
9. 18% grey target (please note, the 18% grey target was produced in Adobe *Photoshop* and its spectral reflectance will be distorted due to the paper stock. For the most accurate colour rendition chart, refer to the Calibrite X-Rite *ColorChecker Passport Photo 2*).

Artefact Modelling for North and South Hemispheres: Workflow

Camera Settings

1. Turn on camera and remove lens cap
2. Turn on all lights in the set up and on-camera flashes (if being used)
3. Set camera to Manual Priority (M)
4. Set shutter speed at 125th of a second, aperture to f/13 and ISO to 1000
5. Take a test shot of object positioned in the setup
6. Check image and adjust settings if exposure is not balanced by adjusting the ISO first

Note: *Avoid shutter speeds below 80th of a sec. High ISO value = brighter image*

White Balance

1. Place white target in the shooting setup.
2. **Canon**: Set camera to Auto white balance, take a photo of the target, set camera to 'Custom White Balance', set white balance to the image of the target. If colour caste is incorrect, return to Auto white balance option, retake the photo and try again.
3. **Nikon**: Set camera to "PRE", take a photo of the white target to set the custom white balance.
4. Remove target from setup.

Information Board

Include the following:

- Name
- Date
- Time
- Shooting location/artefact ID
- Trial #
- Priority setting
- Aperture setting
- Shutter speed
- ISO

Write and photograph a new info board every time you have a new shooting session, artefact or location.

Scaled Photos

Place a scale bar or targets at the base of the artefact to be included in the model,
Or
Measure and record three areas with calipers and transfer them to the model after processing. *Note: This method should be conducted after the shooting stage.*

Camera Positions

1) **High angle**
2) *Connecting*
3) **Close-up horizontal**
4) *Connecting*
5) **Wide**
6) *Close-up connecting*

Turn artefact upside-down

7) **Wide**
8) *Connecting*
9) **Close-up horizontal**
10) *Connecting*
11) **High angle**

1. Quick reference guide to setting up and shooting for close-range photogrammetry

Metashape V2.1 Batch Processing Workflow for Close-Range Photogrammetry

Align Photos

General
- *Accuracy*: **High**
- *Generic Preselection*: **Yes**
- *Reference preselection*: **Source**
- *Reset current alignment*: **No (unless necessary)**

Advanced
- *Key point limit*: **40,000**
- *Key point limit per Mpx*: **1,000**
- *Tie point limit*: **4,000**
- *Apply masks to*: **None (if appropriate)**
- *Exclude stationary points*: **Yes (if appropriate)**
- *Guided image matching*: **Yes**
- *Adaptive camera model fitting*: **Yes (if appropriate)**

Build Point Cloud

General
- *Source data*: **Depth maps**
- *Quality*: **High**
- *Uniform sampling*: **Yes**
- *Point spacing (m)*: **0.1**

Advanced
- *Depth filtering*: **Mild (depending on model quality)**
- *Calculate point confidence*: **No (unless necessary)**
- *Calculate point colours*: **Yes**
- Reuse depth maps: **Yes**
- *Replace default point cloud*: **No (unless necessary)**

Build Model

General
- *Source data*: **Point cloud (if point cloud is made) or Depth maps**
- *Surface type*: **Arbitrary**
- *Depth maps quality*: **High**
- *Face count*: **High**
- *Custom face count*: **200,000**

Blocks (leave as default)

Advanced
- *Depth filtering*: **Mild (depending on model quality)**
- *Interpolation*: **Enabled (default)**
- *Point Classes*: **All**
- *Calculate vertex colors*: **Yes**
- *Use strict volumetric masks*: **Yes**
- *Reuse depth maps*: **Yes**
- *Replace default mode*: **No (unless necessary)**

Build Texture

General
- *Mapping mode*: **Generic**
- *Blending mode*: **Mosaic**
- *Pixel size*: **0**
- *Texture size*: **8,192**
- *Page count*: **1**

Advanced
- *Hole filling* **Yes**
- *Enable ghost filler*: **Yes**

2. Quick reference guide for processing in Agisoft *Metashape*

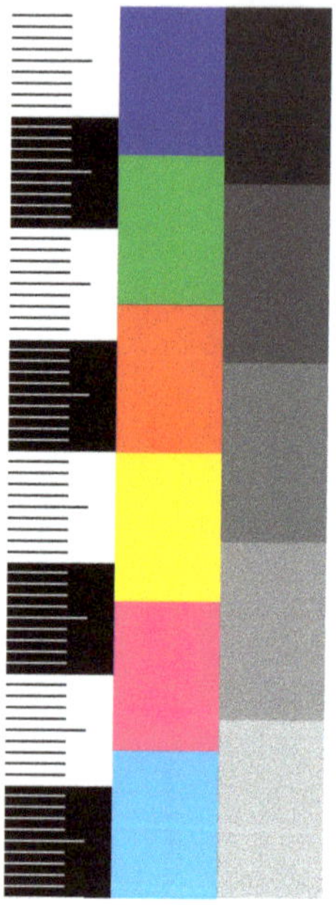

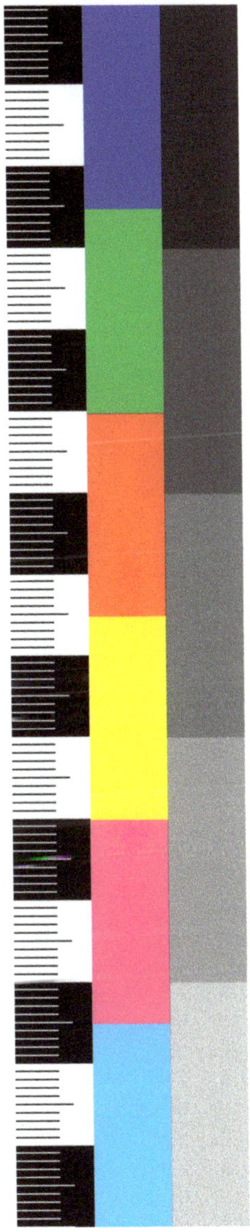

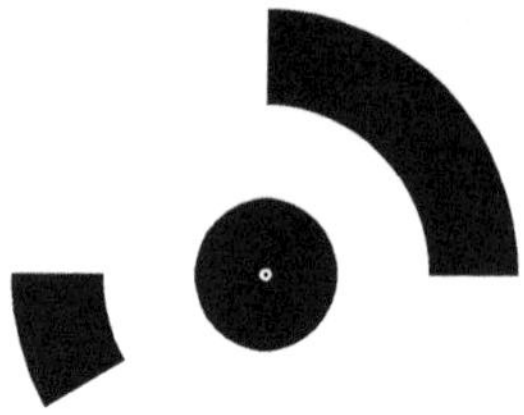

1

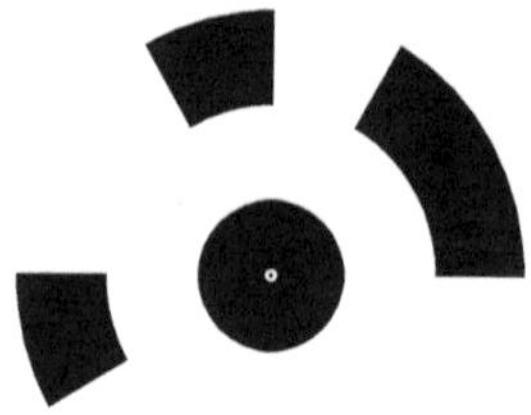

2

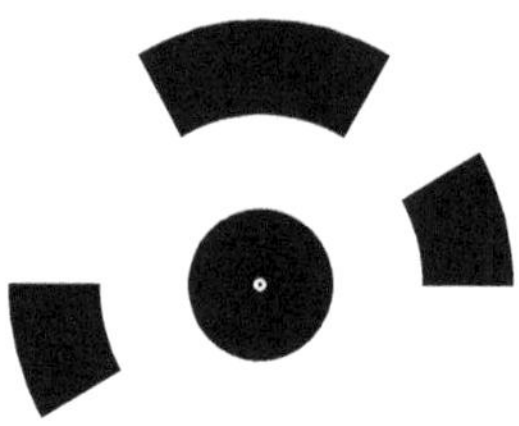

3

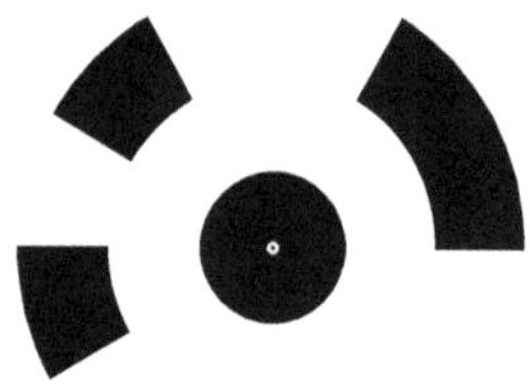

4

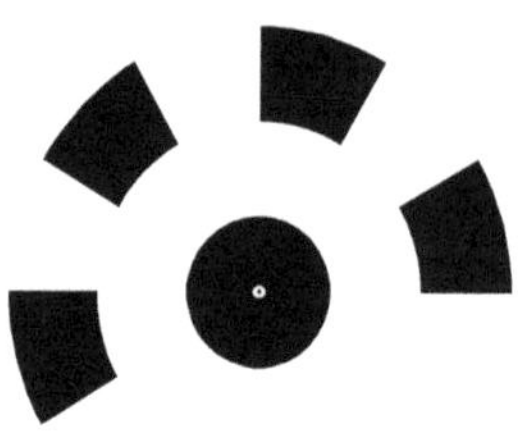

5

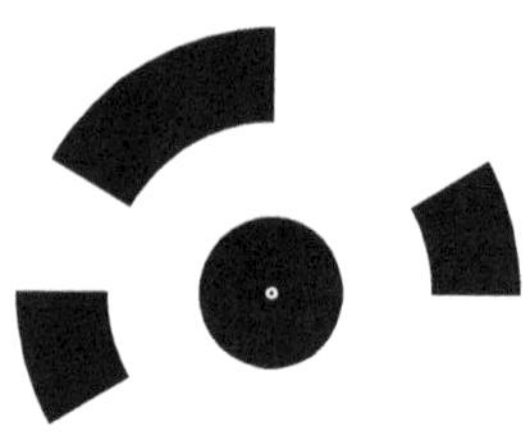

6

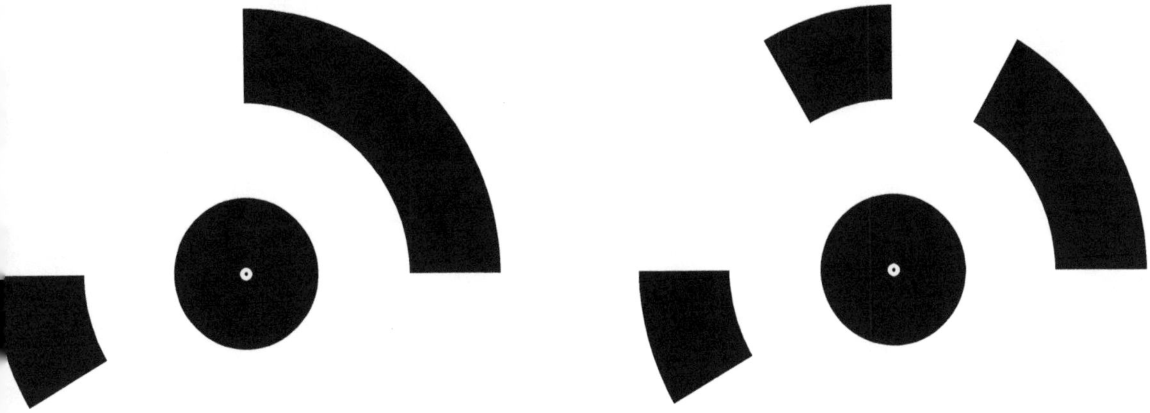

2

4

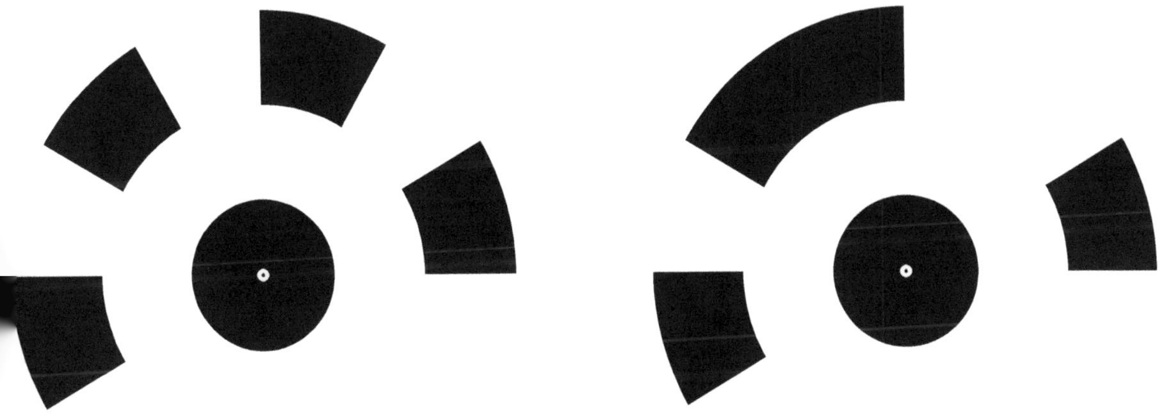

6

www.ingramcontent.com/pod-product-compliance
Lightning Source LLC
LaVergne TN
LVHW070830220926
848486LV00030B/253
9781761540431